Boris Begović • Dušan V. Popović
Editors

# Competition Authorities in South Eastern Europe

## Building Institutions in Emerging Markets

*Editors*
Boris Begović
Department of Law and Economics
University of Belgrade, School of Law
Belgrade, Serbia

Dušan V. Popović
Department of Civil Law
University of Belgrade, School of Law
Belgrade, Serbia

The Conference on Institution Building of the Competition Authorities in South-East Europe held in Belgrade on 2–3 June 2016 was supported by the European Bank for Reconstruction and Development (EBRD). The views expressed in this publication are those of the authors and not necessarily the views of the EBRD.

https://doi.org/10.1007/978-3-319-76644-7

# Foreword

This edited volume is a follow-up of the Conference on Institution Building of the Competition Authorities in South-East Europe, organised jointly by the European Bank for Reconstruction and Development (EBRD) and the Commission for the Protection of Competition of Republic of Serbia (CPC), which was held in Belgrade, Serbia, on 2–3 June 2016.

It was decided in the preparatory stages of the conference, and for the purpose of the conference only, that South-East Europe consists of Albania, Bosnia and Herzegovina, Bulgaria, Croatia, Greece, Kosovo[1], FYR Macedonia, Moldova, Montenegro, Romania, and Serbia. The competition authorities from all these jurisdictions were invited to the conference, and most of them contributed to the success of the event, providing presentations and participating to what was a valuable and productive discussion on competition law enforcement in the Region. These presentations, together with the presentations of invited academics, are the source of the edited papers in this volume. In the process of editing, some of the technical papers were posted to the specialised website (www.stajetokonkurencija.org), rather than being included in this volume.

The views expressed in the papers of this volume are not necessarily the views of the organisers of the conference: the EBRD and CPC. Though some authors in this edited volume are officials and/or staff of the competition authorities in the Region, the views expressed in their contribution are theirs alone and do not represent the views of their competition authorities.

We are grateful to Boris Begović and Dušan V. Popović for the excellent work in editing the volume.

It was our and the editors' pleasure to work with so committed and enthusiastic contributors, so we are grateful to all of them for that. Collaboration with Springer

[1]This designation is without prejudice to positions on status and is in line with UNSCR 1244 and ICJ Advisory Opinion on the Kosovo declaration of independence.

Verlag was flawless and efficient, and our gratitude goes to Katharina Wetzel-Vandai and Martina Nolte-Bohres.

We do hope that this book will prove beneficial to its main audience: competition policy professionals in competition authorities, corporations, law offices, and academia. Feedback from them would be a reward for us.

CPC, Belgrade, Serbia Miloje Obradović
EBRD, London, UK Lorenzo Ciari

# Contents

# List of Contributors

**Boris Begović** School of Law, University of Belgrade, Belgrade, Serbia

**Paolo Buccirossi** LEAR, Rome, Italy

**Lorenzo Ciari** European Bank for Reconstruction and Development, London, UK

**Jelena Grahovac** Commission for Protection of Competition, Belgrade, Serbia

**Yannis Katsoulacus** Athens University of Economics and Business, Athens, Greece

**Dimitris Loukas** Hellenic Competition Commission, Athens, Greece

**Siniša Milošević** Commission for Protection of Competition, Belgrade, Serbia

**Radu Paun** Romanian Competition Council, Bucharest, Romania

**Russell Pittman** US Department of Justice, Antitrust Division, Washington DC, USA

**Andrej Plahutnik** Team Leader of the EU funded project, Podgorica, Montenegro

**Dušan V. Popović** School of Law, University of Belgrade, Belgrade, Serbia

**Jelena Popović Markopoulos** Commission for Protection of Competition, Belgrade, Serbia

**Ivana Rakić** Commission for Protection of Competition, Belgrade, Serbia

**Aleksandra Ravić** Commission for Protection of Competition, Belgrade, Serbia

**Bojan Ristić** School of Economics, University of Belgrade, Belgrade, Serbia

**Danusioa Vamvu** Romanian Competition Council, Bucharest, Romania

# Introduction

**Boris Begović and Dušan V. Popović**

There is nothing simple and straightforward about competition authorities, their design and operations. Even in the most developed countries, those with a long and uninterrupted tradition of market economy and competition policy enforcement, there are dilemmas about the role, organisation, leverage, accountability, and funding of the competition authorities, among other things. There is no blueprint for the first best design of competition authorities, but rather certain guidelines and best practices—and not all of them consistent over time. It is hardly surprising that in South-East Europe the dilemmas are multiplied, as the Region does not have a long tradition of market economy and competition policy enforcement; for most of the countries in the Region competition policy is a novel notion, and rule of law is not exactly a regional hallmark. Clearly, challenges for institution building of competition authorities in South-East Europe are immense.

This edited volume addresses two challenges. The first one is institutional design of the competition authorities, which takes into account specific features of the SEE countries, especially their economic structure and the lack of resources that can be allocated to the competition policy, specifically human capital. The second one is the role of economics in the competition law enforcement—the central job of competition authorities. That role is no longer controversial in the developed jurisdictions, but the introduction of economic methods into the operation of competition authorities of SEE countries is not straightforward.

Within the institutional design domain, three crucial questions were asked. The first one was about the character of the desirable competition policy for SEE countries since that very character greatly affects the design suitable for the given competition authority.

B. Begović (✉) · D. V. Popović
School of Law, University of Belgrade, Belgrade, Serbia
e-mail: begovic@ius.bg.ac.rs; dusan.popovic@ius.bg.ac.rs



B. Begović, D. V. Popović (eds.), *Competition Authorities in South Eastern Europe*, Contributions to Economics, https://doi.org/10.1007/978-3-319-76644-7_1

Paolo Buccirossi and Lorenzo Ciari examined the SEE economies to describe where they stand in terms of these characteristics, and to derive policy implications on how their competition policy should be designed and implemented, affecting the desirable design of the competition authorities. It was demonstrated that the existence of high barriers to entry and poor institutional quality points to the importance of an institutional set-up where the independence and transparency of the competition authorities is maximised within the context of an administrative model. Also, no sector or enterprise, including SOEs, should be excluded from competition law enforcement, and competition law provisions should ensure that the voice of the competition authority is heard whenever new legislation that could potentially affect competition is introduced, i.e. that competition advocacy should be vigorously pursued by the authorities. In terms of competition enforcement, while the role of advocacy emerges as crucial, along with the prosecution of entry-foreclosing abuses, a more lenient approach to merger control can be suggested, in the form of high notification thresholds. In short, a robust and focused competition policy is the recommendation for institutional building the competition authorities in SEE countries.

In his contribution Boris Begović asked, within the conceptual framework of middle-income convergence trap, whether competition policy is good for the growth of SEE countries, taking into account that different levels of economic development influence different engines of economic growth. The answer was that SEE countries are in the middle-income convergence trap and that they should base their growth on innovations and the increase of total factor productivity rather than on accumulation of production factors. Since vigorous competition is a precondition for innovation and productivity growth, there are ample reasons for competition policy to be enforced. Additionally, since most of these countries have a substantial legacy of non-market economy inefficiency, competition policy should be designed so as to enable removing of these efficiencies by restructuring and easing entry and exit. That means that mergers (which are inevitable for effective restructuring) should not be strictly controlled and that competition advocacy should be used for decreasing entry and exit barriers.

The conclusion from these two papers is that the institutional design of the competition authorities in SEE should provide a strong role for competition advocacy, which would make markets more competitive and that would allow for the restructuring of these economies, by focusing on competition law infringements rather than to the merger control.

The second dilemma encountered by the authors writing about the institutional design of competition authorities is related to the functions that the competition authority should encompass—the dilemma between the single-function, i.e. specialised competition authority, and authorities with multiple functions. The most prominent dilemma of than kind in SEE countries is the inclusion of the state aid control function within the competencies of the existing competition authorities.

Dušan Popović examined the institutional design of state aid monitoring authorities in SEE countries and concluded that, regardless of the model chosen, state aid control cannot presently be performed in an entirely independent manner. The reasons for this can be found in the instability of democratic institutions and the limited expertise that exists within the state apparatus, in the area of competition law and state aid. The author compares the current situation in SEE countries with the pre-accession experience of Central and Eastern European countries, and concludes that the efficiency of state aid control will improve only when the SEE countries near the end of their European integration process. Since the SEE countries established their state aid monitoring authorities at the beginning of their (ongoing) European integration process, and enlargement is no longer the European Union's priority, it seems highly likely that the state aid authorities in SEE countries will, for the time being, only continue with their pro forma activities.

In his contribution Andrej Plahutnik analysed the requirements for an efficient competition authority. The author concluded that efficient institutions are not dependent on the number of staff, but on the level of the qualification, good management and full independence from political and economic influence. The author finds that political influence with regard to state aid most likely cannot be avoided. Therefore, merging the competition authority with the state aid authority may lead to greater political pressure even in the area of "pure" antitrust enforcement.

Both authors conclude that, at present level of democratic and economic development, specialised competition authorities are a better option for SEE countries than the establishment of a multifunctional authority.

Finally, as competition policy includes both competition law enforcement and competition advocacy, the third dilemma is about allocation of the competition authority resources between the two. The previous papers demonstrated the significance and effectiveness of competition advocacy, hence the two following papers shed some light on the advocacy efforts and challenges of two specific cases: Greece and Serbia.

In his contribution Dimitris Loukas emphasises that the scope and intensity of the Greek competition authority's advocacy agenda entailed certain risks in recent years. The first risk is related to the over–extension of scarce human resources, often to the detriment of expeditious and effective enforcement. The second risk pertains to the possibility of non-competition policy considerations creeping in to the authority's decision making process in the area of advocacy. Such non-competition policy considerations usually stem from the Government efforts to resolve the difficult economic and financial situation that the country is dealing with.

Similarly, Ivana Rakić analysed the Serbian experience with competition advocacy. The author concluded that the authority's advocacy activities were not fully recognised by policy makers and that it needed to gain more credibility and resources as an effective and impartial advocate for competition. The authority must therefore give continuous attention to building a competition culture, through aggressive public relations activities and dissemination of information. The evaluation of the effectiveness of competition advocacy in Serbia is hampered by the fact that there is no systematic information about implementation experience.

The conclusion is that competition advocacy is a very effective tool for competition policy, which in many cases is more efficient than competition law enforcement. This clears the way for consideration of the role of economics in competition law enforcement.

In his contribution Yannis Katsoulacos focused to the consideration of the extent of economic analysis and evidence in competition law enforcement, i.e. in the operation of competition authorities in this area. It was demonstrated that the extent crucially depends on the legal standard adopted by the competition authority and by the courts in charge of judicial revision of competition legal cases. The contribution examined the factors that influence the choice of legal standards, and hence determine the extent to which economic analysis and evidence are applied in competition law enforcement, focusing on the recent economic literature. A number of explanations were suggested as to why the decisions of competition authorities, in regard to the utilisation of economic evidence, may diverge from the social welfare-maximising decisions, stressing the role of the substantive (or liability) standards adopted. Differences in substantive standards may be used to explain the significant divergence in the type of legal standards adopted in the EU and the USA. The most important segment of this contribution, for the institution building of competition authorities in SEE, is a proposed practical methodology that can be used by authorities for identifying which legal standards minimise decision errors in the assessment of specific conduct.

Russell Pittman provided a non-economist guide to three economist's tools for competition law enforcement, taking into account that the importance of economics in analysis and enforcement of competition policy and law has increased immensely in developed market economies in the past 40 years. Nonetheless, in most SEE countries competition law itself has a history of 20–25 years at most and economic tools that have proven useful to competition law enforcement in developed market economies, by focusing investigations and assisting decision makers in distinguishing central from secondary issues, are inevitably not as well understood. His paper presents a non-technical introduction to three economic tools that have become widespread in competition law enforcement, and especially in the analysis of proposed mergers: critical loss analysis, upward pricing pressure, and vertical arithmetic. The first is used primarily in the context of horizontal mergers for both market definition and the analysis of potential competitive effects of mergers, while the second and third are used primarily in the analysis of potential competitive effects: the second in horizontal mergers, and the third in vertical mergers. All of them are useful economic tools for competition law enforcement by competition authorities in SEE, improving the probability of success of the enforcement.

Virtually all cases of competition law enforcement related to the concentration of enterprises, restrictive agreements, and abuse of dominant position include the definition of relevant markets. Siniša Milošević et al. dealt in their contribution with different quantitative methods for defining relevant markets. It was demonstrated that the selection depends most importantly on the very nature of a specific product market and the availability of data. The paper presents the use of methods that are based on the price movement of the products under consideration: correlation, the stationarity test (unit root test), the cointegration test, and the Granger causality test, and it explores the reliability of these tests in the process of specifying the relevant market. As an example, the practical implementation of price-based tests was demonstrated on an analysis of monthly time-series data related to the price of three products during a 4-year period. The paper presented a set of economic/econometric tools that are rather simple, and therefore can be used even by less experienced competition authorities, such as those in SEE.

The last two contributions in this edited volume are focused on the merger control. In his paper Bojan Ristić developed a merger simulation model based on the application of Cournot's theoretical competition model as a reduced form of two-stage competition in oligopoly markets, in the circumstances with limited capacities. This provides competition authorities a valuable tool for analysing the unilateral effects of horizontal mergers. The outcome of the two-stage competition, where firms chose to have a certain level of capacity, before the price competition, coincides with the outcome of the Cournot quantity competition model. The utilisation of the simulation method could be perceived as a complementary analytical tool for controlling concentrations, capable of decreasing the likelihood of common regulatory mistakes—false positive or false negative conclusions. It does not require significant additional time, data or other resources. If the relevant market was properly specified, all elements are most likely already available. The simulation method certainly allows significant influence of economic theory in merger control, which is in line with the wave of the so-called "more economic approach" in European Commission practice, by incorporating the intensity of the competition and merger efficiencies into one comprehensive economic model. Furthermore, calibration could be seen as a low-cost, and sometimes the only alternative to a full-scale merger analysis, by using econometry in equipping the selected economic model for estimating demand and cost functions. Of course, this does not exclude the possibility of using an econometric approach, when authorities have sufficient time, reliable data and resources for such an endeavour.

Finally, Radu Paun and Danusia Vamvu in their contribution used the difference-in-differences (DiD) methodology to econometrically ex-post assess the impact of a merger on the Romanian retail market in terms of price dynamics. In the merger review process, they identified five potentially problematic locations and accordingly selected suitable and representative time intervals, product categories, as well as the Treated and control groups. The implementation of the DiD technique through regression analysis rendered 55 case estimates, of which 49 match the DiD hypotheses and are thus considered reliable. In each of these cases they estimated the percentage change in the price of a product category in a certain store, due to merger clearance. The results indicate that the approved merger did not lead to general price increases: in 33 of the 49 cases the merger impact on prices is not statistically significant different from zero, and only 3 of the 49 cases show price increases. This example of the econometric ex-post analysis of merger effects proved to be useful for replicating such tests in SEE countries.

There are two main lessons to be learned from all the contributions in this volume. The first one is that SEE countries share some particular institutional and economic features that made institutional building of their competition authorities specific compared to developed jurisdictions, with a prominent role of competition advocacy and rather restricted merger control in the area of competition law enforcement. With substantial barriers to entry, there is ample ground for competition advocacy in SEE. The second lesson is that introduction of economic methods, though inevitable, should not be straightforward, but rather focused on simple solutions and the easy wins in building confidence and expertise of the competition authorities of the Region.

# Western Balkans and the Design of Effective Competition Law: The Role of Economic, Institutional and Cultural Characteristics

**Paolo Buccirossi and Lorenzo Ciari**

## 1 Introduction

In 2001 the International Competition Network was created by the competition authorities of 14 jurisdictions, and today it has 138 members. This rapid growth was due to the introduction of competition law in many countries that previously lacked one. The adoption of anti-monopoly regulation was spurred by the transition from a planned to a market economy, in some areas, and by the general belief that competition could be one of the main drivers of better economic performance. Indeed, there is extensive economic literature that shows that competition can foster productivity growth.[1] More focused literature deals with the relationship between competition policy and economic performance.[2] These contributions indicate that competition policy does play a significant role. However, they also point out that the mere existence of rules intended to protect competition does not suffice to generate the results aimed at. What is needed is a "good" competition policy. So, the policy issue becomes what features a competition policy regime should have in order to effectively pursue its intended goals. Existing literature also shows that the effectiveness of competition policy depends on other characteristics of the given

[1]Among many others, see Aghion et al. (2009), Griffith and Harrison (2004) and Dutz and Aydin (1999). A review of the main empirical literature is Holmes and Schmitz (2010).

[2]See Buccirossi Paolo et al. (2013), Kee and Hoekman (2007), and Konings et al. (2001).

P. Buccirossi (✉)
LEAR, Rome, Italy
e-mail: paolo.buccirossi@learlab.com

L. Ciari
European Bank for Reconstruction and Development, London, UK
e-mail: ciaril@ebrd.com

 
B. Begović, D. V. Popović (eds.), *Competition Authorities in South Eastern Europe*,
Contributions to Economics, https://doi.org/10.1007/978-3-319-76644-7_2

country.[3] Thus, the previous policy question cannot be addressed without considering the wider context in which the anti-trust regime is set. The general normative statement is that the desirable features of a "good" competition policy regime can only be identified taking into consideration the economic, social, cultural, and institutional characteristics of the specific country. This statement needs to be further detailed and limited but growing literature provides attempts to refine the general recommendation.[4] This paper aims at contributing to this research agenda.

In order to establish the desirable characteristics of a competition policy regime, *given* the relevant specific characteristics of a country, one has to perform two operations. First, one must identify the "variables" that warrant a policy decision: we may call it the choice set. It can be thought of as the menu that lists the many models of competition policy regimes from which the decision-maker has to choose. These regimes vary along various dimensions concerning the substantive rules, the institutions entrusted with their enforcement, and the way this enforcement is conducted. Different models can be built by combining these elements in different ways.

The second task is to identify the exogenous characteristics that influence the ability of the previously identified models of competition policy regime to achieve its objectives. These can be thought of as fixed factors that are likely to alter the performance of the regimes in the choice set and are linked to some crucial economic characteristics of the country, its institutions and cultural factors. Once these factors are identified, one has to ascertain which policy model is more likely to perform better, i.e. to better promote and protect competition.

We conduct these analyses in the next two sections of the paper. In Sect. 2 we describe the choice set, i.e. the main elements of a competition policy regime and the alternatives that are available to the policy maker. Section 3 examines the economic, institutional and cultural factors that need to be considered when selecting the model that is predisposed to perform better. In doing so, we focus in particular on those factors that are more likely to characterise emerging economies. This section has normative content and provides some suggestions on what we believe are the best policy choices under the described conditions.

Section 4 presents some indicators reflecting the existing economic, institution and cultural characteristics of the countries in the Western Balkan region.[5] The purpose of this section is to show that the previous recommendations are indeed relevant for the design of the competition policy regime in these countries. The analysis looks at central and south-eastern European countries belonging to the EU as comparators, as well as at some more advanced jurisdictions, to give a sense of the magnitude of the existing gap for the relevant identified characteristics.

---

[3]On this point see also Dutz and Vagliasindi (2000) and Acemoglu et al. (2006).

[4]See the contributions in Michal S. Gal et al. (2015).

[5]The set of Western Balkan countries includes Albania, Bosnia and Herzegovina, Kosovo, FYR Macedonia, Montenegro, and Serbia.

Section 5 concludes and suggests initiatives that can be undertaken to improve the effectiveness of competition policy in the West Balkan region.

## 2 Models of Competition Policy Regime

A competition policy "regime" can be thought as a combination of characteristics that concern the content of the prohibitions or prescriptions set in the law, the institutions entrusted with their enforcement and the way they perform their task. Many combinations exist and competition policy regimes vary significantly across jurisdictions. They have some common traits and a convergence process occurred on some elements. In particular, substantive rules tend to cover similar threats to competition, although the language of the provisions and their interpretation may differ. In a nutshell, antitrust rules prohibit agreements that may distort competition, abusive conducts undertaken by dominant firms, and many jurisdictions prescribe that mergers are ex-ante scrutinised to prevent those that may substantially lessen competition. The exact scope of these rules varies across countries and may even change over time. In the following we set aside this aspect and focus on some of the many other dimensions that shape a competition policy regime.

For the sake of explanation, these dimensions can be roughly divided in two groups. A first group encompasses the choices concerning the institutional set-up; the second group relates to how the main institutions exert their powers, something we may refer to as the "implementation". The institutional set-up includes the following three elements: (1) the position of the competition authority in relation to other public bodies; (2) the scope of the rules whose enforcement is attributed to the authority; and (3) the powers attributed to it. The implementation group includes: (1) the type of analysis used to interpret the substantive rules; (2) the use of sanctioning powers; and (3) the way the agency sets its priorities and goals, and the instruments used to pursue them.

In the following we briefly present the main alternatives that are available for each of these elements.[6]

### *2.1 Institutional Set-Up*

The institutional set-up of a competition policy regime concerns many factors. We focus on three main aspects that we think are particularly relevant. These are: the general model adopted to enforce competition rules, and the independence and accountability of the competition agency; the scope of the enforcement powers

---

[6]For a general discussion of these elements see Buccirossi Paolo et al. (2011).

attributed to the competent authority; and the investigative and sanctioning powers that support and complement the enforcement activity.

### 2.1.1 The General Model and the Independence and Accountability of the Competition Authority

Two basic institutional models can be adopted for the enforcement of competition law.[7] The first one is the administrative model where an administrative authority is responsible for the investigation of cases and makes enforcement decisions that are then subject to judicial control. The administrative model is the most common within the EU. The second option is the judicial or prosecutorial model. In this instance, the administrative authority performs the investigation and then brings the case before a court. The court is responsible for making a decision on substance and on sanctions, or in regards to the imposition of sanctions only. In some jurisdictions, the administrative model has been amended to reap some of the benefits of the separation between *prosecution* and *adjudication*, which is typical of the judicial model. They have adopted a so-called "dual administrative model" where one body investigates the case and a different institution is responsible for making the decision.[8] The choice between the two models affects some important aspects that are generally related to independence and accountability. However, while the choice between the two models bears important implications, the overall level of independence and accountability of the competition law enforcement authority in the two institutional models depends on the more general characteristics of the institutions in a country, in particular on the overall quality of the institutions.

Where the judiciary enjoys a great degree of autonomy from other public powers and from private interests, the *judicial model* guarantees the maximum level of independence of the decision-making body. Yet, this may be achieved only at the expenses of other desirable features. First, to preserve their independence from other powers, courts are less accountable to the general public than administrative authorities, whose leadership is politically appointed. Second, courts generally lack personnel with economic expertise and therefore are not well positioned to conduct more complex economic analyses. Third, even in the judicial model there exists an administrative agency that to a large extent decides which cases to probe and which type of evidence to collect, thus reducing the scope of the independence in competition law enforcement.

The degree of independence that a competition authority enjoys is a trait that distinguishes competition policy regimes within the *administrative model*. Given the

---

[7] A discussion of these models can be found in David Gerber (1998) and Trebilcock and Iacobucci (2010).

[8] Also in this set-up the administrative decision can be reviewed by a court. It should be noticed that the dual administrative model has been abandoned in some EU countries, such as Spain and the UK, mainly for budgetary reasons.

considerable powers that a competition agency exercises in any case, it is important to decide how it should be positioned in the sphere of public powers.[9] At one extreme of the spectrum we may attribute the role of competition agency to the executive branch. This is, for instance, the choice that has (partly) been made in the USA, where one of the two antitrust agencies is a division of the Department of Justice, and at the EU level, where the European Commission (i.e. the Union's executive body) is responsible for the enforcement of competition law. At the opposite extreme, we find agencies that enjoy a maximum level of autonomy, which is guaranteed by formal statutory independence from other public bodies, the lack of supervisory power of other governmental institutions, and the availability of adequate financial and human resources over which the agency has full control, so as to enjoy organisational and financial independence, too. In between there are various options in which the competition authority is subject to general instructions by the government or parliament, or to various degree of supervision, that may include guiding the authority's activities, giving instructions on some general aspects of the law or in regards to the budget or pertaining to wider policy matters.

As the degree of independence of the competition authority varies significantly within the administrative model, so does the degree of the authority's accountability. Especially when the competition authority has a very large degree of independence it becomes important to decide if and which measures should be adopted in order to ensure that it remains accountable to the citizens. This can be achieved by imposing some transparency obligations, and by requiring the authority to submit periodical reports to the parliament or to the government. In some cases, this can be coupled with the obligation to submit plans for upcoming years.

### 2.1.2 Scope of the Enforcement and Other Powers

An obvious important decision to be made in designing a competition policy regime concerns the extent of the enforcement powers attributed to the competition authority. This relates to three different areas: (1) the scope of the competition law, i.e. the conducts that the competition authority can scrutinise to verify their compatibility with the provisions of the law; (2) the exclusion of certain sectors (e.g. defence), or typologies of firms (SOEs), or transactions (e.g. mergers below a certain threshold) from the reach of competition rules or of some of them; and (3) the combination of competition law enforcement with the enforcement of other legislation.

Competition law generally contains three sets of prohibitions, concerning anti-competitive agreements, abusive practices by dominant firms and the ex-ante control of mergers. It is quite striking how the substantive rules of competition law tend to converge on a global scale, notwithstanding the many differences that exist in terms of economic systems and legal and cultural backgrounds across countries. To be clear, the interpretation of these rules is largely influenced by local specificities, an

[9]This topic is discussed by Kovacic and Hyman (2012).

aspect to which we return later. Yet, a less widespread consensus concerns the desirability of including merger control among the enforcement powers of the agency. Historically, even in the most advanced antitrust jurisdictions, a merger control regime was introduced only decades after the first enactment of the competition law. However, countries that have introduced competition law more recently have set up a merger control system from the very beginning, but even in these cases there is some room of manoeuvre as the scope of the merger regulation may be defined by adequately setting the thresholds that trigger the powers of the competition authority.

In many jurisdictions some economic activities are exempted from the applicability of competition law. The rationale for this exemption is that these activities pursue more general interests and require an organization that is not compatible with competition. Moreover, the state assigns to some bodies the objective of pursuing these general interests and does not want other institutions to interfere with the decisions they have to make, aimed at achieving the assigned objectives. This approach makes perfect sense. However, it can be easily distorted to protect vested interests (i.e. rents) in activities that can be efficiently and effectively performed in competitive markets. Thus, the extent of these exclusions is an important policy choice that needs to be made based on careful assessment. Moreover, competition authorities might still act as advocates of the competition principles, even if the law prevents them from enforcing competition rules against the institutions entrusted with these general interest objectives.[10] This is part of the more general advocacy powers that the authority typically can exert to induce lawmakers and policymakers to avoid unnecessary restrictions of competition.

Finally, competition agencies may combine the competition law enforcement task with the enforcement of other rules. For instance, some authorities also act as sectoral regulators, or have supervisory powers over public procurement. More frequently, competition authorities have also the power to enforce consumer protection legislation, which include rules banning misleading advertising and unfair commercial practices.

### 2.1.3 Investigative and Sanctioning Power

In order to ascertain antitrust infringements, the competition authority needs a complex set of powers. These relate to:

- the ability to collect evidence of illegal conduct and data to inform the assessment of the likely impact of a firms' behaviour on the functioning of markets; and
- the possibility to impose remedies that restore competition and sanctions that confer deterrence properties to the enforcement activity.

[10]The competition advocate role of competition authorities, especially in developing countries, is discussed in World Bank, OECD (1988).

Investigative powers range from simple requests for information to far-reaching powers such as the ability to inspect business and non-business premises (dawn-raids). The effectiveness of inspection powers may be further guaranteed by ancillary powers such as the power to seal premises, to collect evidence stored on digital media and to impose sanctions against non-compliant firms. These powers are especially needed to uncover secret violations such as cartels. However, they may be crucial also for abuse of dominance cases where business plans may prove essential to establishing a proper theory of harm.

Once the authority has collected the required evidence, it needs powers to make its enforcement effective. These include the obvious power to adopt prohibition decisions. In some cases, the authority may be given the power to mandate interim measures to avoid irreparable harm to competition or to impose behavioural or structural remedies, as the mere termination of the illegal conduct may not lead to a well-functioning competitive market.

All these powers are pointless if not backed up by an effective sanction system. Sanctions may range from administrative fines on firms to criminal sanctions on individuals. They may stem from the violation of the substantive prohibition of the competition law or from non-compliance with all the other powers attributed to the competition authority, such as the refusal to respond to requests for information, or violations of interim measures, or the unjustified opposition to inspection.

All the powers briefly described so far seem indispensable for the effective enforcement of competition law so that it appears that there is little choice to be made in this respect. However, they should not be taken for granted, as in many jurisdictions the competition authority lacks some or many of them. So, it is worthwhile understanding why and in which circumstances giving the authority a less ample set of power is the proper decision.

### 2.1.4 Implementation of the Rules

Once the body responsible for the enforcement of competition law if identified, the general boundaries of the substantive provisions and the powers that can be exerted by the authority are defined, the competition policy regime depends on the way all this is put into practice. We refer to this aspect as the implementation of the rules, which comprises the main discretionary decisions that the authority has to make to turn the law into a policy.

### 2.1.5 Interpretation of the Substantive Rules

Across jurisdictions, antitrust provisions share the characteristics of being framed in very general terms. The general prohibitions need to be translated in a clear division between licit and illicit behaviour. In the past decades, an effect-based approach has gained popularity. This requires that each conduct is assessed taking into account the legal and economic context in which it takes place, so that a thorough economic analysis can reveal whether it is likely to impair competition or to foster certain efficiencies that justify its adoption. All conducts that do not alter competition or that have efficiency effects that outweigh the anticompetitive effects should be deemed compatible with competition law. Hence, the prohibitions will catch only those conducts that clearly have a potential negative impact on competition and welfare. This effect-based analysis intends to replace a more formalistic approach that aims to classify conducts as prohibited or permitted according to some prominent formal characteristics.

Although the effect-based approach has gained momentum, it would be inappropriate to claim that it has completely superseded the formal approach. Indeed, competition authorities, in all jurisdictions, continue to rely on some formal analyses as well as on precedents. This is understandable, also given that it responds to the need of the business community to have rules that are predictable.

A more nuanced way to describe the options available to a competition authority is to classify them according to the presumptions that are set up and the role that they play. In this respect we can have *per se rules* (generally, per se prohibitions), which establish that a certain conduct (e.g. a cartel) is prohibited irrespective of any economic analysis; when a per se rule is defined, the conduct is presumed to negatively affect competition and this presumptions cannot be rebutted; similarly, a per se legality rule establishes the presumption that the conduct does not restrain competition and, again, such a presumption is unrebuttable.[11]

At the other extreme there is the *rule of reason*; such a rule starts with a presumption of legality and requires that the enforcement authority proves, through a full-fledged economic analysis, its anticompetitive effects and the failure of the possible efficiency benefits to balance out the social cost of an impaired competition.[12]

These presumptions are frequently established through case law. However, competition authorities have other instruments to do so: guidelines, notices, etc. These soft-law instruments have the advantage of being more concise, general and widely known than a specific enforcement decision; moreover, they grant the authority more flexibility because they can revise their position if the need arises, whereas they cannot intervene on their past enforcement decisions.

A competition authority can use these soft-law instruments to clarify presumptions that it will apply in its enforcement activity, the type of evidence it will take into consideration to overcome these presumptions, and the required standard of proof. Hence, they will define the complexity of the economic analysis that needs to be performed to prove either the illegality or the legality of certain practices. Soft-law instruments can cover a number of subject matters, such as the definition of the

[11]In the European tradition there are no per se rule, even for cartels. Indeed, they are presumed to be illegal, but, in principle, the parties can prove that the anticompetitive agreement is justified by efficiency reasons and deserves to be exempted.

[12]A thorough discussion of the properties of per se rules and rules of reasons can be found in: Katsoulacos and Ulph (2009, 2016).

relevant market, vertical agreements, cooperation agreements, unilateral practices, horizontal and vertical mergers, and so on.

For all these dimensions, the choice set is defined by the policy decisions concerning the adoption of *per se* rules or *rules of reason*, and whether the competition authority has to define its position by issuing guidelines or it can rely on its case law.

### 2.1.6 Sanction Policy

In the administrative model, competition authorities may enjoy some degree of discretion in the imposition of sanctions. This discretion can be exerted both in the definition of the harshness of the punishment and in the identification of the circumstances that warrant a more lenient or a more severe attitude. The authority may also identify cases in which the sanction can be strategically traded against some form of collaboration from the parties.

Again, all these aspects of the policy, within the limit defined by law, can be specified through soft-law instruments (e.g. guidelines). The guidelines can cover the general criteria by defining the value of the fine according to the gravity of the infringement and its duration. Moreover, they may define the aggravating circumstances that lead to an increase in the penalty and the alleviating circumstances that allow the party to pay a lower fine. As for the strategic use of the sanctioning power, this may concern: (1) the set up of a leniency programme to obtain information on secret cartels from one or more of the cartel members;[13] (2) special discounts granted to firms that adopt effective compliance programmes in order to encourage their introduction; (3) the adoption of commitment decisions where the authority foresees the possibility of swift resolution of its competition concerns and the opportunity to save resources for other enforcement activities; (4) the definition of settlement procedures so that the competition authority can avoid its decision being challenged before a court.

### 2.1.7 Priority Setting

Competition authorities, as any organization, are resource constrained. Hence, they cannot pursue all cases and need to prioritise their activities. Priority-setting may concern three dimensions. First, competition authorities have to decide whether they want to focus their activity on the anticompetitive conducts undertaken by firms or on the rules set by public authorities that distort competition. The former objective is pursued through the enforcement of the antitrust prohibitions; the latter through the

[13]There are several contributions suggesting that leniency programmes are one of the most successful policy tools for fighting hardcore cartels; see, among others, Buccirossi and Spagnolo (2007).

exercising of its advocacy powers. Second, they may choose the types of infringements that they want to concentrate on. Third, they may want to identify sectors that deserve special attention.

Priority setting can be done through formal strategy and planning documents, which can be even submitted to a public consultation, or through informal statements by the authority's board. In some cases, for example in Turkey, priorities are defined by law.

To summarise: in this section we have identified several elements that define the characteristics of a competition policy regime and that can be fine-tuned to take into consideration the specificities of a country so as build a more effective policy. These elements are presented in Table 1.

**Table 1** Some relevant features of a competition policy regime

| Institutional set-up | Independence and accountability | Scope of the enforcement power | Investigative and sanctioning power |
|---|---|---|---|
| | • Administrative vs. judicial model<br>• Independence of public powers<br>• Organisational and financial independence | • Antitrust prohibitions and merger control<br>• Exclusion of sectors or subjects<br>• Advocacy powers<br>• Other functions (e.g. consumer protection) | • Request for information<br>• Inspection of business and non-business premises<br>• Interim measures<br>• Sanctions for main violations<br>• Sanctions to back up ancillary provisions |
| Implementation | Interpretation of the substantive rules | Sanction policy | Setting priorities |
| | • Guidelines on market definition, and on the interpretation of the substantive rules<br>• Presumptions<br>• Evidence<br>• Standard of proof | • Criteria for fine-setting<br>• Aggravating and alleviating circumstances<br>• Leniency programme<br>• Compliance programme<br>• Commitment decision<br>• Settlement | • Enforcement vs. advocacy<br>• Types of infringement<br>• Sectors<br>• Strategy plans vs. informal statements |

# 3 Emerging Economies and the Shape of Competition Policy

In the previous section we defined the main dimensions that shape a competition policy regime. We now turn to the assessment of the characteristics of emerging economies[14] that affect the optimal design of competition policy. We distinguish three main types of characteristics: economic, institutional and cultural. In the next section we will look at the Western Balkan countries through the lens of the identified relevant characteristics in order to derive the implications for the optimal policy mix that such countries should adopt.

## *3.1 Economic Characteristics*

Several economic characteristics of emerging economies can be identified as having an impact on how competition policy should be designed and implemented. We will focus on three that appear to be particularly relevant: the existence of widespread barriers to entry and government interference in the economy; the sectoral composition of output and domestic consumption; finally, the role of the informal (shadow) economy.

### 3.1.1 Barriers to Entry and the Role of the Government

Emerging economies, especially those with a legacy of central planning or in general those without a tradition of well-functioning markets, are characterised by the presence of strong regulatory and economic barriers to entry, which impede the creation of well-functioning markets. Regulatory barriers have to do with existing laws and regulations that limit entry and operations in markets, such as licensing restrictions, trade rules or more general red-tape regulation that affect the possibility to open and run new businesses.[15] Also—and this is again especially true for formerly centrally planned economies—poorly planned or implemented privatisation processes have led to the entrenchment of legal monopolies instead

---

[14]The literature that explores the link between economic development and the optimal design of competition policy refers in some cases to the notion of *emerging* economies, in others to that of *developing* or *industrialised* economies. We believe that adopting one terminology or another makes little difference, so we will use the different terms interchangeably and we will focus on the description of the economic, political and cultural characteristics that we believe should be taken into consideration when developing the optimal competition policy design.

[15]Industrial policy, defined as the set of policies aimed at encouraging the development and growth of part of or the entire manufacturing sector, as well as other sectors of a country's economy, may also play a role in distorting competition and entry into the market. For a recent review on industrial policy and its rationale see Warwick (2013).

of open and contestable markets, contributing to the creation of artificial barriers to entry by granting dominant players exclusive access to essential inputs.

The existence of regulatory barriers to entry in many developing jurisdictions, especially those emerging from a past of central planning, is combined with a still pervasive role of the state in the economy. The government still retains significant shares in different economic sectors, which tends to alter the playing field especially when inappropriate regulation provides privileges to state-owned companies, for example through exemptions from anti-trust laws enforcement.[16] Even when the legislation does not explicitly foresee exemptions for state-owned companies, political constraints may exist that prevent competition authorities to intervene against companies where governments' stakes are high.

Economic barriers relate to two separate aspects: first, the existence of poor framework conditions that limit the potential for entry and competition (e.g. poor infrastructure, underdeveloped financial markets, geographic barriers);[17] second, the conduct adopted by dominant companies, which actively pursue strategies to foreclose entry of competitors and take advantage of weak enforcement of competition legislation.

The presence of high economic and regulatory barriers to entry and counterproductive government regulation, from the welfare point of view, especially towards SOEs, has important implications for the optimal design of competition policy. Using the classification previously introduced in this paper, we believe that the features of the competition policy regime that should be affected are the independence and accountability of competition authorities; the scope of their enforcement power, the interpretation of substantive rules and the priority setting.

In particular, three main considerations seem to apply. First, in terms of *institutional set-up*, the significant role of the government in the economy and of possibly inappropriate regulation (especially towards SOEs) has important implications. In order to build trust with investors and the business community, competition agencies should not be perceived as favouring state-owned businesses, implying that rules should be defined to maximise transparency and reduce discretion. Transparency of the decisions and of the decision-making process (e.g. by means of publicly available guidelines that define in detail how the competition agency operates, assesses cases, and sets fines), as well as the choice of a legal standard that maximises certainty (even at the cost of a more reasonable effects-based approach) are paramount in ensuring trust in the private sector and also ensuring appropriate investment levels in sectors where the state retains an important role. We will return on this aspect later in this section.

---

[16]In the words of Gal and Fox (2015), state and state-complicit restraints are among the major impediment to competition, which "clog the pathways for initiative on the merits, sometimes almost fully, while reciprocally raising prices". Because of this, the authors emphasize that the law should cover state-owned enterprises and state officials who facilitate illegal cartels or bidding rings by conduct outside the course of their duties.

[17]A detailed description of the economic features that characterise emerging economies and shape competition policy effectiveness and design can be found in Gal and Fox (2015).

Second, in the presence of significant legal barriers to entry, the definition of the *scope of enforcement power* should attribute significant advocacy powers to competition authorities, imposing on policymakers the obligation to fully motivate their decisions when they diverge from the recommendations provided by the competition authority. This would imply that any legislation or regulation potentially affecting competition is scrutinised by competition authorities, whose expert opinion has to be taken into consideration by legislators. Similarly, when it comes to *setting its priorities*, competition authorities may choose to prioritise advocacy over enforcement, or at least the relevance of advocacy should not be underestimated. In countries where well-functioning markets are yet to be formed and significant barriers exist, market creation becomes a more important objective than the protection of competition.[18] Advocacy, both private and public, serves the function of promoting reforms that eliminate or reduce barriers to entry and operations, and creates the appropriate "demand" conditions for more open and contestable markets, by showing the benefits of higher competition for consumers.

Finally, still in terms of *scope of enforcement power* and *priority setting*, the existence of significant economic and regulatory barriers to entry should arguably lead to the prioritisation of abuses of dominance cases,[19] especially those where the potential for foreclosure is greater, precisely because tackling barriers to entry should

---

[18]This conclusion is widely supported in literature. Budzinky and Beigi (2013), "Competition Policy Agendas for Industrialising Countries", *Ilmenau Economics Discussion Papers, No. 81,* underline that while in advanced industrialised countries, sustainable competitive markets exist and "just" need to be preserved or optimised (promoting competition), in industrialising or developing countries, the objective should be to establish working and accepted competitive markets (generating competition). In this context advocacy is identified as the most suitable tool in the hands of competition authorities to help build the market economy by informing the Government's economic policies.

[19]The case for prioritising abuse of dominance cases in the presence of significant barriers to entry does not apply only to exclusionary conduct. Indeed, as discussed in Motta and de Streel (2006), "Excessive Pricing and Price Squeeze under EU Law", in *Ehlermann and Atanasiu (eds), European Competition Law Annual 2003: What is an Abuse of a Dominant Position?, Hart, 91–125*, the authors argue that under two main conditions the prosecution of excessive (exploitative) practices makes sense and the benefits may outweigh the costs of an otherwise dangerous antitrust instrument. The first necessary (but not sufficient) condition is the presence of high and non-transitory barriers to entry. In such cases, it is extremely unlikely that market forces would be able to challenge the dominant firm and that the abusive practices would be self-correcting. The second necessary condition is dynamic and it is that the monopolistic position should be due to current or past exclusive or special rights. In such cases, the traditional argument that monopoly prices should be accepted, to generate incentives to invest, is weaker and non-competitive prices may in principle be tackled with antitrust enforcement, especially in the absence of other effective instruments.

be considered the priority for the competition law regime.[20,21] This does not imply that cartels should be considered less relevant, given the impact they have on consumers, especially in developing jurisdictions where basic goods that represent high proportion of the consumption basket of poorer segments of the population are usually the object of price-fixing arrangements. However, it does imply that when market creation is considered a priority, given the development status of a country, merger control should not absorb significant energies by competition authorities, and legal standards and presumptions should be set in such a way that mergers, which in general contribute to the natural dynamic process of market creation, should be prohibited only in very specific cases (for example when they consolidate existing dominant positions that have been acquired to privileged access to essential inputs).[22]

### 3.1.2 Sectoral Composition of Output/Domestic Consumption

A second relevant feature to look at is the sectoral composition of the gross domestic product and of domestic consumption. For many developing jurisdictions it is typical to observe specific patterns, where, for example, agriculture and food-processing industry still represents a high share in domestic value added, and food products represent a major share in the average consumption basket. The specific sectoral composition of output/consumptions bears direct implications on the

[20]An interesting assessment of the importance of prosecuting abuse of dominance, as a priority, can be found in Gal and Fox (2015). In their view, the "availability of the abuse of dominance prohibition is one of the most important weapons in the antitrust arsenal of developing countries to open up closed markets and thus help make markets work where they have never worked before; where business has been tied up in privilege and cronyism and dominant firms have blocked paths [. . .]." The presence of barriers to entry, especially linked to the legacy of centrally planned economies or more generally to the presence of formerly legalised monopolies, justifies an approach where targeting potentially foreclosing strategies by incumbents becomes a strategic priority for antitrust enforcement.

[21]The case for prioritising abuse of dominance cases in the presence of significant barriers to entry does not apply only to exclusionary conducts. Indeed, as discussed in Motta and de Streel (2006). The authors argue that under two main conditions the prosecution of excessive (exploitative) practices makes sense and the benefits may outweigh the costs of an otherwise dangerous antitrust instrument. The first necessary (but not sufficient) condition is the presence of high and non-transitory barriers to entry. In such a case, it is extremely unlikely that market forces would be able to challenge the dominant firm and that the abusive practices would be self-correcting. The second necessary condition is dynamic—that the monopolistic position should be due to current or past exclusive or special rights. In this case, the traditional argument that monopoly prices should be accepted, in order to generate incentives to invest, is weaker and non-competitive prices may in principle be tackled with antitrust enforcement, especially in the absence of other effective instruments.

[22]An interesting discussion about the relevance of merger control in developing jurisdiction can be found in Begovic (2017). In the paper, the author provides convincing arguments explaining why in the early transition towards market economies merger control should not represent an enforcement priority and notification thresholds should be set relatively high.

implementation of competition law, in regards to the way competition authorities may *set their priorities*. First of all, competition agencies should focus their implementation efforts on sectors that have a large share in the domestic economy and represent a significant portion of domestic consumption, or that have a significant weight in the production structure.[23] This is important not only because focusing on relevant sectors will have the largest effect on the economy's performance (in terms of efficiency and productivity gains), but also because it will help the competition authority to build its reputation as an agency that focuses on addressing issues that matter the most to the citizens and consumers. Second, competition agencies, whose financial and human resources are generally scarce, should specialise in terms of sectoral knowledge in those areas that also appear to be most relevant for the national economy.

### 3.1.3 Informal Economy

Much of the trade in developing countries is conducted by means of the informal sector, where traders are unrestrained by legal obligations such as registration and licensing requirements, as well as health and safety policies, taxation and labour laws. Informality poses challenges to the implementation of a sound competition policy, because of the competition that the informal sector exerts on the formal one. Indeed, the prevalence of informality in markets renders it difficult to assess the existence and impact of anti-competitive conducts, the size of the relevant market, the levels of concentration, the market shares attributable to incumbent players, and the extent to which firms hold dominant positions therein. In essence, the very basic tools of competition law are difficult to implement when informality is prevalent, and this should be carefully considered in the enforcement of all aspects of competition law.[24]

## *3.2 Institutional Characteristics*

Besides the economic characteristics of developing jurisdictions, institutional and governance features have significant impact on the way competition policy works and the way it should be designed. It is clear that competition policy does not operate in isolation, and it is unlikely to work effectively if overall institutions do not function properly. The effectiveness of the courts system is particularly relevant,

---

[23]As suggested by Evenett (2015), one needs to be careful to potential endogeneity issues. For example, the reason why a sector may not be particularly relevant for an economy may have to do precisely with the lack of competition and high barriers to entry.

[24]For a discussion about the impact of informality on the enforcement of competition law, see du Plessis et al. (2011).

as courts have the authority to review agency decisions (in administrative systems) and make both first and second instance decisions (in prosecutorial systems). This implies that the degree of independence and effectiveness of the judiciary plays a key role in ensuring the effective enforcement of competition law. The role of state/governments also has significant implications on competition law enforcement, both directly, through limitations and exemptions often granted to state-owned enterprises, but also (what matters most here) through indirect government interference in the competition authority's decision making, which limits their *de facto* independence.

A number of developing jurisdictions, in particular those that emerge from central planning, are characterised by weak rule of law, widespread corruption and economic structures, where resource allocation is not always driven by market mechanisms. On the contrary, resources are often allocated by governments in non-transparent ways to connected business groups and oligarchs.[25] Weak rule of law manifests itself through an incompetent, ineffective and non-independent judiciary, as well as through regulatory capture by vested interests that influence the activities and priorities of government bodies and *de jure* independent agencies. Weak rule of law is compounded by corruption, which is usually indicated as one the main business obstacles in internationally accredited surveys.

Institutional quality does not have only to do with corruption and vested interests. Even in countries where these phenomena are perceived to be less pervasive, the institutions that support the market require time to set up and start working effectively. This is particularly true for competition agencies, which generally operate with scarce financial and human resources, struggling to recruit people with adequate skills due to low salaries (lower than other civil service jobs) and a low reputation of the agency, at least initially.[26]

Rather than being regarded with pessimism and leading to far-reaching negative conclusions about the desirability of competition policy in the first place, all these

---

[25]The range of relevant institutional characteristics of developing jurisdictions is surveyed in Gal and Fox (2015) who describe the phenomenon of "missing or deficient institutions", which are taken for granted in the industrialized world. The authors stress the role that financial institutions, economic laws and a functioning court system play in guaranteeing the functioning of market economies. While financial institutions provide opportunities for the credit necessary for entering the market, the enforcement of contracts and property rights by the courts enables market players to engage in long-term trading. In the survey, another example of deficient institutions focuses on the inefficiency of the executive branch, which is a feature in many developing jurisdictions.

[26]Several papers insist on this argument. Among others, du Plessis et al. (2011) stress how, even assuming that a developing country could fund the drafting of a suitable competition law policy, its adoption would be rendered useless without properly trained personnel to enforce the legislation in question. The authors rightly remark that many developing jurisdictions often suffer from a severe shortage of trained professionals, especially economists (with quantitative skills) that are qualified to assess the complex competition law concepts. Moreover, there is a lack of available training courses and seminars and scarce funding available to facilitate such training. To the extent that competition law policies are misapplied owing to a failure to understand the underlying concepts, the authors conclude, the adoption of the legislation would be without benefit, and could in fact be detrimental to the economy.

aspects need to be properly acknowledged in the design and implementation of competition law. In particular, we believe that the institutional characteristics of developing jurisdictions should lead to several policy design choices.

The first consideration refers to the *institutional set-up* and the *independence/accountability* of competition authorities. As discussed in Sect. 2 of the paper, lack of judicial independence points to the choice of an administrative model where, in order to protect as much as possible the competition agency from the undue interference of the government and of private interests, maximum independence should be granted by the legislation to the competition authority, which should not formally be part of the government and should not receive any instruction from the government itself. Having a *de jure* independent authority does not ensure an impartial enforcement of competition law—after all, competition authorities can be expected to reflect the positive and negative aspects of the jurisdictions in which they operate. For this reason, once again, it is fundamental that competition agencies operate with full transparency and that their discretion is limited. Transparency concretely means that all decisions should be made available to the public, that the agency should publish annual reports that fully explain its activities and the costs of its activities, as well as its strategy and priorities going forward, be open to scrutiny by third parties and stakeholders, including international organisations. Transparency also means that public and comprehensive secondary legislation should be available, especially in the form of guidelines that clearly describe the way the competition agency operates, including how it assesses cases, conducts investigations, and set fines.

Limiting the discretion of competition agencies is seen as of paramount importance in the context of a weak institutional environment. This limits the possibility of capture of competition agencies ensuring consistency and credibility of its decision making. Simplicity and predictability should be favoured, even if economic theory tells us that a more complex and case-by-case approach is expected to deliver the maximum welfare in normal conditions. In essence, as already highlighted, simplicity and predictability amount to the choice of a per se standard, whereby conducts are identified by clear and well-defined parameters and are allowed or prohibited depending on their characteristics, and not on a case-by-case effects based analysis.

The issue of discretion and transparency becomes more controversial in relation to the investigative power attributed to the competition agency. It may be argued that in a context of potential capture of the agency by the government or vested interests, the faculty to conduct unannounced inspections into business premises (dawn raids) should be limited, as the instrument could be abused, for example, to damage companies in favour of government clientele. This risk, the argument goes, cannot be mitigated by a strict authorisation process under the control of the judiciary, given that the judiciary in weak institutional environment is also subject to capture by vested interests. While we think that these arguments have some merits and we understand the choice adopted by certain competition agencies (e.g. Georgia), where the existence of cartels can only be proved by means of indirect economic evidence, we do not think that this should be the choice taken by developing jurisdictions. As the history of Western Europe and US has proven, the best way to tackle hard-core cartels, is through intrusive investigative techniques, coupled with stiff fines and effective leniency programmes. On the other hand, proving the existence of cartels through indirect economic evidence is an extremely complicated exercise, which requires deep expertise and extremely good data –precisely what is missing in developing jurisdictions. When good data and sophisticated modelling is not available, the analysis usually turns out to be poor, which in turn undermines the credibility of competition authorities. Overall then, the policy rule that we suggest is to attribute clearly defined investigative powers (in terms of conditions under which inspections can be conducted) to the competition authority, which should ensure its accountability through thorough reporting of its activities and of its decisions.

In regard to the sanction policy, a nuanced approach is advisable. High sanctions are necessary for fighting hard-core cartels. They are also needed to increase the effectiveness of a leniency programme, as the advantage of revealing the existence of a cartel is strictly related to the sanction that a cartelist may expect to pay. However, for other potential infringements, at least in an initial phase of operation, a competition authority may prefer to impose less severe sanctions. This is especially appropriate if the enforcement of the antitrust prohibitions is guided by simplified rules that aim to limit the discretionary power of the enforcer and increase the predictability of the interpretation of the law. Indeed, applying simple rules that are largely based on presumptions has the advantage of limiting the risk of the enforcement being distorted by inappropriate interests, but at the same time increases the possibility that some benign behaviours are prohibited and that harmful ones escape prohibition. In other words, simple rules may be over-inclusive, as they may prevent conduct that is competitive, or under-inclusive, as they may allow anti-competitive conduct. In these cases sanctions need to be lower in order to preserve the optimality of the enforcement system.[27]

As mentioned, the effectiveness and independence of the court system is crucial in ensuring the sound implementation of competition policy. In this respect, while the issue of court independence is a complex one, which cannot simply be addressed through competition law, the creation of highly specialised review courts is expected improve the quality of the judicial review, while keeping low the risk of capture by vested political and economic interests.

## 3.3 *Cultural Characteristics*

Along with economic and institutional characteristics, cultural aspects may have a profound influence on the effectiveness of competition policy and should be taken into consideration when designing and implementing competition law. In developing jurisdictions the main relevant feature is the lack of a competition culture.

[27]This is proven in Buccirossi (2010).

Especially in former centrally planned economies, competition is still not fully appreciated as a "positive" mechanism that is capable of favouring an efficient allocation of resources, promoting investment in better products and services, and ultimately delivering more and better jobs. As described extensively in literature,[28] in developing jurisdictions it is difficult to find absolute belief in decentralised economic power, and rules cannot work if the mind-set of a majority does not value the rules and their underlying mentality. In essence, a certain spirit of competition is a precondition for a working, sustainable and accepted competitive market economy. In many cases, competition is perceived with diffidence, as a negative force that may weaken societies by pitting people against each other, at the expense of a more egalitarian and cooperative growth model. Most importantly, the idea that the free market forces, combined with serious ex-post prosecution of unfair and abusive practices, can protect consumers from excessive prices is still difficult to accept. In many cases, the government is still perceived as the sole institution capable of protecting the poor through ex-ante regulation and price control. However, this type of intervention often leads to de facto government promoted cartels, which are unlikely to improve consumer welfare, as argued by competition sceptics.

How should this negative cultural bias against competition be reflected in the design and implementation of competition policy?

A natural response, in relation to the *priority setting strategies* of competition authorities, lies again in advocacy, focused on the private sector, in this context. Competition authorities should invest in educating the public, in particular the consumers and the media, of the benefits of competition. Pointing to the experience of other countries, telling concrete stories of how competition leads to more and better choices for consumers, competition authorities can contribute to the gradual creation of appropriate demand conditions for more competition and less economic control.[29]

A second aspect to stress is that competition authorities need to implement the right strategy to rapidly build their reputation. This implies to select relevant and easy cases, quick wins that can contribute to affirming the role of the competition agency as an institution that is sided with consumers and with the most dynamic and innovative firms in the country. The strategy should involve building alliances with societal players that are receptive to the message, such as (foreign) investors, nascent consumer associations and international organisations. A competition culture cannot be created overnight, but the experience of several countries confirms that much can be achieved by an active and smart competition agency. In regards to the scope of enforcement power, the need for the competition authority to quickly build a

---

[28]See, in particular, Budzinky and Beigi (2013).

[29]Besides the fundamental role of competition advocacy, competition authorities should actively engage in providing guidance to businesses, about how to comply with competition norms. Businesses need guidance whenever a country lacks the appropriate competition culture. As Budzinky and Beigi (2013) notice, lacking spirit of competition implies that a considerable part of the competitors in the market are insecure or ignorant about how to behave in competition and compete on the merits.

reputation of "being on the side of consumers" may suggest attributing to competition authorities functions that go beyond core antitrust and merger control, and encompass consumer protection. This is usually a controversial argument, given that lack of resources and adequate skills, combined with multiplicity of functions, may lead the competition authority to focus excessively on "easy" consumer protection cases that have immediate media and political visibility. This in turn would prevent the build-up of credible skills to prosecute hard-core antitrust infringements. We believe there is merit in this critique, but overall we lean towards the combination of antitrust and consumer protection responsibilities, especially in the early stages of competition law enforcement where pro-competition culture is very weak. This is not necessarily the case of Western Balkan countries, as we will see in the next section.

## 4 Emerging Economies and the Shape of Competition Policy

We now turn to the analysis of the Western Balkan economies, in order to confirm the relevance of the analysis conducted so far and to derive policy implications in terms of competition law institutions and enforcement. In the previous section we defined multiple characteristics that should be taken into consideration when designing and enforcing competition laws. We will now analyse the Western Balkan economies through these lenses. Naturally, a choice has to be made as to which variables one needs to look at, with no ambition to be exhaustive. Our assessment will mainly look at variables and data collected by international organisations such as the World Bank, the IMF and the EBRD. Furthermore, a choice of comparators needs to be made in order to quantify the gap between Western Balkan countries and both peer and more advanced jurisdictions (in terms of economic development). In our analysis, we would normally include as comparators Croatia and Slovenia, both former Yugoslav countries falling outside of the Western Balkan group; Bulgaria, Romania and the Czech Republic, central and south-eastern European countries that have completed the EU accession process; and the more advanced jurisdictions of Germany, Sweden and the US. These reference points should give us a clear picture of the positioning of the Western Balkan countries vis-à-vis countries that are at least in principle at different stages of the transition process towards well-functioning market economies. However, the comparators may differ according to the variable used and the availability of data, which often acts as a constraint to the analysis.

## 4.1 *Economic Characteristics*

In the previous section we identified several economic characteristics as essential to shaping competition law design and implementations. In particular, we focused on barriers to entry and the role of the state, the sectoral composition of the output, and the level of informality. We now present some data to depict the Western Balkan economies.

### 4.1.1 Barriers to Entry, Economic Activity and the Role of the State

As discussed, there are several dimensions that contribute to create barriers to entry and economic activity. We choose here to focus on five indicators that we consider relevant. First, we use the World Bank's Doing Business survey and provide the overall rank of the "ease of doing business" in the Western Balkan countries and the selected comparators. The overall ease of doing business rank captures several dimensions, including regulatory barriers to start (and close) a business, as well as barriers linked to access to electricity, dealing with construction permits, trading across borders, etc.[30] We then look at two specific economic (non-regulatory) barriers to entry and economic activity, namely the quality of the overall logistics infrastructure and the breadth of financial banking markets, as a proxy for access to finance. We measure the former using the World Bank's Logistic Performance Index,[31] a survey based measure of the quality of the overall logistic system in a country, while for the latter we use a simple measure of private credit (by banks) to the GDP, acknowledging the fact that this may be a crude measure of access to finance, especially for more advanced jurisdictions that have access to deeper financial and capital markets.[32] Also, in order to measure the extent to which barriers to entry may be caused by conducts pursued by incumbent dominant operators, we use the World Economic Forum GCI (Global Competitiveness Index) of the

[30]For a description of the data and the methodology used by the WB Doing Business indicators, see http://www.doingbusiness.org/methodology

[31]For a description of the underlying variables and methodology used to measure the quality of logistics, please see http://lpi.worldbank.org/. The LPI is based on a worldwide survey of operators on the ground (global freight forwarders and express carriers), providing feedback on the logistics "friendliness" of the countries in which they operate and those with which they trade. They combine in-depth knowledge of the countries in which they operate with informed qualitative assessments of other countries where they trade and experience of global logistics environment. Feedback from operators is supplemented with quantitative data on the performance of key components of the logistics chain in the country of work." The index is measured on a 1–5 scale, where higher numbers correspond to perceived better quality of performance in logistics. Data on Kosovo is missing.

[32]Data on private sector credit to GDP come from the World Bank's World Development Indicators.

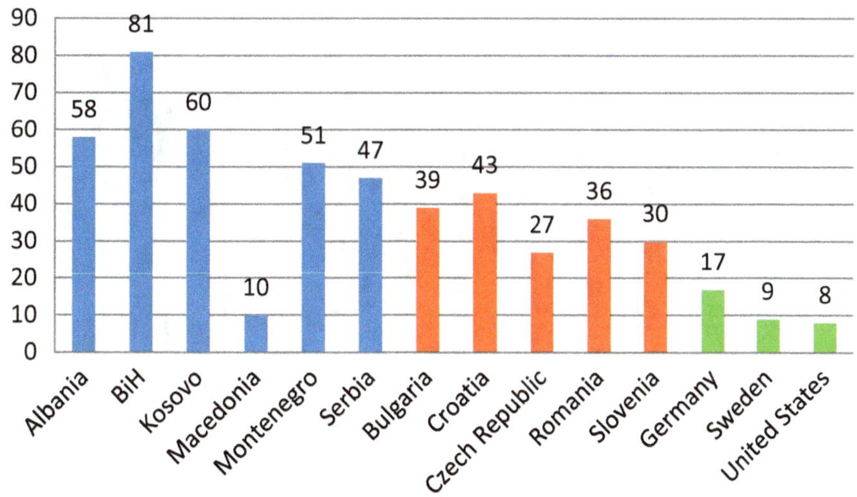


**Fig. 1** The World Bank's Doing Business overall rank. Source: The World Bank's Doing Business report (2016–2017)

perceived "extent of market dominance".[33] Finally, our descriptive section emphasised the role of the state in the economy, as a key economic as well as an institutional factor that should be taken into consideration. In this respect, while a comprehensive measure of state presence in the economy is missing, we look at the quality of government regulation overall, by using the World Bank's Worldwide Governance Indicators of "regulatory quality", which in principle should capture perceptions of the government's ability to formulate and implement sound policies and regulations that permit and promote private sector development. This indicator notably includes, among other aspects, the burden of government regulation, the scope of state subsidies and administered prices.

The graphs presented Figs. 1, 2, 3, 4, and 5 provide, even taking account all the limitations associated with the data,[34] an overall consistent picture. Western Balkan countries, with the notable exception of Macedonia (especially due to lower taxes and low administrative barriers to start a business), rank below EU countries in central and south-eastern Europe in terms of ease of doing business, which is a sign of higher barriers to entry and economic activity. As expected, the gap separating them form more advanced jurisdiction is very big, which clearly suggests that if we

[33]Naturally, dominance is only a necessary but not sufficient condition for the existence of abusive foreclosing conduct. As such, the data provided can only indicate whether existing conditions can be conducive to potential anticompetitive entry-deterrent strategies by incumbent dominant companies. WEF data on Kosovo is missing.

[34]There is an intense debate over the validity of Doing Business data, which led to a thorough review initiated by the President of the World Bank in 2012. For a review of the criticisms addressed to the Doing Business methodology see http://www.doingbusiness.org/~/media/WBG/DoingBusiness/Documents/Methodology/Open-Letter-Review-of-the-Arguments-on-DB.pdf?la=en. Similarly, WEF Global Competitiveness Index has been criticised essentially for being based solely on market participant's perceptions, which in turn can be affected and distorted by cultural bias which would undermine the credibility of the proposed rankings.

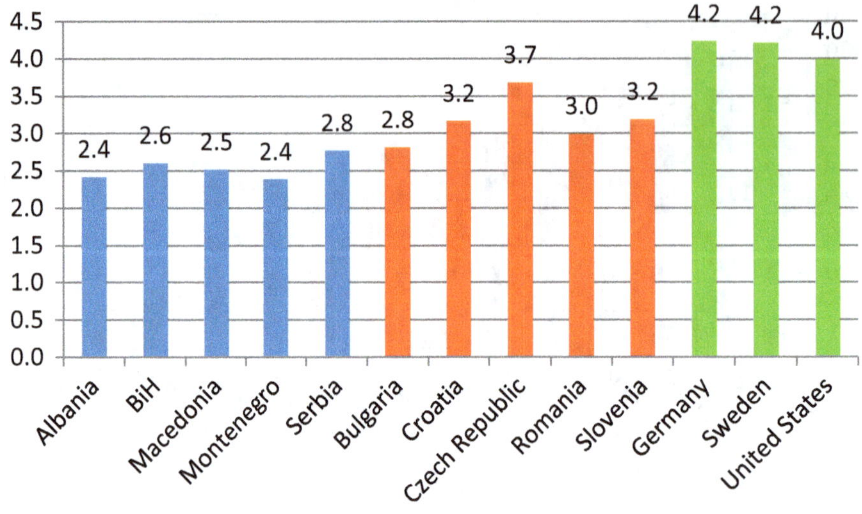


**Fig. 2** The World Bank's Logistics Performance Indicator (LPI). Overall (1 = low to 5 = high). Source: The World Bank's LPI (2016)

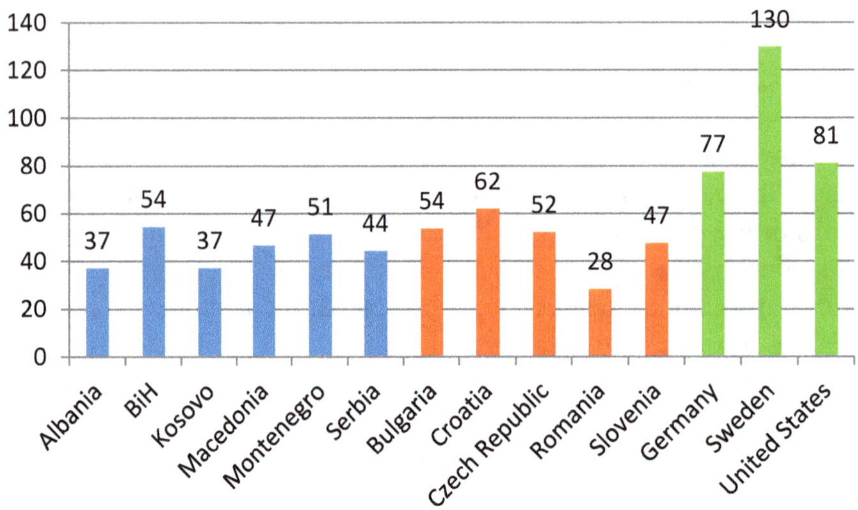


**Fig. 3** Private sector credit (by banks) over the GDP. Source: The World Bank's World Development Indicators (2016)

believe in the theoretical considerations presented in Sect. 3, the design of competition law and its enforcement should take these aspects into consideration, implying a degree of divergence from what is commonly considered "best practice". The gap is confirmed when we look at other aspects measuring overall barriers to entry, including the quality of logistics and level of development of the financial (banking) markets, however the picture is less univocal for these. In particular, while there is a clear infrastructural gap in terms of infrastructure between the Western Balkan countries and developed countries, the gap compared to central and south-eastern EU countries is less pronounced, with the exception of the Czech Republic, for logistics, and Croatia, for access to finance. In terms of access to finance, there is significant variability within the group of Western Balkan economies, with Albania

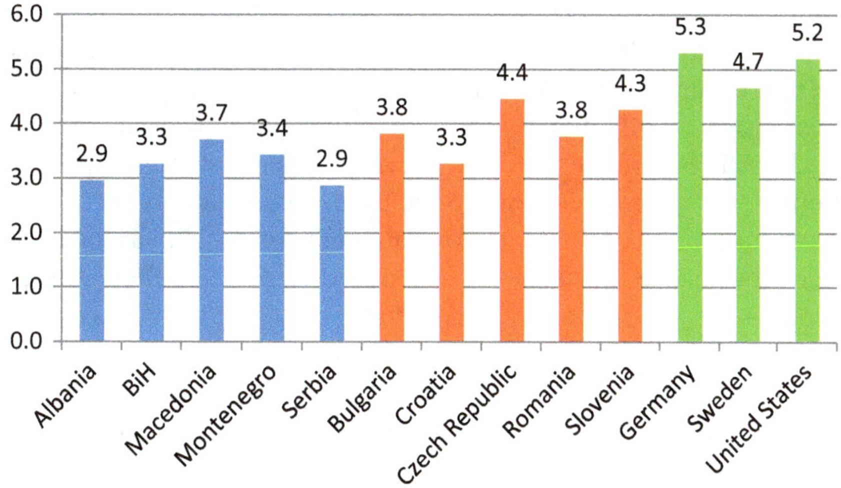


**Fig. 4** WEF indicator of extent of market dominance (The indicator measures the perception of business executives of the extent of market dominance in a given country. The indicator is on a scale of 1–7, with 1 denoting corporate activity characterised by "dominance of a few business groups" and 7 denoting corporate activity "spread among many firms". For a description of the methodology, see the Global Competitiveness Report 2016–2017, Chapter 1.3. https://www.weforum.org/reports/the-global-competitiveness-report-2016-2017-1) (1–7 = best). Source: World Economic Forum (2017), Global Competitiveness Report

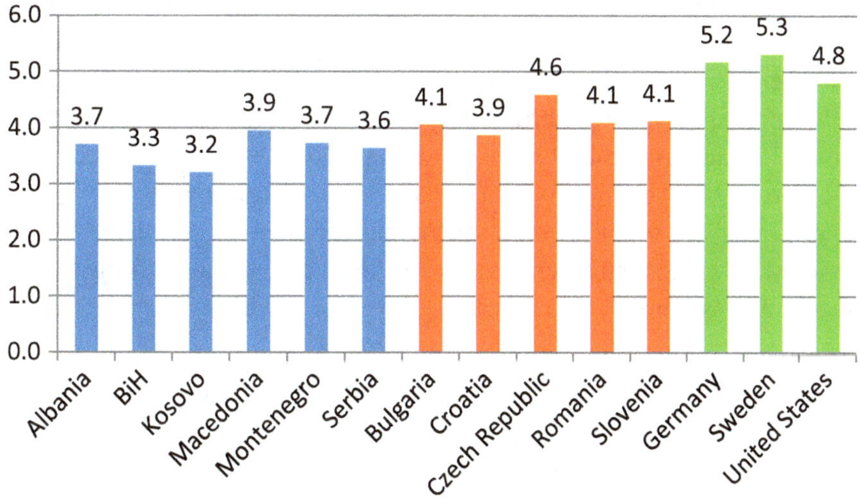


**Fig. 5** Worldwide Governance Indicators—Regulatory quality (normalised 1–6) (The Worldwide Governance Indicators, developed by the World Bank, aggregate a multiplicity of sources and are presented on a −2.5 to +2.5 scale. Here, they are presented on a 1–6 normalised scale to ease reading. For a description of the methodology see: http://info.worldbank.org/governance/wgi/#home). Source: The World Bank (2016), Worldwide Governance Indicators

and Kosovo showing significantly lower private sector to the GDP ratios than other countries in the Region.

Figure 4 further contributes to the understanding of economic barriers in the market, this time linked to the existence of dominant positions in the market, which may lead to potential abuses and foreclosure of competitors and potential entrants.

Again, while the graph suggests the existence of heterogeneity among Western Balkan countries, with Serbia ranking below its peers and Macedonia closer to EU countries such Romania and Bulgaria, on average, the intensity of the perceived dominance is significantly higher in the Western Balkans than in EU members in central and south-eastern Europe, and the gap appears stronger when advanced jurisdictions in Europe and with the US are used as comparators.

The final graph in Fig. 5 shows the overall regulatory quality as measured by the Worldwide Governance Indicators, which, as mentioned, captures aspects of state intervention in the economy and the overall quality of regulations. The graph confirms the analysis so far, with a significant gap between Western Balkans and both EU members in central and south-eastern Europe, (particular large in the cases of Kosovo and Bosnia and Herzegovina), and with the more developed countries included in our sample.

### 4.1.2 Sectoral Composition of Output

In terms of the sectoral composition of the output, aggregate data is reported in Fig. 6. We included a simple repartition of economic activity across three categories: industry, agriculture, and services. Naturally, a more disaggregated analysis would provide more insight, but even at this level, at least two observations can be made. First, compared to more advanced jurisdictions, agriculture still plays a significant role in Western Balkan countries, accounting between 5% and 20% of the GDP. Second, there is significant heterogeneity within the analysed group of countries, with economies such as those of Montenegro and Kosovo largely based on services, while in others, such as Serbia, industry features more prominently. In line with what was discussed in the previous section, the conclusion we should make by looking at this data is that antitrust enforcement should be prioritised accordingly, and appropriate sector assessment skills should be developed within competition agencies,

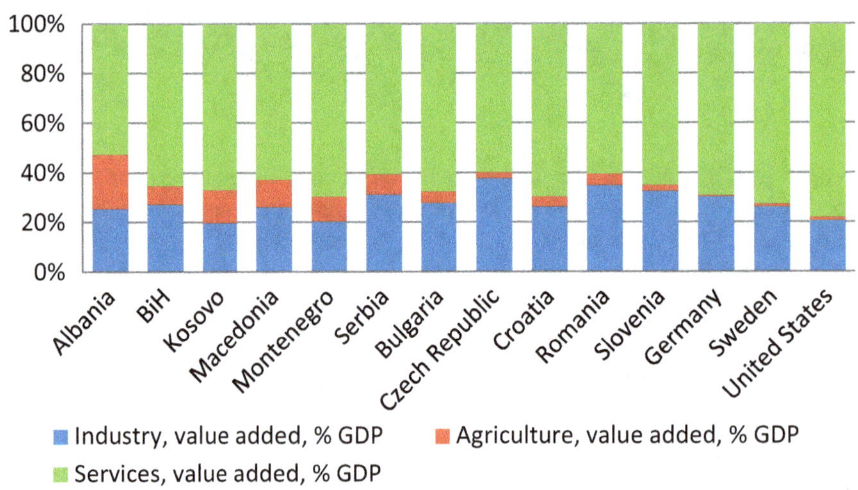


**Fig. 6** Sectoral composition of output. Source: The World Bank (2016), Worldwide Governance Indicators

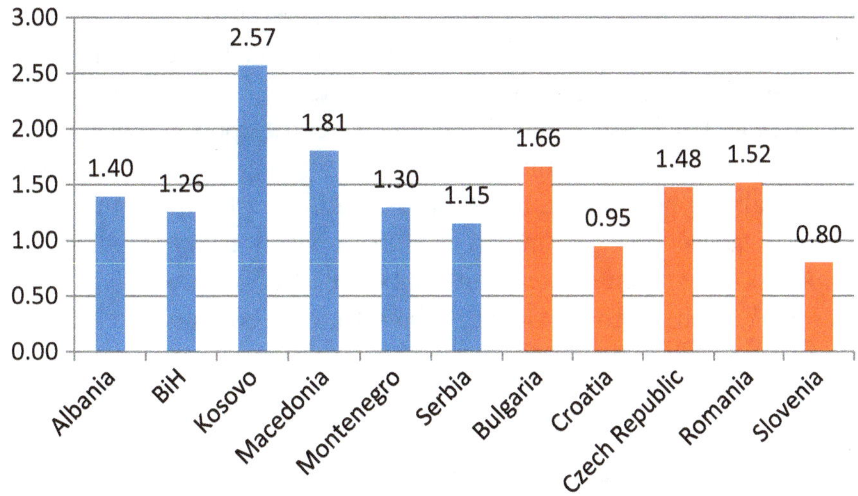


**Fig. 7** (Perceived) Informality as an obstacle to doing business (1–4). Source: BEEPS data, survey prepared by EBRD and the World Bank (2017)

bearing in mind the discussed conceptual caveats, namely the endogeneity of sector composition to competition barriers.

### 4.1.3 Informal Economy

Informality is certainly a pervasive phenomenon in all developing jurisdictions, and Western Balkan countries are no exception. For obvious reasons, measuring informality is a difficult task, and while several attempts have been made to get a sense of the size of the shadow economy, a comprehensive database that includes all the countries explored in this paper is not available. We rely on different data sources to provide an overall assessment of the phenomenon, namely: the BEEPS database assembled by the EBRD and the World Bank, which surveys domestic firms inquiring to what extent informality is perceived as an obstacle to doing business, on a scale from 1 to 4; the database provided by Schneider (2007), which contains a measure of the share of the informal sector in the overall economy and includes more advanced jurisdictions although the data is not up to date; and the ILO dataset, which contains only data for a small subset of the countries we analysed.[35]

Several conclusions could be derived by analysis of these data sources: first, the level of informality in the Western Balkan countries is significantly higher than in more advanced jurisdictions. Broadly speaking, according to Schneider (2007), there is an average difference of 20 percentage points in the share of the informal economy between countries such as the UK and Germany and countries in the Western Balkan region. Second, there is heterogeneity in terms of informality both within the group of Western Balkan countries and when looking at central and south-eastern-eastern European countries currently members of the EU, as reported in Fig. 7 from the

[35]We provide in the paper only some summary reflections. The data used is available from the authors on request.

BEEPS database. For Kosovo, Macedonia, and to a lesser extent Albania, informality appears to be a stronger obstacle to business than in Bosnia and Herzegovina, Serbia, and Montenegro. In turn, informality appears to be more of a constraint in EU countries, such as Bulgaria, Romania, and the Czech Republic, with a much more positive perception in EU countries from the former Yugoslavia (Croatia and Slovenia). Finally, a note of caution should be attached to this data, as confirmed by the ILO database: the gap in informality between countries like Serbia and Albania appears to be much greater than what the BEEPS data suggests, as measured by the estimated share of employment in the informal economy.

### 4.2 *Institutional Characteristics*

We now turn to the quality of institutions in the Western Balkan countries. Several aspects and indicators could naturally be used to provide an assessment of the gaps existing between Western Balkans and the chosen comparators. We focus on three indicators, which in our view can provide an overall understanding of the institutional environment, but can also shed light on two specific aspects, namely the quality of the judiciary and its perceived degree of independence, and the effectiveness of corruption control. As indicated in Figs. 8, 9, and 10, for this purpose we use three indicators: first, the Worldwide Governance Indicators measuring the "overall rule of law"; second, the World Economic Forum GCI index of perceived "judicial

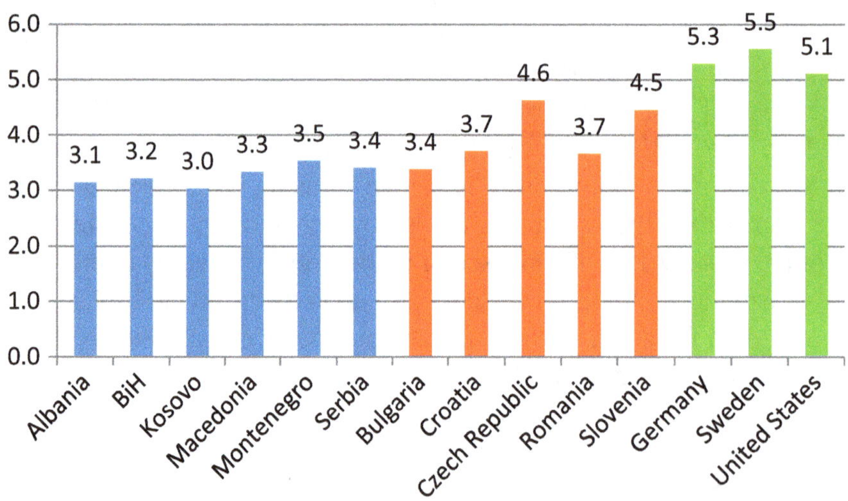


**Fig. 8** Worldwide Governance Indicators—Rule of Law (normalised 1–6) (The Rule of Law indicator "captures perceptions of the extent to which agents have confidence in and abide by the rules of society, and in particular the quality of contract enforcement, property rights, the police, and the courts, as well as the likelihood of crime and violence." As defined above, the scale of the original data is normalised here to ease reading of the graph. The list of sources and variables used by the World Bank to construct the index can be found at: http://info.worldbank.org/governance/wgi/#home). Source: The World Bank (2016), Worldwide Governance Indicators

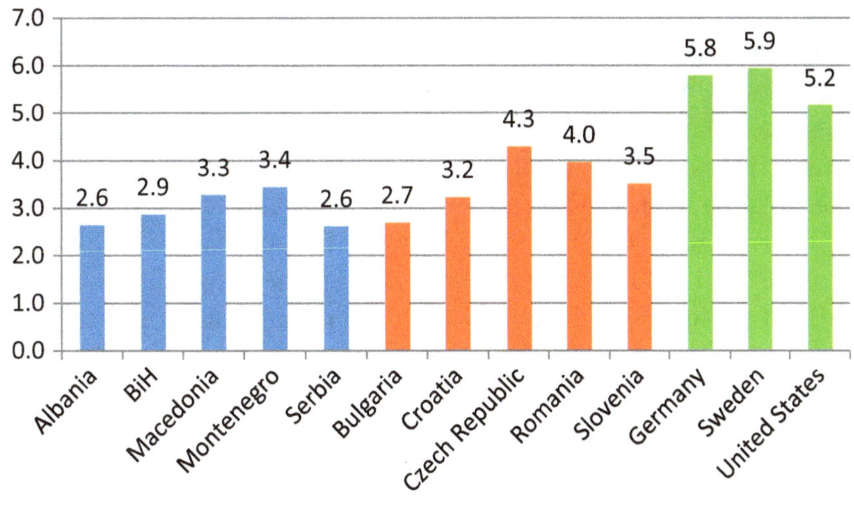


**Fig. 9** Perceived judicial independence (1 to 7 = best). Source: World Economic Forum (2017), Global Competitiveness Indicators. Kosovo missing

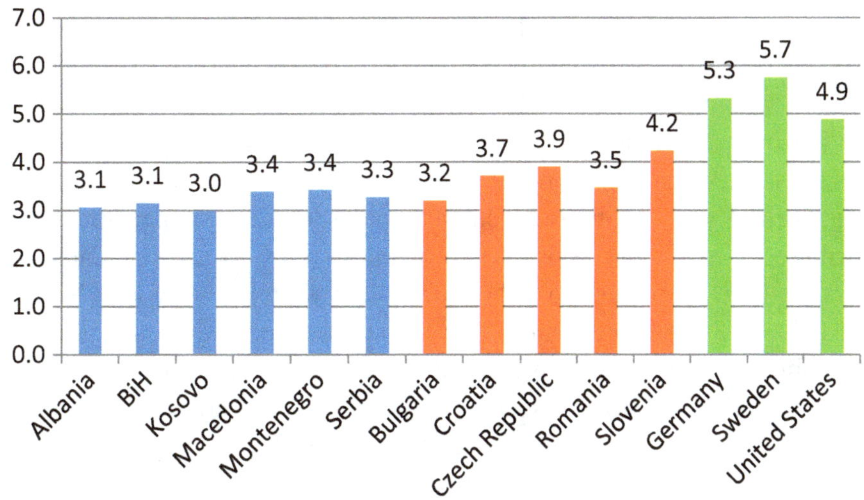


**Fig. 10** Worldwide Governance Indicators—Control of corruption (normalised 1–6) (The Control of Corruption indicator captures "perceptions of the extent to which public power is exercised for private gain, including both petty and grand forms of corruption, as well as 'capture' of the state by elites and private interests". As defined above, the scale of the original data is normalised here to ease reading of the graph. The list of sources and variables used by the World Bank to construct the index can be found at: http://info.worldbank.org/governance/wgi/#home). Source: The World Bank (2016), Worldwide Governance Indicators

independence"; and finally, the Worldwide Governance Indicators of corruption pervasiveness.

The overall picture is consistent with the one described for the economic characteristics, with a significant gap emerging between Western Balkan countries and the more developed jurisdictions of Germany, Sweden, and the US. However, two aspects need to be emphasised, which differentiate the narrative in terms of institutional quality compared to the one on barriers to entry and other economic characteristics. First, in terms of within country heterogeneity in the Western Balkan region, it appears from these indicators that Macedonia and Montenegro stand out as the countries with more effective institutional environment, at least in terms of perceptions. Second, the gap between the Region and EU members of central and south-eastern Europe is evident only in relation to Slovenia and the Czech Republic, while Romania, Bulgaria, and to a lesser extent Croatia, seem to be closer to the Western Balkan region and are far from Western Europe and the US. Overall, if we believe in the theoretical framework provided in the previous section, both the Western Balkan countries and the EU members in central and south-eastern Europe should be carefully considering the institutional and enforcement patterns of their competition laws, possibly diverging in significant terms from the trend currently observed in more advanced jurisdictions.

### 4.3 Cultural Characteristics

We finally look at the cultural characteristics of the Western Balkan region, in particular analysing the perceived attitudes towards the market economy and competition as a stimulus to growth and progress. We saw in the previous section that the lack of a strong competition culture should in principle shape the enforcement priorities of competition authorities, which should favour advocacy and "quick wins", as well as the institutional characteristics of the competition law, which may attribute more visible consumer protection roles to the agencies. The two indicators we used are taken from the Life in Transition Survey (LITS), published by the EBRD. The survey contains two relevant questions addressed to a sample of about two thousand individuals per country. The first relates to the overall attitude towards the market economy; specifically, individuals are asked whether they believe that "the market economy is always preferable to a planned economy", whether they think that "under certain circumstances the planned economy could be preferable" or whether they are "indifferent" to having a planned rather than a market economy. Responses are provided below, in Fig. 11, where the chosen comparators are different to the ones used previously, as Germany and Italy are the only available developed economies. The second indicator, also taken from the LITS, is specific to the notion of whether competition is good or bad, from a cultural point of view. Individuals are asked to rank, on a scale from 1 to 10, whether competition is definitely good as it brings out the best in people (with the most pro-competition answers scored 1) or whether it is bad because it undermines social stability and disrupts social relationships (with the most anti-competition views scored 10). We report in Fig. 12 the percentage of respondents who provided scores between 1 and 3, thus expressing an overall pro-competition attitude.

The results are very interesting and somewhat surprising, and surely would deserve a deeper analysis, which is beyond the scope of this paper. We limit ourselves to two observations. First, the overall pro-competition culture seems to be strong in the Western Balkan countries, broadly in line with other central and

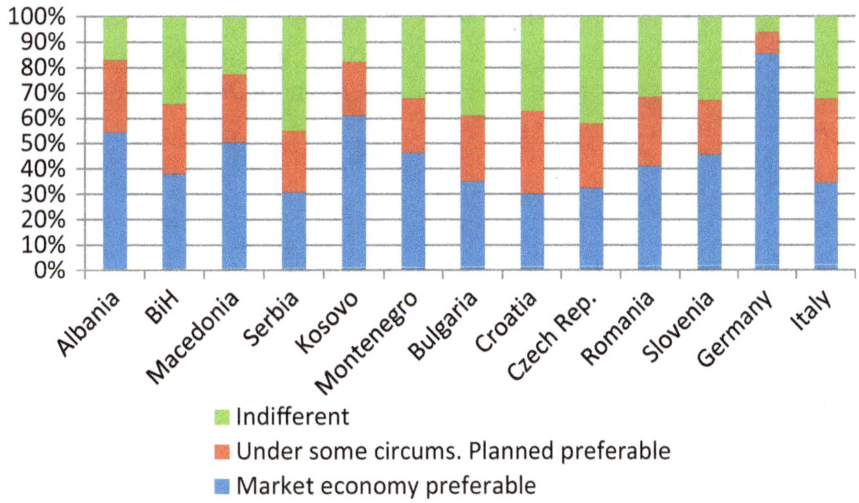


**Fig. 11** Attitudes towards market economy. Source: LITS (Life in Transition Survey), 2016, EBRD

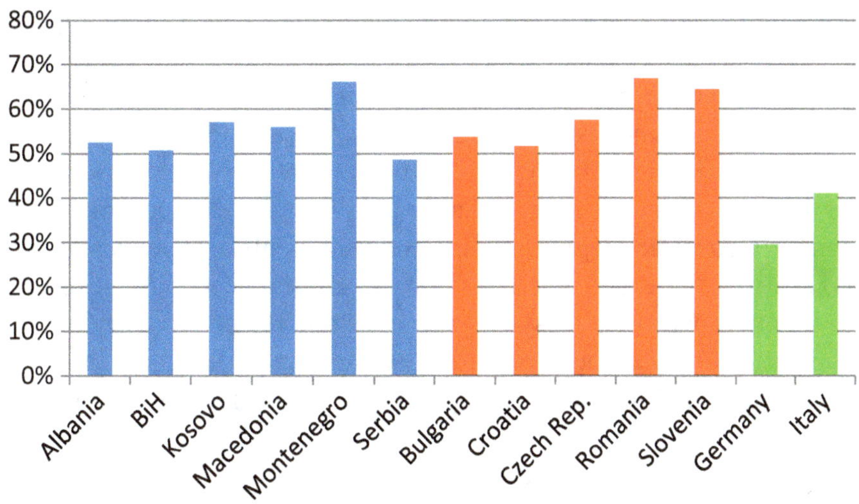


**Fig. 12** Pro-competition culture. Source: LITS (Life in Transition Survey), 2016, EBRD

south-eastern European countries, and more interestingly—significantly higher than in both Germany and Italy. On the other hand, the overall attitude towards the market economy is more heterogenous, with high shares of pro-market respondents in Albania, Kosovo and Macedonia, and much lower shares in other former Yugoslav countries, including the Western Balkan countries as well as Croatia and Slovenia. Interestingly enough, a strong divergence can also be observed between Italy and Germany, with Italians apparently much less favourable towards the market economy. While it is difficult to reconcile these conflicting results, the pattern that seems to emerge for the Western Balkan countries is an overall belief in the merits of competition, while on the other side the perception is that under certain circumstances (possibly in some specific and essential sectors), a planned or regulated system should be adopted. This is indeed consistent with the patterns observed in some developing jurisdictions, where the overall introduction of competition legislation is accompanied by significant exemptions granted to sectors that are considered key or strategic for national interests, independent of whether competition could or could not be introduced to the market.

## 5 Conclusions

In this final section we can try to assemble the pieces of information disseminated throughout the paper and harvest the results of the analysis. To do so we reverse the direction of our journey and start by summarising the main findings on the economic, institutional and social characteristics of the Western Balkan countries. These characteristics are then considered in order to identify the features of the competition policy regime, which seems more in tune with the broader context.

In terms of economic characteristics, a prominent feature that emerges from our analysis is the existence of high and pervasive barriers to entry. These are due to several factors: intrusive and inadequate regulations that limit the scope and dynamism of entrepreneurial initiatives, large-scale direct involvement of the government in many sectors, and the persistence of several markets in which, as a legacy of the previous economic regime, the dominant players may act strategically to prevent the entry of new competitors and defend their market power.

As for the sectoral composition of the economy, we notice a considerable level of heterogeneity across the Region; hence, we cannot offer conclusions of general validity. However, there are clear signs that the informal economy is sizeable in all Western Balkan countries. This suggests the importance of carrying out more focused analyses of each country to identify the sectors that have greater impact on the economy and consumer welfare, and in which informal activities are more pronounced.

The available evidence on the institutional characteristics of Western Balkan countries shows that in all of the vested interests have a strong ability to influence the decision-making process of the government and other public institutions. Of course there are no countries for which the opposite can be said and, furthermore, the situation in the countries under study does not differ significantly from that observed in central and south-eastern European countries that have already joined the EU. However, the gap with respect to more advanced jurisdictions is noticeable. This suggests that some attention needs to be given to this aspect.

Finally, the evaluation of certain indicators of relevant cultural characteristics, seems to provide striking support of the principle of competition and an overall positive attitude towards the market economy.

The design of competition policy in the Western Balkan countries has to take into considerations the factors just summarized. Some robust recommendations are applicable for the definition of the institutional set-up. Overall, the administrative model seems appropriate, given the low level of independence of the judiciary. However, within this model effective measures need to be adopted to fence the competition authority from the interference of the government and interest groups. This can be achieved also by imposing a high level of transparency of the activities carried out by the authority and making it accountable to the general public. For instance, the competition authority may be required to publish and fully explicate all its decisions (not only the decisions to open and close investigations, but also those dismissing complaints), or to publish a periodical report in which it describes past activity and sets the priorities for future actions.

As for the scope of antitrust rules and enforcement powers, it is strongly advisable to eliminate any formal exclusion of SOEs and other public entities from the application of competition law, as they may be a major force against a full deployment of competitive initiatives. Moreover, the competition authority should have the ability to have its voice heard. Its opinions and recommendations cannot replace the normal functioning of the democratic political process. However, the legislator and other decision-makers have to be forced to evaluate the implications of their decisions on competition and be asked to show that other general interests have to prevail and that they cannot be pursued by adopting measures with less anti-competitive impact.

As for the inclusion of ex-ante merger control regulation, we think that international experience has proven that an important gap exists if this is not part of competition law. However, we think that the reach of the merger regulation can be fine-tuned by setting relatively high thresholds that trigger the obligation to notify a merger. This would also allow the competition authority to save resources that can be used more productively in other tasks.

Combining competition law enforcement and other responsibilities, such as sectoral regulation or the enforcement of consumer protection rules, has pros and cons. In the case of the Western Balkan countries the cons seem to prevail. Sectoral regulators are more exposed to the risk of capture, a risk already significant in these countries. Additionally, it is not clear whether the competition authority actually needs the power of enforcing consumer protection rules to build its reputation of being on the consumers' side. Indeed, the available evidence indicates that consumers in the Region already perceive competition as a mechanism capable of defending their interests. Of course, there is a possibility that the used indicators overstate the ability of citizens to fully understand what competition is and the channels through which it fosters consumer welfare. Therefore in this aspect our conclusions have to be taken with extreme caution.

To complete the picture of the institutional setup we have to add a few considerations on investigative and sanctioning powers. We believe that a competition authority will be armless without the possibility of using effective instruments to collect direct evidence of illegitimate conducts and if it does not have the power to inflict adequate sanctions. Moreover, the quality of its decisions may be jeopardized if its decisions have to rely solely on indirect and circumstantial evidence, leading to the deterrence power of sanctions being further diminished by the possibility of higher rates of legal errors. However, in a context in which these powers may be bent toward the protection of vested interests, some prudence is wise. Moreover, this would call for even stronger transparency and accountability requirements.

Some clear indications seem applicable also with respect to the implementation side of the competition policy regime. First, competition authorities in the Western Balkan countries should devote considerable energy to their competition advocate role, as inappropriate regulations appear to be the main source of obstacles to competition. This can be done by performing market inquiries and by acting as an advisor and a constant watchdog of the policy-makers. Sectors that have a significant weight, either in household consumption or in production, should be the preferred target of these activities.

Second, it seems advisable to focus enforcement efforts on abuse of dominance cases especially in markets where ill-conceived liberalization policies have led to the creation of dominant firms that could impede or retard full-scale entry of new competitors.

Third, competition authorities should be encouraged to clarify the interpretation of the applicable rules through soft-law instruments. This approach also has the advantage of making the enforcement less vulnerable to the action of special interest groups. A fast way to achieve this result would be to anchor the interpretation of the applicable rule to the case-law that has been developed in other jurisdictions, such as the EU.

Fourth, it would be advisable to ask the competition authority to state the main priorities of its action in publicly available documents. Of course, this should not compromise the ability of the enforcer to intervene when unexpected news uncovers the existence of serious anti-competitive conducts in sectors that were not prioritized, nor should it oblige the competition authority to reveal information that may put at risk the effectiveness of its investigations. However, an indication of the lines of action that the authority intends to follow increases its accountability and helps improve its performance.

Fifth, at least in an initial stage, competition authorities should use their sanctioning power with caution. Of course, hard-core cartels have to be harshly punished; severe sanctions may also be levied against firms that infringed on competition rules in prioritized sectors, if such priorities had been disclosed to the public. In all other cases more moderate sanctions are justified.

All these suggestions do not form a recipe that guarantees the perfect competition policy. Other ingredients need to be added. The quality of the human resources is of paramount importance, as is the quality of the judicial system and of other public institutions in general. However, this is true in any case: any recommendation in this respect would state the obvious.

To move the analysis one step forward one would need to check the actual features of competition policies in the Western Balkan countries and verify to what extent they match the ones that we believe are desirable and which aspects can be improved. We set this as the subject of future research. Other scholars and practitioners are invited to join.

**Acknowledgement** We are grateful to the participants of the "International Conference on Institution Building of the Competition Authorities in South-East Europe" (Belgrade, Serbia on 2nd and 3rd June 2016), for many helpful comments and suggestions. We are also grateful to Kim Yuni, and Stefano Suardi for excellent research assistance.

## References

Acemoglu D, Aghion P, Zilibotti F (2006) Distance to frontier, selection, and economic growth. J Eur Econ Assoc 4:37–74

Aghion P, Blundell R, Griffith R, Howitt P, Prantl S (2009) The effects of entry on incumbent innovation and productivity. Rev Econ Stat 91:20–32

Begovic B (2017) Competition law and convergence: the case of transition of the CEE countries. Working paper

Buccirossi P (2010) The enforcement of imperfect rules. Lear Research Paper

Buccirossi P, Spagnolo G (2007) Optimal fines in the era of whistleblowers: should price fixers still go to prison? In: Ghosal V, Stennek J (eds) The political economy of antitrust, vol 81. Elsevier

Buccirossi P, Lorenzo Ciari, Tomaso Duso, Giancarlo Spagnolo and Cristiana Vitale, Measuring the deterrence properties of competition policy: the competition policy indexes, J Compet Law Econ, 7 (2011) 165-204

Buccirossi P, Ciari L, Duso T, Spagnolo G, Vitale C (2013) Competition policy and productivity growth: an empirical assessment. Rev Econ Stat 95:1324–1133

Budzinky O, Beigi M (2013) Competition policy agendas for industrializing countries. Ilmenau Economics Discussion Papers, No 81

du Plessis L, Lurie J, van Buuren A (2011) Competition legislation and policy – Is it necessary in a developing economy? Contribution to the fifth annual competition law, economics and policy conference 4 & 5 October 2011

Dutz M, Aydin H (1999) Does more intense competition lead to higher growth? CEPR discussion paper, 2249

Dutz M, Vagliasindi M (2000) Competition policy implementation in transition economies: an empirical assessment. Eur Econ Rev 44:762–772

Evenett SJ (2015) Competition law and the economic characteristics of developing countries. In: Gal MS et al (eds) The economic characteristics of developing jurisdictions. Their implications for competition law. Edward Elgar, Cheltenham

Gal MS, Fox EM (2015) Drafting competition law for developing jurisdictions: learning from experience. In: Gal MS et al (eds) The economic characteristics of developing jurisdictions. Their implications for competition law. Edward Elgar, Cheltenham

Gal MS et al (eds) (2015) The economic characteristics of developing jurisdictions. Their implications for competition law. Edward Elgar, Cheltenham

Gerber D (1998) Two models of competition law. In: Ullrich H (ed) Comparative competition law: approaching an international system of antitrust law. Nomis, Baden-Baden, pp 113–115

Griffith R, Harrison R (2004) The link between product market reform and macroeconomic performance. ECFIN Economic Papers 209, European Commission

Holmes TJ, Schmitz JA (2010) Competition and productivity: a review of evidence. Annu Rev Econ 2:619–642

Katsoulacos Y, Ulph D (2009) Optimal legal standards for competition policy: a general welfare-based analysis. J Ind Econ 57:410–437

Katsoulacos Y, Ulph D (2016) Legal uncertainty, competition law enforcement procedures and optimal penalties. Eur J Law Econ 41:255–282

Kee HL, Hoekman B (2007) Imports, entry and competition law as market disciplines. Eur Econ Rev 51:831–858

Konings J, van Cayseele P, Warzynski F (2001) The dynamics of industrial mark-ups in two small open economies: does national competition policy matter? Int J Ind Organ 19:841–859

Kovacic WE, Hyman DA (2012) Competition agency design: What's on the menu? GW Law Faculty Publications & Other Works. Paper 628

Motta M, de Streel A (2006) Excessive pricing and price squeeze under EU law. In: Ehlermann C-D, Atanasiu I (eds) European competition law annual 2003: What is an abuse of a dominant position? Hart, pp 91–125

Schneider F (2007) Shadow economies and corruption all over the world: new estimates for 145 countries. Economics: The Open-Access, Open-Assessment E-Journal, vol 1, nr. 2007–9

Trebilcock MJ, Iacobucci EM (2010) Designing competition law institutions: values, structure, and mandate, 41 Loy U Chi L J 455

Warwick K (2013) Beyond industrial policy: emerging issues and new trends. OECD science, technology and industry policy papers, no. 2. OECD, Paris

World Bank, OECD (1988) A framework for the design and implementation of competition law and policy, Chapter 6

# Middle Income Convergence Trap and the Role of Competition Policy in SEE Countries

**Boris Begović**

## 1 Introduction

Economic growth is the paramount objective of the SEE countries.[1] That is quite understandable: the Region is still the poor side of Europe, as it has been for decades. Rosenstein-Rodan (1943), in his seminal contribution to the theory of development, declared the main reason of underdevelopment in SEE as an "international depressed area".[2] Over the past century, there was no real convergence of the SEE countries towards Western European productivity and living standards. Maddison (2007) demonstrated that the per capita income differences between the two regions have even increased during that period.[3]

Accordingly, in this paper the role of competition policy is evaluated only from the perspective of speeding up the long-term economic growth of the SEE countries. It is presumed that there is no other aim of competition policy but to increase the economic growth rate to the optimal one.[4] Although a dynamic notion, growth rate optimisation can be compared to social welfare criteria, which is a static notion, commonly used as the standard in competition law enforcement.

---

[1]For the purpose of this paper, SEE countries are: Albania, Bosnia and Herzegovina, Bulgaria, Croatia, Greece, FYR Macedonia, Moldova, Montenegro, Romania and Serbia.

[2]Even though the author considers SEE together with East Europe, as a single region: "everything between Germany, Italy and Russia".

[3]According to Maddison (2007), Western Europe per capita income was 2.04 time higher than per capita income of Eastern Europe in 1913. This ratio increased to 3.07 in 2003. Although there is no separate calculation for the SEE, it is presumed that the ratio is even higher. Begović (2013) provided some political economy explanation for the lack of the convergence.

[4]The economic growth rate optimisation is based on the "Golden Rule" (Phelps 1966), specified as the saving rate that maximises steady state consumption.

B. Begović
Faculty of Law, University of Belgrade, Belgrade, Serbia
e-mail: begovic@ius.bg.ac.rs



B. Begović, D. V. Popović (eds.), *Competition Authorities in South Eastern Europe*, Contributions to Economics, https://doi.org/10.1007/978-3-319-76644-7_3

The aim of the paper is to explore whether and what kind of competition policy is desirable for SEE countries using growth rate optimisation as the criterion. Taking that into account, the possibility of SEE countries being caught in the middle income convergence trap must be explored. The structure of the paper is devised accordingly. First, the mechanics of the middle income convergence trap is explored. Next considered is the hypothesis about different competition policies being suitable for different levels of economic development. The answer to the question about whether SEE countries are in the middle income convergence trap follows. A key segment of the paper follows, with a suggestion regarding the desirable elements of competition policy for the SEE counties. Conclusion ends the paper.

## 2 Engines of Economic Growth: The Mechanics of Middle Income Convergence Trap

There are basically two engines of economic growth: the accumulation of production factors, i.e. their investment into production, and the increase of total factor productivity (TFP) due to improvements of efficiency and due to the technological progress, i.e. innovations.

Accumulation of the production factors is crucial for growth at lower levels of economic development (measured by lower levels of per capita income), i.e. for growth of the countries that are far from the technological frontier. Many production factors, especially labour, are not utilised at all, capital is scares due to the low income and low saving rate, and within such a framework, marginal productivity of investments is rather high. That is good for both economic growth and for investors, since high returns provide strong incentives for investments to materialise. The problem with this mechanism of growth is that it is not sustainable. As it has been demonstrated even by early models of exogenous growth (Solow 1956), accumulation of production factors can achieve only transitory economic growth. When the steady state is achieved, due to the inevitable equalisation of the investment rate and the deprecation rate, i.e. when capital per labour is constant, economic growth depends only on the increase of the TFP due to the technological progress that is exogenous to the model.[5]

A crucial prerequisite for this type of economic growth, i.e. investment based growth, is high expected investment returns, as only such returns provide incentive for investment. If returns are low or if the probability of returns and/or investments expropriation is high, then expected returns are low, providing weak or no incentive for investors to invest physical capital. Since capital is a mobile production factor, it is welcomed in other industries and/or countries with higher expected returns. On the

[5]This insight is based on the implicit assumption that efficiency is maximised (Solow 1956), i.e. that there is no way to improve the efficiency and increase TFP on that basis. Accordingly, all the transitional economic growth in this model is based on production factor accumulation.

one hand, product market competition is a strong mechanism for eliminating market power and the ability of incumbent firms to appropriate economic rent, hence decreasing expected returns in this way. On the other hand, rule of law provides protection of private property rights, decreasing the probability of expropriation, either by private or government predators, consequently increasing expected returns.

As previously pointed out, the increase in the TFP has two main sources. One is inefficiency that can be removed for a given technology, such as production inefficiency (with the endogenous average cost not being minimised) and allocative inefficiency (with prices above marginal costs). Both efficiencies can be eliminated or at least minimised by incentives created by competition, especially product market competition. A special type of inefficiency is inefficient industrial structure with substantial resources engaged in low-productivity activities. Competition, including production factors market competition and high mobility (due to low barriers) of the production factors, can provide for inter-industry reallocation of resources from low-productivity to high-productivity activities, consequently increasing of the TFP.

Like the above-described inter-industry reallocation of resources, competition provides for intra-industry reallocation of resources, due to the market selection among incumbents (Aghion et al. 1997; Aghion and Schankerman 2004), as it generates a larger market share for low-cost firms, at the expense of high-cost firm (with some of them exiting the industry). This leads to a decrease in average costs—the same outcome as improvement of production efficiency.

The main issue with increased efficiency as the source of TFP growth is that it is a one-off event; the reallocation of resources from low-productivity to high-productivity activities can be done only once—it is not sustainable. The only sustainable increase of the TFP is based on technological progress, i.e. innovations that improve the technology that is used in production. If a stead state is achieved, then growth rate is equal to the technology progress rate. Modern economic growth theory considers technological progress to be endogenous, based on research and development (R&D) or, only locally, based on adoption of existing but superior technology—technology from the technological frontier. For a country/industry that is close to the technological frontier, the only means of technological progress, and in that way improved TFP, is own R&D, and technological innovation as its outcome. For a country/industry that is far from the technological frontier, imitation, i.e. adoption of advance technology is an option, which not available to the former.

Investment based growth is the dominant engine of growth for poor countries, i.e. countries that are far from the technological frontier. This is quite expected, considering that scarcity of capital and low level of capital per worker provide for increasing returns in production and high returns for the investors. Furthermore, a substantial segment of the labour force is not engaged, hence accumulation of production factors is the inevitable first stage of economic growth of poor countries. Nonetheless, there is substantial room for improvement of efficiency in countries with a low level of per capita income. Accordingly, increased TFP due to the increased efficiency can substantially contribute as an additional engine of growth for these countries.

The thesis that investment based growth, i.e. capital accumulation, is a prerequisite for economic growth of the countries that are far from the technological frontier has been challenged. Both Hall and Jones (1999) and Easterly and Levine (2001) pointed out that production factor accumulation is not crucial for economic growth of poor countries. They pointed out that difference in productivity, both in TFP and labour productivity, can successfully explain the differences in per capita income between the countries. In other words, it is not production factor accumulation that made now developed countries rich, but rather the increase of the TFP. Furthermore, a substantial part of the difference in productivity between the countries can be explained by different technologies that they use: modern, cutting-edge technology used by the countries that are on the technological frontier and traditional, obsolete technology used by countries that are far from the technological frontier. The only way for this gap to be closed is imitation, i.e. adoption of the modern technology in the poor countries. As substantial part of these technologies is embedded in physical capital, investments are needed for adoption of the modern technology that would improve the TFP. At the end of the day, it is investment based growth that is an indispensable engine of growth for the poor countries, although it is not the only one.

Innovation based growth is the dominant engine of growth for rich countries, which are close to the technological frontier. Investment based growth is not an option for them, since, due to diminishing returns of capital, they have already achieved steady-state in which growth depends only on innovations based on the technological progress. As these countries are on the technological frontier or very close to it, there is no way for them to imitate, i.e. to adopt technology from the countries that are technological superior—such countries do not exist. Furthermore, most of the inefficiencies have already been eliminated, hence there is very limited room for increasing TFP on that basis.

Acemoglu et al. (2006) pointed out that institutions suitable for investment based growth are not suitable for growth based on innovations. In principle, the success of investment based growth depends on the incentives to invest. That can, in principle, be subsidised by the government or government policy, based on the lack of competition policy and substantial legal barriers to entry, which provide for substantial rents appropriated by incumbents. As it was indicated (Acemoglu et al. 2006), it is rather difficult, or even unfeasible for less developed countries, those that need investments, to provide subsidies from their modest budgets, inevitably due to their limited income, and competing needs in provision of public goods. The only feasible institutional option is a lax or even absence of a competition policy and substantial legal barriers to entry. In that way excessive profits, created by market power and preserved by barriers to entry, turned into rent for investors, providing incentive for investment.[6]

[6]This approach does not consider rule of law, which provides universal protection of private property rights, as an institutional option for increasing expected returns on investment that would create incentives for investment. The justification for such an approach, if any, can be found in the insight that rule of law does not have a negative effect on innovation based economic growth.

This institutional option has a substantial drawback because the lack of competition that it produces eliminates incentives for efficiency, and there are substantial inefficiencies in the countries that are on the low level of both economic and institutional development. Hence with such an institutional option, the prospect for a TFP increase contributing to growth is very slim. Furthermore, with no competition there is no incentive for adoption of modern technology, i.e. imitation of innovations, as no "escape competition" motive exists.

The situation is much more difficult in the case of developed countries, which are close to the technological frontier, because their growth depends only on innovations and only competition provides incentives for them. With no competition, with substantial market power enjoyed by undertakings, there is no incentive for any incumbent to invest in R&D, an activity that creates technological innovations. This cannot be changed in situations with substantial legal barriers to entry, as there is no pressure from potential competition, and no new entries that can bring in innovations based on technological progress. With no resources allocated to R&D, there is no technological progress, and no movement of the technological frontiers. Accordingly, institutions that are appropriate, at least up to a point, for low per capita income countries are entirely counterproductive for high per capita income countries, which are close to the technological frontier.

This is the foundation for the middle-income convergence trap.[7] Investment based economic growth, established on the appropriate institutions, brings the country to the higher per capita income and closer to the technical frontier. Both real income and technological convergence starts. Nonetheless, by achieving that success, economic growth undermines its foundation—it is not sustainable any more, as the engine of investment based growth runs out of steam and can no longer produce results at the higher level of economic development, i.e. closer to the technological frontier. No further convergence, neither income nor technological, can be achieved. As theoretically demonstrated (Aghion et al. 2005), divergence follows, as growth continues in developed countries, those close to the technological frontier.

Innovation based growth should take over growth sustainability and further convergence. New, quite different institutions are needed, which produce incentives for innovations, i.e. for R&D which produces these innovations. The most important institutions are those that produce strong competition and enable free entry of newcomers. Intensive competition provides incumbent firms with strong incentives to invest in a pre-emptive decrease of production costs to obtain market power, i.e. "escaping competition" motive, and to prevent new, more efficient entries that

[7]Middle income trap in this paper is considered only as the middle-income convergence trap, i.e. the situation in which real income and technology convergence stalls. This trap is sometimes referred to in the literature as "non-convergence trap" (Aghion et al. 2005). Im and Rosenblatt (2013) provided an extensive review of various concept of middle-income traps, as well as other notions of traps in economic growth and development literature common parlance, some of them rather far away from the notion used in this paper. Without a clear specification of the main mechanism of the middle-income trap, empirical testing of the hypothesis produced mixed results (Han and Wei 2017).

can undermine the rent that is appropriated by incumbents (Aghion et al. 2001; Aghion and Howitt 2006). Free entry, i.e. low barriers to entry, provides a classic Schumpeterian model of growth situation: a new, technologically superior, i.e. more efficient entry replaces the incumbent, which exits the industry. Furthermore, it was demonstrated (Aghion et al. 2009) that free entry also provides incentives for incumbents to innovate and increase their efficiency, although that incentive proved to be effective predominantly for the incumbent that are close to the technological frontiers, not so for those far from it.[8] This leads to the equilibrium distribution of firm, including both incumbents and new entries (Acemoglu and Cao 2015).

The right timing of the shift from investment to the innovation based growth is essential for escaping middle income convergence trap. If the institutions suitable for innovation based growth are introduced too early, then investment based growth, the one that still enables convergence, is undermined. The absence of investments that is generated through the shift will not be compensated by increased innovations and growth will slow down—the convergence would come to an end. Contrary to that, if the institutions suitable for innovation based growth are introduced too late, then the engine of innovation based growth is constrained and investment based growth cannot compensate for that, so growth would slow down; convergence would again come to an end.

From the theoretical perspective, the model is symmetrical (Aghion et al. 2005): the threat of premature institutional reform is equal to the danger of delayed institutional reform. Since competition policy is an essential part of the institutions appropriate for the different engines of growth, the question is whether this is true for such a policy. Is the threat of premature introduction of competition policy greater than the danger of introducing it too late?

## 3 Different Competition Policies for Different Per Capita Income Levels?

Building on the insight related to the concept of dual engines of growth, it is possible to advocate different competition policies for countries at different per capita income levels, i.e. countries featuring different distances from the technological frontier.

Singh (2002) suggested that competition policy was counterproductive for poor countries, since their growth is based on investments and high returns on them, due to the market power, would be undermined by competition policy. Not only are the incentives for investment compromised in this way, but he also suggested that low retained earnings, due to the eliminated/limited market power, could not provide

---

[8]This finding, theoretically explained by Aghion and Howitt (2006), assumes that the new entries' technologies are on the technological frontier and was supported empirically by the case of the UK (Aghion et al. 2009). Some empirical support for this finding, in the case of the FDI in CEE, has been provided by Sabirianova et al. (2005), although not in China (Lu et al. 2017).

sufficient funds to be reinvested. This argument, based on insights of imperfect or even missing capital markets and financial intermediation in poor countries (Laffonte 1998; Acemoglu et al. 2006), reinforces the recommendation against competition policy in countries far from the technological frontier. It is evident that a substantial legal barriers to entry should be introduced, as a necessary condition for the lack of competition policy effectiveness, since the economic profit of the incumbents, the main incentive for investment, would otherwise dissipate; free entry kills economic profit.

This argument against competition policy countries that are far from the technological frontier should be evaluated by taking into account a several insights. The first one is that the crucial incentive for investment is an expected value of their returns, not their magnitude, meaning that probability of the appropriation of the returns matters. It was empirically demonstrated (Akhtaruzzman et al. 2017) that protection of private property rights, i.e. protection of the investment as well as its returns, is much more important for expected returns on investments than the magnitude of the returns themselves, although the results are restricted to the FDI.[9] Accordingly, introduction of rule of law, which decreases the probability of investment/capital expropriation, is much more important for investment decisions than the sheer magnitude of the returns, depending on the market power and ultimately on competition policy. It is rule of law that is a crucial incentive for investors, not the lax competition policy, or rather the lack of it. Hence, building institutions that provide rule of law and universal protection of private property rights is a priority in speeding up investment based economic growth.

The second insight is that increasing TFP, by increasing the efficiency of the incumbent firms and intra- and inter-industry reallocation of the resources from low-productivity to high-productivity activities with given technology, is an important source of growth for countries far from the technological frontier. With these inefficiencies being widespread there is substantial room for improvements of this kind and it takes time for the one-off improvement to materialise. Hence, the increase in the TFP, due to the improved efficiency, can contribute to economic growth for some time. A crucial incentive for improved efficiency is competition; with lax competition policy or rather without it, and the consequent substantial market power, this incentive would diminish, and there would be no restructuring or both intra- and inter-industry resource allocation from high-cost to low-cost activities. Economic growth would inevitably slow-down due to no contribution from the increase in the TFP. This effect countervails the effect of speeding up growth due to the higher expected returns and higher investment rates achieved by abandoning competition policy.

[9] Akhtaruzzman et al. (2017) considered expropriation risk as only one of the political risks that investors faced. The other two are redistributive taxation, and regulatory burden and government inefficiency. Accordingly, only expropriation by the government is considered and not expropriation by private predators. All explanatory variables proved to be highly statistically significant and robust in the econometric analysis encompassing 83 developing countries over 32 years in dynamic panel with fixed effects.

Finally, the economic growth of countries far from the technological frontier depends on the speed of adoption of modern technology through international technology transfer. It is crucial to analyse the incentives for firms in these countries to adopt modern technology. An important insight for this analysis is that adoption of technology creates ex ante certain fixed costs, which are far below the size of the fixed cost of the R&D that should produce innovation, and there is no uncertainty regarding the outcome of the process, unlike in the case of R&D, but the fixed costs of technology transfer are still substantial and unavoidable since they provide the firm with adoption capacity. Accordingly, they can be compared to R&D costs, by their character if not magnitude. Taking this into account, competition is a strong incentive for adoption of modern technology, similar to the "escape competition" mechanism of the Schumpeterian model of economic growth. A market power that would be created through adoption would provide rents that would compensate the fixed costs of that adoption.[10] If there is no competition, there is no "escape competition" motive for adoption of modern technology, at least not for incumbent firms; they already have market power due to the absence of competition policy and the high barriers to entry.

Obviously, there are countervailing effects of the competition policy on the economic growth of the countries that are far from the technological frontier, so the question is which effect is dominant. The ultimate answer to this question is empirical. For the time being, there is no specific empirical research that directly addresses the issue, but there are some results that can provide clues about it. Empirical research has provided evidence that competition policy is good for economic growth without specifying whether it is good for the investment based or innovation based growth. Since the sample does not consist only of countries that are far from the technological frontier, the obtained results should be interpreted with caution. Dutz and Hayri (2000) used a cross-section the effective competition policy of 53 countries, demonstrating a statistically significant relationship between competition policy, as an explanatory variable, and economic growth, in the way that more competition policy accelerates economic growth. Petersen (2013) used panel data for 154 countries, from 1960 to 2005, and tested whether the introduction of competition law had an effect of economic growth. He found that there was a statistically significant and robust positive effect with a lag of 10 years. The explanation of the result is intuitive: the lag effect is both due to the lag on the part of the national competition agencies (NCAs), on account of making competition law enforcement more effective through learning-by-doing, and the part of undertakings, as it takes time for the deterrent effect of competition law enforcement to become effective.

[10]There are some substantial differences between the two "escape competition" mechanisms. In the case of innovation market power is specified in time, with protection of intellectual property rights, mainly patents. In the case of adoption of existing technology, there is no protection. Hence, expected values of rent in the case of adoption are smaller, although in the case of innovation the rent is uncertain, due to the uncertainty regarding the product of R&D. The costs of adoption of existing modern technology are also fixed, but the smaller than the fixed costs of R&D.

The only research that focuses at least on some countries that are far from the technological frontiers, selected transition economics as the sample (Dutz and Vagliasindi 2000). It was demonstrated that effective competition policy had a positive effect on the growth of these countries, as more competition policy implementation led to the expansion of more efficient private firms, which was good for growth, not only because reallocation of resources from high-cost to low-cost firms, but also because of investment in the low-cost firms.

Indirect evidence that competition is good for the growth in countries that are far from the technological frontier is provided through analysis of the effects of foreign trade liberalisation, as a way of introducing competition. Tybout (2000) demonstrated that in the manufacturing sector of the developing countries the growth of output and productivity is mainly due to the liberalisation of foreign trade. Obviously, competition can be introduced this way only in the case of industries producing tradable good, but what is more important, in the case of manufacturing, increased competition produces increased output, i.e. economic growth in countries that are far from the technological frontier.[11]

Competition policy should not be mistaken for competition. Competition can be provided by many instruments other than competition policy, especially competition law considered separately from advocacy. Kee and Hoekman (2007) demonstrated the substantial effect of import liberalisation on competition (measured as price mark-ups), using an empirical model, cross-industry, cross-country, time series regression (sample of 28 industries, 42 counties and 18 year). It was demonstrated that the impact of competition policy is not statistically significant when control variables are imports and the number of firms in industry. Nonetheless, the number of firms is considered an outcome of competition policy—lower legal barriers to entry.

Alesina et al. (2005) provided both theoretical arguments and empirical support (in the case of OECD countries) for the thesis that deregulation based on the liberalisation of entry, i.e. removing legal barrier to entry barriers, provides an increase in investments. Although the analysis focused on heavily regulated industries (transportation, communications, and utilities), insights into the mechanism that increases the level of investments by removing the entry barriers and introducing competition are highly relevant for all industries.[12]

There is no controversy whether competition is good for innovation based growth, or more general, for the increase of the TFP, as an engine of growth. The more relevant the TFP increase is for economic growth, the greater the need for

[11]In a specific case-study, Pavcnik (2002) demonstrated that in Chile import the liberalisation of manufactured good produced a significant and sustainable increase in productivity of the manufacturing industry, partly due to the selection effect, i.e. reallocation of resources from high-cost to low-cost firms. Nonetheless, the level of investments, as the consequence of liberalisation, was not analysed.

[12]An additional important insight is that massive deregulation is needed for increasing investments to materialise—Alesina et al. (2005) found small changes in heavy regulated environment were not likely to produce the results.

competition. There are several empirical studies that provide confirmation of the positive impact of competition on the TFP level and growth. Voigt (2009) empirically demonstrated (cross-section analysis, 107 countries) a statistically significant relationship between competition policy and the TFP, with more competition policy leading to an increase in the TFP. This relationship was demonstrated not only for the entire sample, but also for the subsample of countries that are far from the technological frontier, providing evidence that competition speeds up economic growth of such countries by reducing inefficiencies and improving productivity. Buccirossi et al. (2013) provided empirical evidence of a positive impact of competition policy on the increase of the TFP at the industry level (22 industries) in twelve OECD countries, over the course of 10 years. Furthermore, Aghion et al. (2004) empirically demonstrated in the case of the UK that more entry, due to the institutional reform that reduced legal barriers to entry, provided an increased TFP of incumbent firms and led to faster TFP growth of both incumbent and aggregate. New entries were on the technological frontiers (US FDIs), but domestic, although lagging, were not far behind—a situation described as "neck-and-neck competition". Obviously, such a constellation provided strong incentives to innovate both to the new entries and incumbent firms.

It is evident that for countries that are close to the technological frontier strong competition is favourable for economic growth, hence institutions that encourage and protect competition are desirable. Accordingly, effective competition policy is inevitable, consisting of both competition law enforcement and advocacy. The latter is important because free entry is a key prerequisite for keeping high competitive pressure on the incumbents and enabling new entries to bring their innovation to the market. Competition advocacy for import liberalisation and low barriers to entry should be an integral part of the competition policy.

Bearing all these insights in mind, the middle income convergence trap can be reconsidered within the framework of competition policy. Is the error of introducing competition policy too early greater than the error of introducing it too late? Is the damage done to investment based growth by introducing competition policy greater than the damage done to innovation based growth by not introducing it?

The answers to these questions should be based on two findings. The first one has already been considered in this paper: competition has substantial positive effects on the economic growth of countries that are far from the technological frontiers due to the incentives that it creates for improvement of efficiency and for imitation, i.e. adoption of modern technology. Furthermore, it was demonstrated that rule of law is more important for creating incentives for investments that high returns on account of market power. Contrary to that, lack of competition has no positive effect whatsoever on the economic growth of countries that are close to the technological frontier. Undoubtedly, there is a strong asymmetry regarding these relationships. Based on this asymmetry the conclusion follows: the error of introducing competition policy too early is much smaller than the error of introducing it too late.

There is an additional insight, from the political economy prospective, which supports the conclusion on asymmetrical danger. As pointed out by Aghion and Schankerman (2004), the lack of competition policy, including high legal barrier to entry, creates very specific winners: incumbents with substantial market power, appropriating substantial rents, who have every incentive to use theses rents to bribe legislators not to introduce competition policy, especially not to remove legal barriers to entry. Powerful incumbents, established within the framework without competition, are determined to prevent the increase of competition. This creates a specific institutional trap: lack of competition policy creates further lack of competition policy. Because of this trap, competition that is weak cannot become strong. As a consequence, if a country decides to start down the path of prosperity, without competition policy and with high legal barriers to entry, then it could end up in a low-competition trap.[13]

This finding is just a specific case of the political economic model created by Aghion and Schankerman (2004). Assuming that there is cost heterogeneity in the economy and that there are low-cost and high-cost firms, there are basically two institutional equilibriums: low competition and high competition. The comparative statics of the model demonstrated that countries that are most vulnerable to the low competition trap are those with a low initial level of competition, a low initial degree of cost asymmetry, and office holders more driven by their private interests than by social welfare concern. This is exactly the situation in many countries that are far from the technological frontier.

Accordingly, it is not only that the error of introducing competition policy too early is much less dangerous for convergence than the error of introducing it too late, but there is a substantial danger of the institutional trap if the country decides to move forward without competition policy and with high legal barriers to entry. Taking that into account, is there a way to detect the right timing from the ongoing macroeconomic development? More specifically, could a growth crisis be a cue for the institutional shift that will take a country away from the convergence trap? Could a government wait for the growth crisis in order to conclude that the growth model is obsolete, that the engine of growth has run out of steam, and then to initiate reforms, shifting from institutions that support investment based growth towards institutions that support innovation based growth?

For this strategy to be applied, there are two principal problems that should be kept in mind, and both are related to timing. The first is linked to the timing of the diagnosis of the growth crisis. Negative growth rates are not sufficient condition for such a diagnosis. These rates could be the consequence of output fluctuations within business cycles, i.e. a recession due to the temporary slump in demand. Or in the case in economies that do not have diversified output, negative growth rates could be the consequence of a drop in the prices of the main export commodities and deterioration of the country's terms of trade. It inevitably takes time, even for unbiased, non self-

[13]Similar to this trap is the high legal barriers to entry trap in oligarchic societies (Acemoglu 2008). In an oligarchy the political elite is accountable only to the business elite protected by legal barriers and earning substantial rent. Sharing of that rent provides a strong incentive for both elites not to remove those barriers. In this paper the character of political institutions is not considered as a factor or outcome of competition policy, although there are some attempts in that direction (Petersen 2013; Ma 2016).

delusional governments to realise that there is a growth crises and that the growth model should be changed. The likelihood is high that it will already be too late for that.

The other timing is the one related to the institutional reform. Such a reform takes time to materialise. First it must be designed, then implementation institutions need to be developed, including training the staff, followed by a period of learning-by-doing, and finally time is needed for the deterrence to be established, before the new competition institution is fully effective.

In short, not only is the error of introducing competition policy too early much smaller, and less dangerous than the error of introducing it too late, but the probability of the error of introducing it too late is much greater. Both danger and probability are asymmetrical.

This finding clears the way for consideration of the case of SEE countries and their competition policy.

## 4 SEE Countries: In the Middle of the Convergence Trap?

Are SEE countries in the middle of a convergence trap? What is the main engine of growth of the SEE countries? Is competition good for the growth of these countries? Do they need competition policy and what kind?

A framework needs to be established in order for these questions to be answered. Part of that framework is based on the answer regarding the main features of the economies of the SEE countries, especially taking into account that, with the exception of one, all of them were once socialist countries, with administrative decision-making and compulsory mobilisation of the production factors, including the labour force. Investment rates were high and investments were allocated to manufacturing (heavy industry concept) and infrastructure. A rather high level of human capital has been achieved. Due to the legacy of the past (no market allocation of resources, no private property, no free foreign trade), most of these economies feature inefficiency and significant distance for the technological frontiers. As to the industrial structure, rather inefficient manufacturing is dominant, with some agriculture and very limited service industries. The beginning of the transition introduced market allocation of the resources, private property and created a dual economy: one segment made up of modern, greenfield, private and low-cost firms, mainly new entries, and the other made up of obsolete, incumbent, frequently state-owned, and high-cost firms—a heterogeneity with a considerable cost difference.[14]

The bottom line is that accumulation of the production factors was substantial, its allocation rather inefficient, and the technology used lagging behind the technological frontier, although not as much as most of the less developed countries.

[14]A socialist legacy of the transition economies, as well as the first transition moves, including liberalisation and privatisation, has been thoroughly analysed in Aaslund (2007).

**Table 1** Median distance to the technological frontier in 2014

| | GDP per capita | Output per worker |
|---|---|---|
| SEE countries | 13 | 16 |
| EU-15 | 88 | 92 |
| USA | 100 | 100 |

Source: World Bank database

**Table 2** Growth accounting for CEE and SEE countries: Contribution of the production factors and TFP

| | 1997–2001 | | | 2002–2006 | | |
|---|---|---|---|---|---|---|
| | Capital (%) | Labour (%) | TFP (%) | Capital (%) | Labour (%) | TFP (%) |
| EU 10 | 2.9 | 25.6 | 77.3 | 10.6 | 21.3 | 58.1 |
| WB | 13.9 | 10.4 | 75.7 | 30.6 | −17.8 | 87.3 |

Source: Borys et al. (2008)

Notwithstanding substantial methodological issues, approximation of the distance to the technological frontier is estimated as the distance from the USA in terms of GDP per capita (Madsen et al. 2015) and output per worker (Begović et al. 2017). The median distance of the SEE countries and EU-15 are in the Table 1.

Taking all this into account, one could assume that the increase of TFP is the main engine of growth of the CEE economies. Simple growth accounting results for CEE and SEE countries (Borys et al. 2008) provided confirmation of this conjecture (Table 2).[15]

It is evident that the greatest source of economic growth in SEE Europe has been TFP growth, rather than production factors accumulation.[16] Accordingly, competition, which is undoubtedly good for TFP growth, should be achieved through effective competition policy in these countries.

There is missing information on the structure of the of the TFP growth in the SEE countries, due to the inherent limitation of the methodology: it is not known which part of the TFP is due to technological progress and which is due to improved efficiency. From the dynamics of the TFP in the two regions, as well as from the economic features of the SEE countries and their distance from the technological frontier, it can be corroborated that most of the growth of TFP is due to the increase in efficiency, provided by the privatisation and subsequent restructuring, reallocation of resources from low-productivity to high-productivity activities (mainly from inherited manufacturing to service industries) and reallocation from high-cost to

[15]These results, related to the contribution of the TFP to economic growth, have been confirmed by Iridian (2007) and World Bank (2008). The considerable difference in the growth of TFP between "Old" and "New" Europe, being much higher in the latter, indirectly confirming the presented results, has been recorded by Burda and Severgnini (2009).

[16]This is entirely different from the case of the Southeast Asia "tigers" in the period of their intensive growth (1966–1990). The contribution of the TFP growth to the economic growth was: 30% for Hong Kong, −5% for Singapore, 12% for South Korea, and 20% for Taiwan. The contribution of capital accumulation was much higher: 42% for Hong Kong, 73% for Singapore, 46% for South Korea, and 40% for Taiwan (Young 2005).

low-cost firms within the same industries, with exits of high-cost firms. A smaller part of the TFP increase is due to the technological progress, mainly due to the adoption of modern technology from countries close to or at the technological frontier.

Indirect confirmation of this conjecture is a drop of the TFP growth share in the case of ten EU countries. After initial restructuring that was carried out prior to 2002, there are fewer activities that can be restructured and an increase in capital accumulation is needed for new technology to be introduced. This means that the share of TFP growth in the case of the economic growth of SEE countries will probably continue to decrease, but that is irrelevant for the finding on desirability of competition policy, since competition is good for both (local) innovation, i.e. adoption of modern technology, and for firm restructuring, and both intra- and inter-industry reallocation. Competition is a necessary precondition for TFP growth, both for the restructuring of incumbent firms and for the adoption of new technology, both by incumbents and new entries, FDIs and other investments.

Effective competition policy includes competition advocacy aimed at and improving the business environment, primarily in the direction of facilitating new entries. The business environment in the SEE countries could be analysed using three available indicators: indexes of economic freedom by The Heritage Foundation and The Wall Street Journal, and by the Fraser Institute, and ranking according to the Cost of Doing Business survey (Table 3).

It is evident that the level of economic freedom and the quality of the business environment in the median SEE country is lagging behind the median EU-15 country ("Old Europe") and, especially, behind the best score/rank. Competition law enforcement cannot do anything about that, but competition advocacy can, focusing especially to the issues of effective foreign trade liberalisation and elimination of legal barriers to entry.

Substantial trade liberalisation occurred in the process of accession to the EU. Some of the SEE countries are members of the EU (customs) union, and some have FTAs with the EU. Furthermore, there is a regional FTA arrangement in the Western Balkans, connecting non-EU member states. Accordingly, substantial barrier to trade across the border, especially tariffs and quantitative restrictions, have been eliminated. Nonetheless, there are still substantial hidden barriers to trade that should be removed and the limited capacity of the local customs administrations should be improved to increase competition through importing, and competition advocacy should focus on those barriers.

**Table 3** Median indexes and ranking of the business environment in SEE countries in 2014

| | Heritage-WSJ index | Fraser institute index | Cost of doing business (rank) |
|---|---|---|---|
| SEE countries | 62 | 74 | 47 |
| EU-15 | 81 | 84 | 25 |
| Best score | 100 | 100 | 1 |

Sources: The Heritage Foundation, Fraser Institute, and The World Bank Doing Business

In the case of barriers to new entry, competition advocacy should focus not only on the registration of new firms, which is usually swift in SEE countries, but on all effective barriers of entering the market in a specific industry. This, for example, includes the process and permissions regarding land development, provision of the infrastructure to new facilities, as well as operations of the tax administrations (compliance costs) and judicial protection of private property rights. In the globalised economy with capital being a mobile factor, all these elements create effective barriers to entry, not only strictly speaking legal barriers. The smaller the number of new entries, whatever of these reasons may be, the smaller the competitive pressure on the incumbents and the lower the prospects of adoption of new technology.

Competition advocacy should be carried out by NCAs for two obvious reasons. The first is the NCAs are knowledgeable about the mechanisms and effects of competition, and that makes them effective and efficient in competition advocacy (Ghosal 2013). The second is the economy of resources within a NCA. Not only is there a substantial economy of scope (with competition law enforcement and competition advocacy being carried out together), but there is a complementary in resource allocation: the more resources that are allocated to advocacy, with advocacy being effective, i.e. increasing competitiveness of the environment, the fewer resources will be needed for competition law enforcement. The expected effectiveness of advocacy in the SEE countries should take into account the assumption of advocacy substantial and perhaps increasing marginal returns. This assumption is based on the insight that competition culture in SEE countries is not very developed, not very widespread in the public, and that its achievements, however modest, have a rather short tradition. Competition advocacy is not the panacea for improving competition in the SEE countries, but it should definitely be a very important segment of the efforts.

## 5 Elements of Competition Policy for the SEE Countries

Most of the SEE countries have already adopted EU-style competition policy, with competition law regime very similar and in many cases identical to the EU provisions. Such a choice provided huge benefits: clear readymade solutions, a framework for training the staff that enforced the law, and, not least, a long history of case law that can be used. The problem with the EU-style competition policy adopted in the SEE countries is that it is focused to the law enforcement, not to the competition advocacy. That is quite appropriate for the old EU member states, or the core of the EU, countries with a long tradition of capitalism and market economy, but that is a disadvantage for countries where there is no long tradition of competition culture.

Accordingly, the priority for the SEE countries should be competition advocacy, focusing on two areas: foreign trade effective liberalisation and freedom to entry. As to foreign trade, substantial liberalisation has already occurred in the early transition and the process of EU accession, with removing tariff barriers and quantitative restrictions. Nonetheless, there are still hidden barriers to trade, especially in the Western Balkan countries, preventing foreign trade from achieving its full potential in creating substantial import competition.

As to the barriers to entry, there is a lot of room for improvement regarding various legal statutory and sub-statutory texts. Competition advocacy should address every effective legal barrier to entry, not only those barriers linked to the registration of new companies—usually they are quite limited. Substantial barriers exist in the development of the property (obtaining town-planning and development permits for new facilities), registration of the property, providing infrastructure services, and many other barriers to entry. The cost of doing business, like costs of compliance with tax regulations (efficiency of tax administration) and costs of protection of own private property rights (efficiency of the judiciary in litigations) are also effective barriers to entry, especially in the case of FDIs, which are an important vehicle for technology transfer. By removing barriers to entry, potential competition would be created, providing incentives to the incumbents to improve their efficiency, and new entries would materialise, increasing the TFP on average and speeding up the economic growth of the SEE countries.

SEE countries lag behind the EU-15 countries in both economic freedom and costs of doing business; their business environment is not beneficial for competition as it is the EU-15 countries. Institutional convergence of that kind can be achieved only through vigorous competition advocacy and public pressure created by that advocacy. This is the only way to achieve the results in institutional convergence, taking into account that private interest groups are rather well-organised in SEE countries, with high stakes in the institutional reform game. Economic freedom harms rents crated by various barriers to entry and there is strong incentive for all those appropriating these rents to prevent the institutional reforms that would increase economic freedom.

It should also be taken into consideration that the economies of the SEE countries are in the middle of the restructuring process, both in terms of intra- and inter-industry reallocation of resources. Not only is competition a crucial prerequisite for this (the selection effect of competition, moving resources from high-cost to low-cost firms), but this process is carried out to a great extent through mergers and acquisitions. For that very reason it is important that merger control in SEE countries be lenient: merger control should not be a substantial barrier to restructuring in SEE economies, which would lead to a TFP increase. The best way forward would be to increase the notification thresholds. In that way, many mergers that are now obliged to be notifies and that are cleared in the first stage of the review, would not require notification at all. The costs of mergers, both in terms of resources and time, would decrease and that would speed up the restructuring process and boost the TFP increase.

## 6 Conclusion

Competition is good for the economic growth of the SEE countries. Their growth is based on the increase in the TPF, mainly on account of the restructuring process and reallocation of resources, but also due to the adoption of modern technology. Competition provides key incentives for this type of economic growth and no disadvantage of competition has been recorded for the TFP based growth. Accordingly, effective competition policy in the SEE countries is essential for these countries to continue restructuring their economies and avoiding the middle income convergence trap. After all, from the prospective of this trap, the danger of introducing competition policy too early is much smaller than the danger of introducing it too late. In that respect, the SEE countries are on the safe side of introducing competition policy.

Taking into account that the business environment in the SEE countries still lags behind the business environment of "Old Europe", that economic freedom is somewhat curtailed, and that there are still important legal barriers to entry, advocacy should be a priority of the competition policy. Since EU-style competition policy has been widely adopted in the SEE countries and since it is not well equipped for advocacy, additional efforts are needed for designing a suitable competition advocacy strategy, allocating resources needed for effective advocacy, and changing some of the legislative provisions to grant more power to the NCAs to conduct their advocacy activities.

Competition legislation enforcement should not be neglected in the SEE countries. Nonetheless, taking into account that restructuring contributes significantly to the economic growth of these countries, and that mergers and acquisitions facilitate that process, merger control should not be an obstacle to this process. For that very reason it is important that merger control in SEE countries be lenient. The best way forward would be to increase the notification thresholds. Such a move would save some NCA resources, which can be allocated to competition advocacy.

**Acknowledgment** The author is grateful to Milan Kostić and Russell Pittman for their helpful comments and suggestions. The support of the Swiss National Science Foundation, program SCOPE IZ73Z0_152730, and cooperation with the Department of Economics, University of Zurich is gratefully acknowledged. Naturally, none of them is to be held accountable for possible remaining errors and value judgments in this paper.

## References

Aaslund A (2007) How capitalism was built: the transformation of Central and Eastern Europe, Russia and Central Asia. Cambridge University Press, Cambridge

Acemoglu D (2008) Oligarchic versus democratic societies. J Eur Econ Assoc 6(1):1–44

Acemoglu D, Cao D (2015) Innovations by entrants and incumbents. J Econ Theory 157:255–294

Acemoglu D, Aghion P, Zillibotti F (2006) Distance to frontier, selection, and economic growth. J Eur Econ Assoc 4(1):37–74

Aghion P, Howitt P (2006) Joseph Schumpeter lecture – appropriate growth policy: a unifying framework. J Eur Econ Assoc 4(2–3):269–314

Aghion P, Schankerman M (2004) On the welfare effects and political economy of competition-enhancing policies. Econ J 115(498):800–824

Aghion P, Harris C, Vickers J (1997) Competition and growth with step-by-step innovation: an example. Eur Econ Rev 41(3-5):771–782

Aghion P, Harris C, Howitt P, Vickers J (2001) Competition, imitation and growth with step-by-step innovation. Rev Econ Stud 68(3):467–492

Aghion P, Blundell R, Griffith R, Howitt P, Prantl S (2004) Entry and productivity growth: evidence from microlevel panel data. J Eur Econ Assoc 2(2–3):265–276

Aghion P, Burgess R, Redding S, Zilibotti F (2005) Entry liberalization and inequality in industrial performance. J Eur Econ Assoc 3(2–3):291–302

Aghion P, Blundell R, Griffith R, Howitt P, Prantl S (2009) The effects of entry on incumbent innovation and productivity. Rev Econ Stat 91(1):20–32

Akhtaruzzman M, Berg N, Hajzler C (2017) Expropriation risk and FDI in developing countries: does returns of capital dominate returns on capital. Eur J Polit Econ 49:84–107

Alesina A, Ardagana S, Nicoletti G, Schiantarelli F (2005) Regulation and investment. J Eur Econ Assoc 3(4):791–825

Begović B (2013) The political economy context of economic growth in South East Europe. In: Anastasakis O et al (eds) Defining a new reform agenda: paths to sustainable convergence in South East Europe. St Antony's College, Oxford, pp 7–24

Begović B, Mladenović Z, Popović D (2017) Democracy, distance for the technological frontiers and economic growth: some empirical results, CLDS Working Paper #0217, April 2017, Center for Liberal-Democratic Studies, Belgrade

Borys MM, Polgar EK, Zlate A (2008) Real convergence and the determinant of growth in EU candidate and potential candidate countries: a panel data approach, ECB Occasional Paper Series, No. 86, European Central Bank, Frankfurt

Buccirossi P, Ciari L, Duso T, Spagnolo G, Vitale C (2013) Competition policy and productivity growth: An empirical assessment. Rev Econ Stat 95(4):1324–1336

Burda MC, Severgnini B (2009) TFP growth in Old and New Europe. Comp Stud 51(4):447–466

Dutz MA, Hayri A (2000) Does more intense competition lead to higher growth? Policy Research Working Paper 2320, World Bank

Dutz MA, Vagliasindi M (2000) Competition policy implementation in transition economies: an empirical assessment. Eur Econ Rev 44(4-6):762–772

Easterly W, Levine R (2001) It's not factor accumulation: stylized facts and growth models. World Bank Econ Rev 15(2):177–219

Ghosal V (2013) Resource constrains and competition law enforcement. Theoretical considerations and observations from selected cross-country data. In: Sokol DD, Cheng TK, Lianos I (eds) Competition law and development. Stanford University Press, Stanford, pp 90–114

Hall RE, Jones CI (1999) Why do some countries produce so much more output per worker than others? Q J Econ 109(1):83–109

Han X, Wei SJ (2017) Re-examining the middle-income trap hypothesis: what to reject and what to revive? J Int Money Financ 73(A):46–61

Im FG, Rosenblatt D (2013) Middle-income traps: a conceptual and empirical survey, World Bank Policy Research Working Paper WPS6594, World Bank

Iridian G (2007) Rapid growth in transition economies: growth-accounting approach, IMF Working Papers, No. 07/164

Kee HL, Hoekman B (2007) Import, entry and competition law as market disciplines. Eur Econ Rev 51(4):831–858

Laffonte JJ (1998) Competition, information, and development. In: Pleskovic B, Stiglitz J (eds) Annual World Bank conference on development economics. The World Bank, Washington, DC, pp 237–257

Lu Y, Tao Z, Zhu L (2017) Identifying FDI spillovers. J Int Econ 107:75–90

Ma TC (2016) Antitrust and democracy: perspectives from efficiency and equity. J Compet Law Econ 12(2):233–261

Maddison A (2007) Contours of the world economy, 1-2030 AD: essays in macro-economic history. Oxford University Press, Oxford

Madsen J, Raschky P et al (2015) Does democracy drive income in the World, 1500–2000? Eur Econ Rev 78(1):175–195

Pavcnik N (2002) Trade liberalization, exit, and productivity improvements: evidence from Chilean plants. Rev Econ Stud 69(1):4245–4276

Petersen N (2013) Antitrust law and the promotion of democracy and economic growth. J Compet Law Econ 9(3):593–636

Phelps ES (1966) Golden rules of economic growth. W.W. Norton, New York

Rosenstein-Rodan PN (1943) Problems of industrialisation of Eastern and South-Eastern Europe. Econ J 53:202–211

Sabirianova K, Svejnar J, Terrell K (2005) Distance to the efficiency frontier and foreign direct investment spillovers. J Eur Econ Assoc 3(2–3):576–586

Singh A (2002) Competition and competition policy in emerging markets: international and developmental dimension. G-24 Discussion Paper Series, UNCTAD, Geneva

Solow RM (1956) A contribution to the theory of economic growth. Q J Econ 70(1):65–94

Tybout JR (2000) Manufacturing firms in developing countries: how well do they do, and why? J Econ Lit 39(1):11–44

Voigt S (2009) The effects of competition policy on development: cross-country evidence using four new indicators. J Dev Stud 45(8):1225–1248

World Bank (2008) Unleashing prosperity: productivity growth in Eastern Europe and the former Soviet Union. The World Bank, Washington, DC

Young A (2005) The tyranny of numbers: confronting the statistical realities of the East Asian growth experience. Q J Econ 110:641–680

# Institutional Design of State Aid Authorities in South East Europe: The Unfit Legal Transplant and Its Ramifications

**Dušan V. Popović**

## 1 Introduction

All countries in South East Europe (hereinafter, SEE)[1] aspire to join the European Union. This political aim has been confirmed and strengthened by these countries participating in the Stabilization and Association Process, established by the EU. The Process, launched in 1999 and re-affirmed at the Thessaloniki European Council meeting in 2003, sets out common political and economic goals to be achieved by the participating countries. The Process rests on the Stabilization and Association Agreements (hereinafter, SAA), signed by the European Union with each of the participating countries, and the EU's financial assistance, aimed at strengthening the rule of law, institutional development of a market economy, and structural adjustment. The SEE countries have reached different stages in the European integration process. Albania signed the SAA in 2006 and was granted EU candidate status in 2014. Bosnia-Herzegovina signed the SAA in 2008 and submitted its application to join the EU in 2016. The FYR Macedonia signed the SAA in 2001 and was granted EU candidate status in 2005. Kosovo*[2] signed the SAA in 2014 and the EU has been facilitating the high-level dialogue between

[1]The term South East Europe shall be used to designate Balkan countries that are candidates or potential candidates for membership of the European Union.

[2]The asterisk refers to the following footnote: "This designation is without prejudice to positions on status, and is in line with UNSC 1244 and the ICJ Opinion on the Kosovo Declaration of Independence."

D. V. Popović
Faculty of Law, University of Belgrade, Belgrade, Serbia
e-mail: dusan.popovic@ius.bg.ac.rs



B. Begović, D. V. Popović (eds.), *Competition Authorities in South Eastern Europe*, Contributions to Economics, https://doi.org/10.1007/978-3-319-76644-7_4

Kosovo* and Serbia since 2012.[3] Montenegro signed the SAA in 2007 and was granted EU candidate status in 2010. Serbia signed the SAA in 2008 and was granted EU candidate status in 2012.

As an important prerequisite for accession to the European Union, the SEE countries are required to introduce a national system of state aid control. The obligation to introduce state aid monitoring systems stems from the Stabilization and Association Agreements, but also from the Central European Free Trade Agreement and the Energy Community Treaty; the latter two initiatives may be observed as part of the wider European integration process. The national state aid control systems are envisaged as transitional mechanisms, since the monitoring of state aid will be carried out by the European Commission once the SEE countries accede to the Union. As demonstrated by the experience of countries in Central and Eastern Europe, effective enforcement of the national state aid rules is one of the essential requirements concluding the negotiations on the competition policy chapter.

This paper analyses the reasons for the introduction of state aid control in SEE countries (Sect. 2) and the types of institutional design of these authorities (Sect. 3). It concludes by considering the reasons for the observed inefficiency of state aid monitoring authorities in the region of South East Europe (Sect. 4).

## 2 Duty to Introduce State Aid Control

The Stabilization and Association Process draws on the experience of pre-accession agreements of Central and East European countries (hereinafter, the CEEC). The association agreements[4] concluded with CEECs required that each of these countries establish a temporary monitoring authority in charge of state aid control pending the country's accession to the European Union.[5] Once the country accedes to the Union, the competence is transferred to the European Commission. In the same manner, the Stabilization and Association Agreements concluded with the SEE countries set a general obligation for candidate or potential candidate countries to adopt national state aid legislation and establish a state authority competent for the enforcement of the said rules. The SEE countries need to ensure that their legislation is aligned with

[3]Kosovo* declared independence from Serbia in 2008. Although its independence is not recognized by all EU Member States, Kosovo* participates in the Stabilization and Association Process separately from Serbia.

[4]The association agreements concluded between the EC and its Member States, and the Central and Eastern European countries that joined the EU in 2004/2007 were usually referred to as the "Europe agreements".

[5]See: the Europe Agreement establishing an association between the European Communities and their Member States, of the one part, and the Republic of Poland, of the other part, Art. 63 (4) (b) and (7), and Art. 68. Under these articles, Poland had to ensure transparency in the area of public aid and to approximate the country's existing and future legislation with that of the EC.

the EU *acquis* and properly enforced by the competent authority. Regarding state aid, each of the Stabilization and Association Agreements concluded with the SEE countries provides that any "(...) state aid which distorts or threatens to distort competition by favouring certain undertakings or certain products, as they may affect trade between the Community and [associated country], shall be incompatible with the proper functioning of the Stabilisation and Association Agreement".[6] This definition is modelled upon the definition of incompatible state aid laid down by Art. 107, para 1 TFEU. The agreements concluded with SEE countries also provide that suspected practices shall be assessed on the basis of criteria arising from the application of the competition rules applicable in the Community, in particular from Art. 107 TFEU and interpretative instruments adopted by the Community institutions.[7] Therefore, the associate countries have to assess the state aid schemes on the basis of criteria arising from the application of secondary legislation, frameworks, guidelines and other relevant administrative acts that are in force in the EU, and those that will be adopted following the entry into force of the SAA, as well as on the basis of the criteria developed in the case law of the EU courts, and from any decision taken by the Association Council. The advancement of each country participating in the Stabilization and Association Process is assessed in annual Progress Reports, published by the European Commission.

Following the conclusion of the SAA, the countries in South East Europe adopted comprehensive legislative frameworks for state aid control, which are generally harmonised with EU law.[8] A detailed analysis of the national state aid rules reveals that further approximation with EU law is needed with respect to secondary legislation (Popović and Caka 2017; Botta 2013). For example, in most SEE countries the notion of *de minimis* aid or aid for restructuration is not conceive in line with the General Block Exemption Regulation[9] and the *de minimis* Regulation.[10] Simultaneously with the adoption of the first national state aid acts, the SEE countries established their state aid monitoring authorities, in line with the requirements of the

---

[6]See: SAA with Albania, Art.71 (1) (iii); SAA with Bosnia-Herzegovina, Article 71 (1); SAA with the FYR Macedonia, Art. 69 (1) (iii); SAA with Kosovo*, Art. 75 (1); SAA with Montenegro, Ar.73 (1) (iii); SAA with Serbia, Art.73 (1) (iii).

[7]See: SAA with Serbia, Art.73 (2).

[8]Since the Kosovo* proclamation of independence was not recognized by five EU Member States and Serbia, the EU signed the SAA with Kosovo* only in 2014, when the EU-sponsored negotiations between Belgrade and Pristina made progress. Kosovo* adopted its national state aid legislation and established the monitoring authority in 2011, several years before the entry into force of the SAA. Therefore, the establishment of the state aid authority was not the result of compliance with the SAA but a reaction to criticism expressed in the European Commission Progress Reports for 2008, 2009, and 2010.

[9]Commission Regulation (EU) No. 651/2014 declaring certain categories of aid compatible with the internal market in application of Articles 107 and 108 of the Treaty (hereinafter, GBER), Official Journal of the European Union n° L187/1, 26.6.2014.

[10]Commission Regulation (EU) No. 1407/2013 on the application of Articles 107 and 108 of the Treaty on the Functioning of the European Union to *de minimis* aid (hereinafter, *De minimis* Regulation), Official Journal of the European Union n° L352/1, 24.12.2013.

Stabilization and Association Agreements. All SAAs in (almost) identical manner prescribe the duty to establish such monitoring authorities: "[The associated country] shall establish an operationally independent authority which is entrusted with the powers necessary for the full application of [the state aid rules] within one year from the date of entry into force of this Agreement. This authority shall have, inter alia, the powers to authorise state aid schemes and individual aid grants (. . .) as well as the powers to order the recovery of state aid that has been unlawfully granted."[11] The SAAs do not further specify requirement for operational independence of the national state aid authorities. Logically, this requirement should be understood as excluding any instruction or interference by other state bodies in the activities of the state aid authority.

The "neutral" position of the European Union towards the choice of the appropriate institutional design of the national state aid authority in SEE countries does not come as a surprise since it is in line with the earlier EU approach in other areas of competition law enforcement. For example, when the European Union introduced decentralised competition law enforcement, the European Commission merely prescribed that the national competition authorities (hereinafter, NCA), henceforth competent to enforce Arts. 101 and 102 TFEU, should be designated in such a way that they effectively comply with the provisions of Regulation 1/2003.[12] The choice of the institutional design of NCAs was therefore left entirely to the discretion of the Member States, which is in line with the principle of institutional and procedural autonomy of the EU Member States. As a result, NCAs take different forms in different Member States, ranging from administrative bodies to judicial authorities. Furthermore, in a number of Member States a specific form of government intervention exists in merger cases. It usually entails that the government may intervene on grounds of public interest after the NCA has analysed the impact of the merger on consumers and businesses.[13]

In addition to adopting national state aid rules and establishing the monitoring authority, the duty to introduce state aid control includes the task of establishing an inventory of state aid schemes and drafting a state aid regional map for each SEE country. Under the SAA, within 4 years from its entry into force, the state aid authority should complete a comprehensive inventory of the aid schemes existing in the country. The establishing of the inventory is the first activity that the authority

[11]See: SAA with Montenegro, Art. 73 (4).

[12]Council Regulation (EC) No 1/2003 of 16 December 2002, on the implementation of the rules on competition, laid down in Articles 81 and 82 of the Treaty, Official Journal of the European Community n° L1/1, 4.1.2003, Art. 35. Regulation 1/2003 revolutionised the enforcement of EU competition law by abandoning the notification system and decentralising enforcement of Arts. 101 and 102 TFEU (ex Arts.81 and 82 TCEU).

[13]Commission Staff Working Document SWD (2014) 231/2, Enhancing Competition Enforcement by the Member States' Competition Authorities: Institutional and Procedural Issues, accompanying the document Communication from the Commission to the European Parliament and the Council Ten Years of Antitrust Enforcement under Regulation 1/2003: Achievements and Future Perspectives, COM (2014) 453.

should carry out. By the end of the transition period (4 or 5 years, depending on the country), the state aid authority is required to draft a state aid regional map for the country, indicating the maximum aid intensity per region of the country, on the basis of the data concerning the GDP per capita in each region. The regional aid map is then assessed by the European Commission.

As it has already been underlined, the duty of SEE countries to establish a national state aid legal framework does not stem only from their participation in the Stabilization and Association Process, but also from the Central European Free Trade Agreement (hereinafter, CEFTA), to which these countries are parties. The original CEFTA agreement was concluded in 1992 by the members of Visegrad Group: Poland, Czech and Slovak Federative Republic and Hungary. CEFTA was conceived as a free trade agreement, the purpose of which was to facilitate the transition of former communist Central European countries to market economies of a West European style. The membership in CEFTA is supposed to be of a temporary character: once the participating country joins the European Union, its CEFTA membership ends. The original agreement was amended several times in order to allow other Central and East European countries to join. Slovenia joined CEFTA in 1996, Romania in 1997, Bulgaria in 1999, Croatia in 2003 and the FYR Macedonia in 2006. Following the 2004 enlargement of the EU, the CEFTA membership ended for most of the participating countries. Therefore, the new "enlarged" CEFTA agreement[14] was signed in 2006, to which Albania, Kosovo*, Moldova, Montenegro, Serbia and Bosnia-Herzegovina adhered.

Article 21 CEFTA lays down a general prohibition on state aid: "*Any aid granted by a Party or through State resources in any form whatsoever which distorts or threatens to distort competition by favouring certain goods shall, in so far as it may affect trade between the Party concerned and other Parties to this Agreement, be incompatible with the proper functioning of this Agreement.*" CEFTA also requires the Parties to the Agreement to assess state aid schemes under the conditions laid down by Art. 107 TFEU. The Parties are required to ensure transparency in the area of state aid, *inter alia* by reporting to the CEFTA Joint Committee on the total amount and the distribution of the aid and by providing to other Parties information on aid schemes. Although there is a direct reference to Art. 107 TFEU in the Agreement, CEFTA state aid framework differs significantly from the one provided under SAAs. CEFTA Member States are not explicitly required to establish a national state aid control authority. Instead, CEFTA provides for a system of mutual withdrawal of the trade concessions, inspired by the WTO Dispute Settlement Understanding.[15] This system is initiated only if a Party to the Agreement decides

[14]Agreement on Amendment of and Accession to the Central European Free Trade Agreement, also referred to as CEFTA 2006.

[15]The dispute settlement procedure is laid down in Art. 24 CEFTA. The Parties should first attempt to resolve any differences between them through direct consultations. Nevertheless, a party may decide to refer the case to the Joint Committee. The Joint Committee examines the case without delay and may make any recommendation needed to put an end to the difficulties notified. In the absence of such recommendation and if the problem persists, the complaining Party may adopt

to challenge another Party that allegedly does not comply with the duty to prohibit state aid (Dangerfield 2006). The complaining Party may also take countervailing measures in accordance with the relevant Articles of GATT and the WTO Agreement on Subsidies and Countervailing Measures or related internal legislation.

Finally, the requirement to introduce a state aid control stems from membership of the SEE countries in the Energy Community, an international organization dealing with energy policy. This international organization was established by the European Union, and it brings together the EU, the SEE countries (Albania, Bosnia-Herzegovina, Kosovo*, the FYR Macedonia, Montenegro, and Serbia), and countries from the Black Sea region (Moldova, Ukraine).[16] One of the aims of this organization, established by an international treaty in 2005, is to enhance competition at the regional level and to exploit economies of scale.[17] Under Article 18 of the Energy Community Treaty (hereinafter, EnCT), any public aid which distorts or threatens to distort competition by favouring certain undertakings or certain energy resources shall be incompatible with the proper functioning of the Treaty. Any such practices should be assessed on the basis of criteria arising from the application of the rules of Article 107 TFEU.

Similarly to CEFTA, EnCT does not explicitly require from Contracting Parties to establish a state aid monitoring authority. However, a Party which does not comply with EnCT requirements (e.g. by favouring its national energy producers and distributors), may face sanctions. Under the Rules on dispute settlement, the Energy Community Secretariat may start an investigation if one of the Contracting Parties does not properly implement the EnCT. The Secretariat may bring the case to the Ministerial Council, which can withdraw the voting rights of the Contracting Party. The EnCT Rules on dispute settlement were amended in 2015 to introduce a fast-track procedure, allowing the Secretariat to directly submit a reasoned request to the Ministerial Council without preliminary procedure (i.e. without first issuing a reasoned opinion). The EnCT Rules on dispute settlement were enforced in several state aid related cases. For example, in July 2016 the Secretariat sent an opening letter to the Republic of Serbia for its failure to comply with the Energy Community

---

appropriate measures necessary in order to remedy the situation. At present, any dispute between CEFTA members arising out of competition issues and any dispute in which only one of the parties is also a WTO member must be resolved by the CEFTA internal dispute resolution mechanism (Biukovic 2008).

[16]Georgia, Armenia, Norway and Turkey participate as observers. Georgia is presently in the process of joining the Energy Community as a full-fledged member. The ministers took the decision on Georgia's accession in October 2016. As of January 2017, Georgia is in the process of completing its internal procedures for approval of the accession to the Energy Community.

[17]Up until 1992, there was lack of clear competence of the European Community to take measures on energy matters. It was only the Treaty of European Union (Art. 3 (1) u) that empowered the EU to take measures in the sphere of energy. Prior to the adoption of the said Treaty, the measures in the sphere of energy were taken on the legal basis of other EC competences, such as the internal market or competition policy (Karova 2010: 2). At present, the EU is not only competent to take internal measures on energy issues, but may also influence the energy policy of the candidate and potential candidate countries *via* the Energy Community.

state aid *acquis*. The Republic of Serbia failed to comply with its obligations under the EnCT, in particular Articles 18 and 19 thereof, because the national state aid authority either did not assess or incorrectly assessed the compatibility of state aid granted to Elektroprivreda Srbije (public enterprise Electric Power Industry of Serbia) for the Kolubara B power plant project.[18] In September 2010, the Secretariat sent an Opening Letter to Bosnia-Herzegovina, expressing the preliminary view that this country had failed to fulfil its obligations under the EnCT, by not adopting legislation prohibiting state aid and enforcing that prohibition.[19] Following the opening of a dispute settlement procedure, in 2012 Bosnia-Herzegovina adopted an act on state aid control and established the monitoring authority.

## 3 Types of State Aid Authorities in SEE Countries

The analysis of the institutional design of state aid monitoring authorities has revealed that SEE countries largely chose to establish an authority with close links to the government. In Albania, Bosnia-Herzegovina, Kosovo*, Montenegro and Serbia, the state aid authority takes the form of a unit either within the ministry of finance or the ministry of economy, or of a collegial body formed by representatives of different ministries, but formally separated from the Government. Only the FYR Macedonia has chosen to design its state aid authority in a different manner, by entrusting the existing competition authority with the task of state aid control. The first type of a state aid authority was actually "transplanted" from countries in Central and Eastern Europe. Similar authorities existed in the majority of CEECs in the pre-accession period (e.g. in Estonia, Slovenia, Estonia, Hungary, and the Czech Republic). The second model of a single competition and state aid authority also existed in certain CEECs. In Poland, for example, the president of the NCA was in charge of authorising state aid (Piszcz 2011:42).

### *3.1 Authority Closely Linked to the Government*

The Albanian Law on State Aid[20] provides for the establishment of the State Aid Commission and the State Aid Directorate, as bodies put in charge of controlling the granting of state aid. The State Aid Commission is responsible for authorising state aid, under the proposals of the State Aid Directorate.[21] The Commission is the main

[18]Case ECS 11/14: RS/State aid.

[19]Case ECS 01/10: BH/Competition.

[20]Albania, Law 9374 On State Aid, 21 April 2005, Official Gazette No 36, 1311.

[21]Albania, Government Decision n° 182, 21 March 2006, Official Gazette No 0, 30.

decision-making body responsible for the control of state aid.[22] The Commission's proclaimed independence from the Government may be called into question given the composition of this body and the rules on the appointment of its members. The Commission is chaired by the minister of economy, who is member of the Commission *ex officio*. Three other members of the Commission are appointed by the government, nominated by the minister of finance, the minister of European integration, and the minister of justice, in view of their "proficiency and experience in the area of economy". One member is nominated by civil society.[23] The State Aid Commission reports annually to the government.[24] On the other hand, the State Aid Directorate[25] represents a special department within the Ministry of Economy, which provides the State Aid Commission with all the necessary input for its decision-making process. It identifies and analyses the legal and economic aspects of state aid schemes and individual aid, prepares investigative reports, and drafts the guidelines, which are subsequently approved by the State Aid Commission. Given the fact that the members of the State Aid Directorate are employees of the Ministry of Economy, there is undoubtedly a substantial conflict of interests each time the Directorate assesses the state aid granted by that ministry.

In Bosnia-Herzegovina, the authority charged with state aid control is the State Aid Council. The members of the State Aid Council are appointed by the Council of Ministers of Bosnia-Herzegovina and the governments of the country's three units (Republic of Srpska, Federation of Bosnia-Herzegovina, District of Brčko). The Council members are appointed from among "renowned economic or legal experts" and must not exercise any duty that may expose them to conflict of interest.[26] Each of the three constituent peoples of Bosnia-Herzegovina must be represented by at least two members in the Council. The constituency of peoples as a collective political right of ethnic communities in Bosnia-Herzegovina (Serbs, Croats, and Bosniaks) was provided as a constitutional category by the Washington and Dayton peace agreements which put an end to the war, in 1995. However, such rule precludes BH citizens who do not belong to any of the constituent peoples from running for a particular government office (Begić and Delić 2013). The independence of the State Aid Council is under threat from not only the manner in which its members are appointed, but also the irregular and insufficient financing of its activities.[27]

---

[22]Albania, Law on State Aid, as amended by Act No 21/2016, 10 March 2016, Official Gazette No 47, 3140, Art. 16 (2).

[23]Albania, Law on State Aid, Art. 16 (2).

[24]*Ibid*, Art. 16 (3–4).

[25]*Ibid*, Art. 18.

[26]Bosnia-Herzegovina, Law on the System of State Aid, Official Gazette of Bosnia-Herzegovina No 10/12, Art. 7.

[27]The European Commission warned in several Progress Reports that the Secretariat of the BH state aid authority was not yet fully operational. See *Bosnia-Herzegovina 2015 Progress Report*, SWD (2015) 214 final, 41–42.

In Kosovo*, the competence for monitoring the state aid is split between the State Aid Commission and the State Aid Office. The system of state aid control in Kosovo* is thus very similar to the Albanian system. The State Aid Commission consists of the minister of finance, the minister of European integration, the minister of trade and industry, the chair of the Association of the Municipalities of Kosovo, and one representative from civil society.[28] The members of the Commission are appointed by the Government of Kosovo, nominated by the minister of finance, for a period of 4 years. The Commission shares its competence in the area of state aid with the State Aid Office, an administrative unit within the Kosovo Competition Authority. The Office is responsible for receiving and analysing notifications and other data concerning aid schemes and individual aid. The Office prepares assessment reports and decisions for the State Aid Commission. The Office reports to the Kosovo Competition Authority. The Office is not yet fully operational (Ceku 2015: 121–122), which has regularly been criticised by the European Commission in its Progress Reports. In the most recent Report, the Commission concludes that the activities of the State Aid Office have so far been limited to distributing notification forms to potential aid granters and that the Office does not have the capacity to screen existing aid schemes, as required by the SAA. No decisions on state aid have been issued in the past 3 years.[29]

In Montenegro, the members of the Commission for the Control of State Aid are appointed by the Government, following nomination by the Ministry of Economy, the Ministry of Sustainable Development and Tourism, the Ministry of Transport and Maritime Affairs, and the Association of Employers. The candidate for the president of the Commission is proposed by the Ministry of Finance. This creates potential for conflict of interest, given the fact that the majority of aid schemes and individual aid are granted by the ministries represented in the Commission. This has also been noted by the European Commission in its 2015 Montenegro Progress Report.[30] Furthermore, the members of the Montenegrin state aid authority need not necessarily be specialists in the area of competition law. The Law on State Aid Control only prescribes that the member of the Commission "must have a bachelor degree in economics or law".[31] The lack of expertise in competition law and/or state aid control may make the members of the state aid authority easily influenced by the Government and businesses. The current enforcement record of the Commission for State Aid Control does not demonstrate that the body has the necessary credibility, powers and resources for the full application of state aid rules.[32]

In Serbia, the Commission for State Aid Control was established under the auspices of the Ministry of Finance. The members of the Commission for State

---

[28] Kosovo, Law on State Aid, No 04/ L-024, Official Gazette 13/2011.

[29] See *Kosovo 2016 Progress Report*, SWD (2016) 363 final, 47–48.

[30] See *Montenegro 2015 Progress Report*, SWD (2015) 210 final, 36.

[31] Montenegro, Act on State Aid Control of, Official Gazette of the Republic of Montenegro No 74/09 and 57/11, Art. 11.

[32] See *Montenegro 2015 Progress Report*, SWD (2015) 210 final, 36.

Aid Control are appointed by the government from among persons who possess "expert knowledge in the field of state aid, competition, and/or EU legislation",[33] nominated by the ministries of finance, economy, infrastructure and environmental protection, as well as the Commission for the Protection of Competition. The member nominated by the Ministry of Finance is the chairperson of the Commission for State Aid Control, while the representative of the Commission for the Protection of Competition serves as a deputy chairperson. The Law on State Aid Control attempts to resolve potential conflict of interest by prescribing that a member of the Commission who is at the same time the representative of the aid grantor may not take part in the decision-making process, although he/she may provide additional information within the state aid control procedure.[34] The European Commission has on several occasions criticised the potential for conflict of interest within the Serbian state aid authority. For example, in its 2015 Progress Report, the European Commission emphasised that the operational independence of the Commission for State Aid Control still remains to be demonstrated.[35] The similar finding has been repeated in the latest Progress Report: "The Republic of Serbia has to take steps to make the Commission for State Aid Control more independent and effective."[36] Further to the issue of composition of the Commission for State Aid Control, its ambiguous legal status may also generate its increased dependency on the executive branch. The Law on State Aid Control does not define the legal status of the Commission, aside from stating that the latter shall be "operationally independent in performing its duties".[37] Consequently, the Commission cannot be classified as the Government's working group, an independent agency, or an administrative organization within the meaning of the Law on General Administrative Procedure. The proclaimed operational independence of the Commission is additionally compromised by its financial dependency on the Ministry of Finance, since the Commission does not have a separate budget.

## 3.2 *Independent Authority Accountable to Parliament*

As our analysis has demonstrated, the large majority of SEE countries (Albania, Bosnia-Herzegovina, Kosovo*, Montenegro, Serbia) have decided to entrust the competence of enforcing competition and state aid rules to two different authorities. While the competition law enforcement is entrusted to an administrative agency

[33]Serbia, Act on State Aid Control, Official Gazette of the Republic of Serbia No 51/2009, Art. 6 (4).

[34]*Ibid*, Art. 21 (2).

[35]See *Serbia 2015 Progress Report*, SWD (2015) 211 final, 36.

[36]See *Serbia 2016 Progress Report*, SWD (2016) 361 final, 38.

[37]Serbia, Law on State Aid Control, Art. 6 (7).

accountable to parliament,[38] the enforcement of state aid rules has been assigned to an administrative body of doubtful independence from the executive power. Further to the jurisdictions we already analysed, the latter model of a state aid authority closely linked to the government was followed by the FYR Macedonia until 2006. In this country, the state aid control was first exercised by a separate authority—the Commission for State Aid Control, established under the 2003 Law on State Aid.[39] The members of the Commission were appointed by the government and administrative support for its activities was provided by the Ministry of Economy. Following the 2006 amendments to the Law on State Aid, the competence for state aid control was transferred to the existing Commission for the Protection of Competition. The Commission, which was already in charge of enforcement of other competition rules (prohibition of anti-competitive agreements and abuse of a dominant position, control of concentrations) was established as an independent state agency, with full operational autonomy. Its members are appointed by parliament.

The institutional design of a state aid authority that the FYR Macedonia opted for in 2006 is certainly preferable to the one chosen by other countries in South East Europe, for at least two reasons. First, there are very few experts in the area of competition law and state aid in the SEE countries, especially among civil servants, so their concentration into a single authority would be beneficial to the quality of market analysis. Second, a single "enlarged" authority is not only formally protected from the government's direct influence, but it would also be better prepared to deal with the tactics of informal influence employed by both the executive power and businesses. Unfortunately, both the Government and the Parliament of the FYR Macedonia failed to provide adequate conditions for the smooth performance of the "enlarged" authority, which remains understaffed and under budgeted. As noted by the European Commission, the administrative capacity of the state aid division within the Macedonian Commission for the Protection of Competition is inadequate, as it lacks staff and equipment. It only has three staff members to deal with a growing number of cases and outdated equipment.[40] The Macedonian experience of merging the state aid authority with the NCA reminds us that, regardless of the clear benefits of having a single authority, there is also a danger of neglecting one of its functions. In such multiple function authority it is of the outmost importance to provide adequate conditions for the proper exercising of each of the authority's competences.

[38]As a rule, the members of a collegial decision-making body are appointed by parliament from among experts in competition law and policy. The national competition authority is accountable to parliament, to which it reports annually.

[39]The FYR Macedonia, Law on State Aid, Official Gazette 24/2003.

[40]See *The FYR Macedonia 2016 Progress Report*, SWD (2016) 715 final, 39–40.

## 4 Concluding Remarks: The Reasons for Inefficiency

All countries in South East Europe met the basic requirements under the Stabilization and Association Agreement, CEFTA, and the Energy Community Treaty in the area of state aid—they adopted national state aid rules and established a state aid monitoring authority. However, the enforcement record of these authorities is unsatisfactory. Analysis of the annual reports of state aid authorities in SEE countries reveals that they tend to adopt only decisions approving the notified state aid. There are very few examples of the contrary; for example, the Albanian State Aid Commission adopted only one negative decision between 2006 and 2016.[41] Decisions ordering the recovering of unlawful state aid are seldom passed. One of the rare examples of a decision ordering the recovery of granted state aid is the decision of the Montenegrin Commission for State Aid Control in the case of the Aluminium Plant Podgorica (KAP).[42] Additionally, regarding the lenient approach of state aid authorities towards notified aid, one should understand that an important number of state aid grantors fail to notify the aid schemes. Since the SEE state aid authorities rarely initiate *ex post* control, a significant volume of granted aid is left out of the monitoring regime. Should one blame the institutional design of the SEE state aid authorities for their unsatisfactory enforcement record? It seems that the answer to this question should be negative, for four reasons, at least.

First, regardless of the model chosen—a state aid authority under the auspices of the government, broadly speaking, or a single competition and state aid authority accountable to parliament—the control of state aid in SEE countries cannot presently be performed in an entirely independent manner. The reasons for this can be found in the instability of democratic institutions in the region of South East Europe and the limited expertise within the state apparatus in the area of competition law and state aid. One would intuitively expect that a state aid authority accountable to parliament would be more immune to political influence. Still, one has to conclude that the establishment of a state aid authority, which is accountable to parliament instead to the government, does not necessarily prevent the influence of the executive power over the authority's activities. In SEE countries, the national parliaments have not yet fully developed as an independent branch of government. Instead, they are generally dominated by the executive branch and do not fulfil their role as the controller of the government (e.g. Stojiljković 2015). Therefore, both types of state aid authorities in SEE countries are still quite receptive to direct and indirect Governmental influence.

Second, the statistics does not support the hypothesis according to which a state aid authority accountable to the Parliament would be more efficient than the one established under the auspices of the Government. The enforcement record of the Macedonian state aid authority, for instance, is equally unsatisfactory as the results

[41] According to the authority's annual reports.

[42] Montenegro, Commission for State Aid Control, Kombinat Aluminijuma Podgorica (KAP), decision No 01-33/1, 1 June 2012.

of state aid control in the countries that preferred the first type of institutional design of the monitoring authority. So far, the Macedonian state aid authority did not adopt a single decision prohibiting a state aid.[43] The same "result" is achieved by the Serbian Commission for control of state aid—an authority which is accountable to the Government.

Third, we are of the view that the governments in the SEE countries do not sincerely support the activities of their state aid authorities. The majority of state aid authorities are understaffed and do not have the sufficient financial capacity to fulfil their mission in its entirety. Since state aid rules are a relatively novel element of the national legal regime, even the basic rules remain unknown to a significant number of state aid grantors. The monitoring authorities should therefore allocate sufficient resources to engage in advocacy activities. The latter are particularly important, given the fact that in all SEE countries large amounts of granted state aid are not being notified. This is especially the case with the aid granted by local authorities, which seem not to fully understand the system of state aid control. The central governments, on the other hand, generally do notify the state aid schemes and individual aid, but employ certain "avoidance strategies" in cases where it might be anticipated that a specific aid would not meet the criteria for approval; such aid is either intentionally not being notified (e.g. state aid provided for air transport in the FYR Macedonia)[44] or gets authorised in a non-transparent procedure. For example, in the sensitive case of the takeover of the Serbian national air carrier Etihad Airways/Jat Airways (Air Serbia), the Serbian Commission for State Aid Control merely described the notified scheme and concluded that the latter conforms to the rules, without providing any in-depth reasoning behind such a conclusion (Popović and Caka 2017).[45]

Fourth, at the moment the achievement of efficient state aid control in SEE countries is not treated as a high priority requirement in the European Commission's pre-accession agenda. The support of the national governments in SEE countries for the activities of their state aid authorities would certainly be greater had the European Union exposed the candidate and potential candidate countries to more intensive political pressure in the area of state aid. The inefficiency of state aid authorities is in fact noted in the annual Progress Reports the European Commission adopts. For example, in the 2016 Montenegrin Report the Commission emphasised that the operational independence of the state aid authority has yet to be ensured and that the effectiveness of its control of state aid at all levels must be improved. However, it is also true that in the current, rather initial phase of the enlargement process, the efficiency of state aid control is not a requirement that the European Commission insists on being met. Given the EU's economic and political problems, it is evident that the SEE countries will not accede to the Union in the near future. Therefore, the

---

[43] According to the authority's annual reports.

[44] See *The FYR Macedonia 2016 Progress Report,* SWD (2016) 715 final, 40.

[45] Serbia, Commission for State Aid Control, Etihad Airways/Jat Airways (Air Serbia), decision No 142/2/2013-38, 21 February 2014.

pre-accession process will last longer than in the case of the countries in Central and Eastern Europe. Judging from the experience of CEECs, the efficiency of state aid control will improve only when the country approaches the end of its European integration process (Atanasiu 2001; Birnstiel and Heinrich 2011; Cremona 2003; Evans 2004). The CEECs adopted state aid rules in the mature phase of the pre-accession process[46] and their monitoring authorities started operating efficiently only when the EU accession date was (practically) determined. The efficient work of the national state aid authorities thus demonstrated that the countries in Central and Eastern Europe are prepared for the EU accession. Since the SEE countries established their state aid monitoring authorities at the beginning of their (ongoing) European integration process, and since the enlargement is no longer the European Union's priority, it seems highly likely that the state aid authorities in SEE countries will, for the time being, only continue with their *pro forma* activities, exposed to mild criticism of the European Commission.

**Acknowledgment** The author is grateful to Fjoralba Caka, Assistant Professor at the Faculty of Law, University of Tirana for assistance in researching and analysing Albanian and Kosovar legal sources.

## References

Atanasiu I (2001) State aid in central and eastern Europe. World Compet 24:257–283

Begić Z, Delić Z (2013) Constituency of peoples in the constitutional system of Bosnia and Herzegovina: chasing fair solutions. Int J Const Law 11(2):447–465

Birnstiel A, Heinrich H (2011) State aid in the accession states. In: Szyszczak E (ed) Research handbook on European state aid law. Edward Elgar, Cheltenham, pp 44–63

Biukovic L (2008) The new face of CEFTA and its dispute resolution mechanisms. Rev Cent East Eur Law 33:253–294

Botta M (2013) State aid control in South-East Europe: The endless transition. Eur State Aid Law Q 12:83–94

Ceku OM (2015) Competition law in Kosovo: problems and challenges. Yearb Antitrust Regul Stud 8(12):101–127

Cremona M (2003) State aid control: substance and procedure in the Europe agreements and the stabilisation and association agreements. Eur Law J 9:265–287

Dangerfield M (2006) Subregional integration and EU enlargement: where next for CEFTA? J Common Mark Stud 44:305–324

Evans A (2004) Enlargement and state aid in CEECs. ClaSF Working Paper 4

Karova R (2010) Rationale behind the establishment of the energy community. EUI Working Paper Law 14

[46]Latvia and Hungary adopted national state aid rules in 1997, Estonia in 1998, Lithuania, Slovenia and Poland in 2000. These countries joined the European Union in 2004. Romania adopted its Law on State Aid Control in 2001 and joined the EU in 2007.

Piszcz A (2011) Competition law in comparative perspective. Bialystok Law Books, Temida 2
Popović DV, Caka F (2017) State aid control in South-East Europe: waiting for a wake up call. Eur Bus Org Law Rev 18:333–349
Stojiljković Z (2015) Moć i nemoć parlamenta. In: Stojiljković Z, Lončar J, Spasojević D (eds) Parlament i demokratija. Fakultet političkih nauka Univerziteta u Beogradu, Belgrade, pp 7–20

# Antitrust, Mergers, State Aid and Consumer Protection Under the Same Roof: Does Political Compromise Prevail over the Expert Approach?

**Andrej Plahutnik**

## 1 Introduction

This contribution discusses complementarities and tensions between competition policies and consumer protection policies, with the occasional reasonably critical view on various ideas on organising different policies, such as competition (antitrust and merger control), state aid, and consumer protection, under the same roof. The focal point of the organization of any authority should be to reach the best possible result, which could be identified as efficient implementation for the sake of public interest, using necessary but not excessive funds. This contribution will try to briefly elaborate on different models, specific advantages of the authorities that are in charge on one or more policies, with specific regard to either functional independence and real autonomy, or political influence that may affect the level of expertise in the authorities being exposed to political pressure. The contribution has no intention to suggest or propose one model of institutional organization or another; the aim of this contribution is to identify different challenges as seen by the author, based on relevant practical experience in different jurisdictions.

Establishing an efficient organizational system for each authority, especially the ones that may be described as reasonably new, such as the authorities in charge of competition law and policy, state aid control and consumer policy, should be the basic goal of every country, for the sake of political and economic stability, national competitiveness, economic growth, and the benefit of the citizens. A functioning market economy cannot exist without efficient competition. A transparent,

---

Team Leader of the EU-funded project Strengthening the Capacities of the Montenegrin Authorities for the EU Accession Process and IPA II Instrument—EuropeAid 137894/DH/SER/ME. The opinions expressed in this presentation are those of the author and do not express or reflect views or opinions of any institution to which he is affiliated.

A. Plahutnik
EU Funded Project, Podgorica, Montenegro

 
B. Begović, D. V. Popović (eds.), *Competition Authorities in South Eastern Europe*, Contributions to Economics, https://doi.org/10.1007/978-3-319-76644-7_5

user-friendly and non-discriminatory legal framework, credible institutions and implementation, represent the basic preconditions for an efficient competition (Bellamy and Roth 2001; Bishop and Walker 2007; Faull and Nikpay 2014). Bearing in mind the Treaty of Rome, it can be observed that the main principles of competition and the substantial provisions that identify competition philosophy and competition protection have remained unchanged. The list of "famous" five articles, i.e. stipulations regarding national monopolies of a commercial character, restrictive agreements, abuse of a dominant position, granted special and exclusive rights and state aid, covering the broad field of competition, has changed several time times, but the substantial stipulations have remained unchanged. Almost all jurisdictions around the world have included provisions similar to the ones previously mentioned; in the broader European area substantial provisions equivalent to the EU competition *acquis* can be found in all jurisdictions. This provides for transparency and legal predictability, especially when the competition authorities publish their decisions.

Regarding the task of publishing decisions, it is worth noting that the enforcement records of the competition authority reveal its orientation, priorities and enforcement abilities. The greater the number of antitrust cases that are handled, the more competent the competition authority is considered to be, by the professional society, international partners and the stakeholders whose interest it is efficient competition in the market. If the enforcement record consists to a high extent or almost exclusively of merger control, it can be considered that the priority is not to the fight against cartels and abuses of dominance.

Merger control is of course not something that is not necessary, nonetheless its importance is sometimes overestimated and focusing on potential competition harm, in form of mergers, may be wrong, especially when the fight against traditional breaching of competition, e.g. cartels and abuses of dominant position, are not given proper importance. It can be understood, although not supported, that (especially) in the case of small competition authorities human and financial resources are limited and such authorities do not have at their disposal sufficient resources to tackle demanding antitrust cases, which need to be analysed using sophisticated techniques, and had to deal with strong economic and legal teams of the companies under investigation, whereas in merger control the companies involved are very keen to provide all the necessary data in order to have the merger cleared in a short time. Although merger control also provides for introduction of economic analysis, relevant market definition, and potential harm estimation, that is not enough; the basic goal of competition protection is detection of infringements and that is not an easy task. Special know-how is an absolute must, including special knowledge of investigative techniques, using specific economic and econometric analyses, IT forensics, etc.

Institutional capacities represent an important element for the implementation, either in form of the competition law enforcement or in the form of competition advocacy, which represents an important although sometimes overlooked element of a higher level of competition culture.

## 2 Institutional Capacities

Although the competition authorities should be granted the sole competence for competition protection, there are other institutions that have a very significant role in providing the conditions for efficient competition in the market. Sector regulators, which have a significant role in providing conditions for competition for the market and in the market, are sometimes not exposed to critical analysis regarding their positive (and sometimes negative) impact on competition efficiency. In some industries (sectors), especially those that are either dependent on infrastructure or have only recently been open to competition and/or privatization, the competitive pressure may not be as strong as in the markets that have been open to competition for years.

The situation in (especially) infrastructural sectors, as well as in sectors or markets where state monopolies of a commercial character exist(ed), and/or exclusive and special rights are granted, can be considered not in favour of efficient competition and competitive market economy. It is very important to identify the rules of the game in the market and the potential obstacles for efficient competition, and then decide what institutional capacities, either general or specialised, are needed to provide the conditions that are necessary for a competitive market.

The first element is to have a transparent and non-discriminatory legal framework that provides for level playing field. Regarding the legal framework, sometimes a basic mistake may occur when considering that competition framework in the narrow sense (i.e. antitrust, merger control and state aid) is enough.

Sector legislation (especially, although not exclusively in the sectors dependent on infrastructure, financial services, etc.) represents an important element for either opening the relevant markets to competition or preventing such markets from having competition. One of the important elements of such legislation is to precisely determine the scope and level of authority as well as accountability of the sector regulators, in order to provide the necessary elements for efficient regulation, on one hand, and not to allow a selective negative approach by regulators, on the other.

Providing the sector regulators with some sort of authority with regard to competition control means a specific advantage of these sectors, compared to other sectors.

In some countries, such as Italy, Croatia, Serbia, etc., in the past the central banks had the competence over competition control in these countries; to a certain extent, especially regarding fines, sectors such as banking were in a more favourable situation than other sectors. A typical example for such differentiated approach can be seen in Serbia, where the central bank could impose much lower fines than the competition commission for the same kind of infringement. Having in mind the *ne bis in idem* rule, the banks and insurance companies may wish to be fined by the central bank and not by the competition commission.

It is very important to take into account that a development of a specific sector and/or specific company should not be identified as a public interest; the development of the national economy and its competitiveness should always be identified as a public interest and international competitiveness of a "national champion" cannot be an excuse for a non-competitive environment in the domestic market. Nonetheless, incumbents have a historically privileged position in the market, and all institutions, i.e. sector regulators, competition authorities and the courts, should pay a special attention in this regard.

Although economy of scale and scope is a very important issue, the creation and support of "national champions", referring to international competitiveness of such undertakings and economy of scale and scope, cannot be an excuse for monopolization of a domestic market or for the privileged treatment of "national champions".

When talking about competition and its protection, special attention should be given to the courts and the scope of their authority. Judicial review in competition cases is a very important element for two reasons—it provides a very clear indication of whether the decisions of the competition authorities on merits and sanctions are correct, and with transparency it provides for legal predictability); therefore, it may create an incentive for effective leniency program, of course provided that the competition authorities issue rulings with rigorous fines, having deterrent effect. Transparency of enforcement, in the form of publication of non-confidential versions of decisions, is a must for both competition authorities as well as the courts. Such transparency provides for very clear understanding of the authority's policies, as well as a kind of a guideline how to define relevant markets, how to apply different instruments of competition law, like leniency, direct settlement, commitments, etc.

In addition to judicial review, the courts have another, very important, role in the competition law enforcement. Private enforcement is an efficient model that undertakings suffering damages from competition infringements may choose however in the EU, save the UK, the cases of private enforcement are still quite rare. There are different reasons for such a situation: on one hand, awareness of all the possibilities that competition law provides is still at a low level and the courts in some jurisdictions are still not providing the quality of decisions that is desired and absolutely necessary. This might be because competition law was fully introduced in many jurisdictions in early 1990s and that the courts, if not specialised, such as the European Court of Justice and the Competition Appeal Tribunal in the UK, still require time to get familiar with the very specific infringements that cause significant economic harm. Legalistic approach is neither an advantage nor the future development that would lead to efficient judicial review, nor to a more active approach of both undertakings in the market and the courts. It is still necessary to raise public awareness about the benefits of competition law and policy, and especially about credible institutions, on a daily basis, and this applies to all institutions: competition authorities, sector regulators, and the courts. In some jurisdictions, especially in the Western Balkans, administrative courts are given the competence for the judicial review in competition cases. This is possible due to a wrong understanding that competition authorities are administrative bodies and that the administrative court judges are properly qualified for such review. The question whether such understanding is the best possible one remains open. Nevertheless it should be pointed out that judicial review should be much more focused on the merits, on type of infringements and economic harm, and not on potential procedural mistakes (almost exclusively).

Competition authorities are *sui generis* institutions, much more "quasi courts" than administrative bodies. In administrative disputes, the administrative bodies pass down decisions regarding the rights of the parties; in antitrust judicial reviews the courts pass either decisions on the merits or decisions on procedural mistakes, nevertheless the challenged decisions of the competition authorities are always based on infringements for which the parties may be accountable. The decisions of the competition authorities on the merits are therefore not decisions about the rights of the parties, on the contrary, the decisions are based on infringements; more precisely—the competition authorities do not decide about the rights of the parties, they are entitled to bring decisions if the parties break the law. Another important element that may cast doubts on the competence of the administrative courts in cases of judicial review of competition the authority's decisions is the competence of the competition authorities to impose fines; such decisions, based on the decisions on merits, are not administrative decisions at all.

An additional reason the administrative courts are not the best placed institutions for judicial reviews in competition cases can be found in the level of fines that are as per rule set at up to 10% of the annual turnover, which exceeds the level of fines that are prescribed in specialised laws regarding criminal liability of legal persons. Typical proof for such a statement can be found in the Menarini judgment in which the court upheld the decision of the relevant competition authority (Autorità Garante della Concorrenza e del Mercato, the Italian competition authority). The court found that the fine, which exceeded the level of fine as stipulated by the relevant criminal code for such infringements, was based on procedure in which the procedural standards, and thus the rights of the party against which the procedure was initiated, are significantly lower than in criminal procedure. The European Court of Human Rights then held that it was not incompatible with the European Convention on Human Rights for the sanction to be imposed initially by an administrative authority, provided that the decision was subject to control by a court having full jurisdiction.

## 3 Competition Authorities: What Should They Protect

As previously mentioned, competition law and policy is quite a new category in all SEE jurisdictions. Following early understandings of how markets work, especially bearing in mind Lex Mercatoria and Adam Smith with the recognition of potential anticompetitive behaviour, the first institution, the U.S. Federal Trade Commission, was established in 1914, and the Treaty of Rome, which introduced the five competition rules, was signed 60 years ago, on 25 March 1957. Bearing in mind these facts, it is no surprise that there are still some misunderstandings of competition rules.

There is a wrong understanding that consumers should be protected under competition law, although the incumbent Competition Commissioner Margrethe Vestager correctly emphasised that "competition is a consumer issue" at BEUC General Assembly, on 13 May 2016 (Vestager 2016). Former Competition Commissioner Mario Monti pointed out that "consumers in Europe expect, need and deserve a strong and ambitious competition policy" at the International Cartel Conference in Berlin in 2001, however it should not be understood that the competition law and policy exist for the sake of consumer's benefit only, usually identified as better choice and better price/quality ratio (Monti 2001). Competition policy should be understood as the vision that consumer benefits should also be taken into account. It is evident that consumers are not directly protected by competition law and policy. Consumers benefit from efficient competition, which is achieved by efficient competition law and policy; nevertheless, they are legally protected under the comprehensive general civil legal framework. It is even remains unknown to what extent the consumers need a specific law on consumer protection, if they are properly protected by the general, non-specific legal framework. Much more importantly, consumers are properly informed about their rights, about the possibilities that the general legal framework provides. If consumers are properly informed, then it can be expected that they will not be regarded as average consumers, exposed to consumer fraud, etc., but as reasonable consumers, knowing their rights and able to protect them. Regarding the effects that competition law and policy may have on consumer benefits, it is undisputed that consumers will benefit if competition authorities, sector regulators and courts are able to perform efficient enforcement. If consumers need a specific legal framework with regard to competition law and policy, it is worth considering introducing (if it has not been introduced already) possibilities of class actions (collective redress) in private enforcement of the competition law; such introduction would provide consumers with better chances to recover damages from possible competition infringements (Kroes 2009).

Another common misapprehension is that competition law and policy should protect the competitors. Again, competition law and policy cannot protect one or more competitors in the market; competitors/undertakings should have the best conditions in the market and enjoy full support of their business activities when the proper conditions are fulfilled: having a transparent and non-discriminatory legal framework that provides a level playing field and institutions that perform efficient enforcement. Both dilemmas regarding consumer benefits (and not protection) and the competitors' lawful interests were addressed by former Competition Commissioner Mario Monti in his prominent remark that the European Commission and all national competition authorities should perform "consumer oriented competition policy" and that all jurisdictions should provide is a level playing field for all market participants (Monti 2004). Efficient competition should be protected by competition law and policy, which should be achieved by fighting cartels and abuses of dominance, and by prohibiting mergers that would significantly impede effective competition.

## 4 How Should Competition Authorities Be Organised?

There is no "one size fits all" rule. Competition authorities and other institutions, as authorities that are in charge of antitrust, merger control, state aid (monitoring), sector regulation, consumer policy, trade defence instruments, etc., clearly identified as guardians of public interest, may be organised in different ways according to size and development, both economic and institutional, depending on the jurisdictions concerned. There are no detailed rules on how the institutions should be organised; nevertheless, there is a very simple rule that should always be respected—all institutions should be granted functional independence and should in no way be exposed to political influence.[1]

There are different conditions for providing functional independence; however, two of them are inevitable for supplying this kind of independence and thus a reasonable level of autonomy. First, the authority should have the competence to issue final decisions, subject to judicial review only. Any kind of administrative review significantly jeopardises functional independence. Second, the authority should have the right to decide on the necessary financial and human resources on its own. Limiting resources directly affects the enforcement record and the level of expertise.

This is more easily said, even stipulated in the legal framework, than provided in practice. The judiciary has a specific position and is not subject to the comments regarding autonomy and independence in this paper.

As for other institutions, such as competition authorities and sector regulators, the question of independence and accountability remains a special challenge to be discussed. Most of competition authorities are formally independent, their administration appointed in different ways, either by parliament, executive government, president, etc., for a specific, mostly renewable period of time. In competition law, the conditions for extraordinary dismissal are quite similar and in line with the general legal system(s), nevertheless there are different ways of how to violate the spirit of the regulation and abuse the extraordinary dismissal instrument. One of the models is to amend competition law for some other reasons, e.g. more precise elaboration of procedural rules, alignment with the EU *acquis* or including provisions that would *prima facie* appear as constructive upgrading of the current legal system. If in such cases the transitional provisions do not provide for the current administration of the respective authority to retain the current term of office until the end of the given mandate, then it is obvious that such a model represents a typical political influence on appointments.

A more sophisticated model of negatively influencing the independence of the institutions is the limitation of financial resources. If the authorities are not provided sufficient financial resources, they cannot afford to recruit and train the experts that are absolutely necessary for efficient enforcement.

The staff of competition authorities and sector regulators can provide their service at a high professional level only when such experts are properly trained and motivated.

[1]Indeed, as it stems from the Communication (Commission 2014) and Working Documents (Commission 2014a, b) adopted on the occasion of the tenth anniversary of the Regulation 1/2003, the European Commission does not provide clear guidance to the Member States on the issue of competition authority organisation.

(De)motivating such experts, who must have specific interdisciplinary knowledge, by equalising them with administrators that are engaged in "classic" administrative tasks, is the perfect way for high staff turnover, thus weakening the institutions. If the human resources are lacking, then the enforcement records are hardly credible and we can ask ourselves whether the philosophy of the EU Competition Commissioners can actually be implemented in practice. In small jurisdictions and in jurisdictions that have only recently initiated sound competition law and policy, the challenge of recruiting, training and especially retaining experts, who are scarce, is high and sometimes also not in the interest of partisan politics and political horse trading.

If there is a proper political consensus, the competition institutions should be provided with sufficient financial resources in order to provide credible enforcement and sound competition advocacy. Competition advocacy is very important as it provides relevant information to the authorities on how to ensure conditions for competitive market, a level playing field, and how to prevent state (government) induced competition distortions. In small jurisdictions and ones that had only recently introduced market economy and competition law and policy, competition advocacy is very desirable. It should be aimed at all relevant stakeholders, lawmakers or those who have executive powers for legal implementation. It should also provide awareness raising activities in order to raise the level of competition (and general legal) culture. A brief overview of the enforcement records of the competition authority can show whether an authority has set the proper priorities and/or whether it possesses sufficient human and financial resources.

Another challenge, especially in EU candidate countries, is what competence competition authorities should be granted. Should such authorities have the competence for antitrust and merger control only; should they also be in charge of state aid monitoring; should they also focus on consumer protection; should all sector regulators be merged into one institution, etc.

## 5 Antitrust, State Aid and Consumer Protection Under One Roof

Following the model of the DG Competition of the European Commission, the authorities in certain jurisdictions, especially in some current candidate countries, have been granted jurisdiction over antitrust, merger control and state aid control. The question is whether such a model is good. There are some reasons *pro* and *contra* such model, as is the case for different models available.

European Commission is the guardian of the internal market, without any borders, (however some limits, especially with regard to free movement of labour force, still exist), level playing field, common trade and competition policy, etc. It is logical and inevitable that the EU has monopoly over state aid control, otherwise the conditions in the internal market would be distorted as it cannot be expected that all member states will provide the same standards regarding state aid, for different reasons: political stability, social compromises, and (potentially) better results in elections at the state and local level.

Of course, the EU member states are not prohibited to provide state aid, however this must be done according to the rules and under strict control of the EC (DG Competition).

EU member states do have the right to design and implement their state aid policy, although with the burden of responsibility, even though there is a feeling that the state aid grantors sometimes do not really care, or do not have enough related knowledge, for a transparent, non-discriminatory state aid policy, with all the potential negative consequences.

The authorities, state aid grantors, should bear in mind that the undertakings that have been granted unlawful state aid, should recover such aid or go bankrupt (e.g. British Aerospace and/or Rover). The grantors are also especially accountable to the citizens, since as taxpayers they contribute to the budget, and the unlawfully dispensed state aid funds should be used properly, for the common good.

To provide common, transparent, and efficient state aid policy and its control, the authority is given exclusively to the European Commission, in order to avoid conflict of interests and political economy pitfalls. The question is whether the national competition authorities are the best placed authorities for the control of state aid.

It should also be noted that specific challenges regarding human and financial resources appear already when competition authorities implement their tasks in the domain of antitrust and merger control, when the parties in the procedures are undertakings that are active in the market, and not state authorities. Can we imagine what would happen (in the context of available human and financial resources) if the competition authority were to constantly warn the "master" of their financial (and subsequently human) resources of what is proper and what is not.[2]

Competition authorities should provide expert view of competition distortion, without any political influence. Deciding about competition infringements and related fines is strictly an expert decision. Deciding about mergers should also be strictly an expert decision, which should not be exposed to any political influence. If the undertakings concerned are not happy with the decision and if they feel that their rights were violated, judicial review is always a possibility. If the competition authority has erred, the courts can pass a decision that will recover (potential) damages of the undertaking(s) concerned.

Even in Germany, where the Federal Minister of Economy can challenge the decision (prohibition of a merger) of the Bundeskartellamt (German Federal Cartel Office), this can be done only through court procedure, on the basis of proven public interest (a very limited choice of economic and social policy elements) and it is in no

[2]The very sensitive question of state-aid induced distortions of competition is not elaborated in this specific contribution, however, non-transparent and unlawful state aid policy is in fact a state-induced distortion of competition.

way a “classic” case of over-ruling. Spain has followed the same model for competition law since 2007.

The situation with state aid monitoring is a bit more complicated. The monitoring institution has to be the guardian of the state aid rules and has to have the power to inform the state aid grantors how to design and implement the state aid policy, and also should have the power not just to inform, but also to block the decisions of the state on different levels. This kind of decision has a political dimension and if state aid monitoring and “classic competition” are organised under the same authority, the question remains open whether political influence, based on different interests related to state aid policy, extends also to antitrust and merger control enforcement.

Decisions in antitrust cases are primarily expert decisions; the influence of politics is rare and usually does not represent a major influence on decisions. It is presumed that a bit more political influence appears in cases of merger control, however it is unclear how strict merger control should be, having in mind the dynamics of the markets, especially in economies in transition, having only recently opened their borders.

However, state aid policy and implementation (granting, monitoring, evaluation, recovery) represent a specific challenge. It is always in focus of daily politics for different reasons; buying social peace, ensuring better starting positions for elections at state and local levels, using public funds for separate (sometimes strictly individual) interests represent very specific challenges and obstacles for a sound, transparent and non-discriminatory approach.

Regarding state aid policy and implementation, as well as control, political interests and influence are constantly present, sometimes less intensively, sometimes with direct influence on specific decisions.

Political influence regarding state aid is most likely unavoidable. Giving antitrust (and merger control) to the same authority with the state aid control may lead to political influence and also have a spill-over effect on expert decisions in antitrust and merger controls fields.

There is another issue that should be mentioned. The exclusive authority over state aid control in the European Union is granted to DG Competition. The EU member states therefore do not have any decisive (control) power.

In the case of candidate countries, it is convenient to have separate authorities, as one (antitrust and merger control) will continue operation also after EU accession, whereas the other (state aid control) will have to be reorganised as a contact point only.

It was already mentioned what kind of data collection problems competition authorities encounter in antitrust cases. The competition authorities request data, and may even impose procedural fines if the data are not submitted on time, however ministries have the best overview of the relevant data, overseeing either granting the aid and/or financial transfers, and the ministry responsible for finance.

The idea of having an inter-ministerial commission for state aid control is perhaps a much better idea than to incorporate state-aid monitoring into the competition authorities, for at least three reasons: (1) such a commission would include representatives from different sectors (state aid grantors) and other institutions whose interest should be transparent state aid policy (having influence over market structure, competition, and macroeconomic policy), as well as the ministry in charge of finance, where all relevant data is controlled; (2) such a commission should have only administrative support from the ministry responsible for finance, which should not have dominant influence; and (3) the decisions of the commission could be subject to a "gold anchor", effectively a veto right, granted (possibly) to the representative of the competition authority and/or representative of the institution in charge of macroeconomic policy and development.

Another important element not supporting vesting state aid control in the competition authority is the fact that following the EU accession the competence over state aid control will rest with the European Commission; the coordination unit of the new member state, for coordination and transferring data, should be placed in the institution that has the best overview over relevant data and an additionally very important element, according to the EU Progress Reports for all candidates, the field of antitrust is not as strictly observed and evaluated as the field of state aid; however, this means that the focus will be on state aid. Bearing in mind all the challenges related to scarce human and financial resources in the field of antitrust, state aid policy will represent a top priority, with antitrust enforcement suffering accordingly.

If state aid policy is a very detailed and clear element of comprehensive economic and competition policy, consumer protection represents a completely different category. As already briefly elaborated, it is a question of how we understand the term *consumer protection*: is it protection from consumer fraud, is it a policy of comprehensive information of consumers, and of course the question who should implement it?

The state administration has the firm obligation to adopt and implement laws that will not harm consumers. There are different institutions, such as inspectorates: market surveillance authorities, phytosanitary inspectorates, etc. that are tasked with controlling the market conditions, in order to provide the required standards to consumers. Competition authorities, if they are efficient in their enforcement, provide consumers with a better choice and better price-quality ratio, as a result of efficient competition in the market.

What kind of additional protection still needed, in addition to the one originally provided by the general legal framework and credible enforcement of the institutions concerned? And from whom to protect the consumers? The state institutions, relevant authorities, should provide their services in the interest of the public, bearing in mind that they are financed from the budget, they should always have in mind that the taxpayers, and in broader sense consumers, provide the financial resources for their operations. The fact is that if the consumer rights are not respected, or even infringed, the general civil framework exists to provide the rules, and the courts are there to provide the protection.

The role of consumer organizations is very important in providing proper information in order to promote average consumers to reasonable consumers.

It is unclear what kind of consumer is the focus of our interest: the average consumer or the reasonable one. The reasonable consumer is a properly informed consumer, knowing her/his rights and the consumer policy can be a subject of different models. Nevertheless, the combination of different policies and different goals under the same roof, the one of competition authority, bearing in mind that some policies have only recently been introduced, may not always lead to the desired results.

## 6 Concluding Remarks

There are different models of implementation for different policies. Even for antitrust and merger control there is not necessarily just one institution in each jurisdiction, and the scope of competence of some institutions may be broad. The choice of the best institutional model is still the relevant dilemma in many jurisdictions.

One should not follow the populist approach according to which it would be less expensive if two or more institutions were merged to cut costs. Cutting costs is not the way to introduce efficient institutions. Efficient institutions are not dependent on the number of staff, but on the level of their qualification, good management, and full independence, and that model cannot be considered as a cheap solution. Without investments (in human resources) good results cannot be expected. Although investments may be considered expensive, it can be said that the most expensive investment is the one you do not make.

## References

Bellamy C, Roth PM (2001) Bellamy & Child European community law of competition. Sweet & Maxwell, London

Bishop S, Walker M (2007) Economics of EC competition law: concepts, application and measurement. Sweet & Maxwell, London

Commission Staff Working Document (2014a) Ten years of Antitrust enforcement under regulation 1/2003. SWD 230/2

Commission Staff Working Document (2014b) Enhancing competition enforcement by the Member States' competition authorities: institutional and procedural issues. SWD 231/2

Communication from the Commission (2014) Ten years of Antitrust enforcement under regulation 1/2003: achievements and future perspective. COM 453

Faull J, Nikpay A (2014) The EU law of competition. Oxford University Press, Oxford

Kroes N (2009) Collective redress – delivering justice for victims. Speech/09/88. http://europa.eu/rapid/press-release_SPEECH-09-88_en.htm?locale=en (20 May 2017)

Monti M (2001) Competition and consumers: innovation and choice. Speech/01/275. http://europa.eu/rapid/press-release_SPEECH-01-275_en.htm?locale=en (15 May 2017)

Monti M (2004) Competition for consumers' benefit. Speech 2004/16. http://ec.europa.eu/competition/speeches/text/sp2004_016_en.pdf (22 April 2017)

Vestager M (2016) Competition is a consumer issue. Speech https://ec.europa.eu/commission/commissioners/2014-2019/vestager/announcements/competition-consumer-issue_en (30 May 2017)

# Realigning Competition Advocacy Priorities in the Context of Economic Adjustment Programmes: The Greek Case

**Dimitris Loukas**

## 1 Introduction

This contribution aims to describe the realigned advocacy role of the Hellenic Competition Commission (thereinafter: HCC) and, in particular, its continued efforts to considerably diversify and expand advocacy and outreach activities in recent years, in order to promote structural reforms,[1] pledged in the context of Greece's Stability Support Programme (thereinafter: Adjustment Programme).[2] On this occasion, the contribution also aims to provide a high-level overview of Greece's reforms in the area of product and services markets, and the perceived progress achieved since the inception of the economic crisis (2009), to the extent that the HCC played a direct or indirect role with respect to it.

The HCC's increased focus on advocacy was essentially prompted by specific conditions included in Greece's Adjustment Programme (see Sect. 3). Indeed, the

---

The views expressed in this contribution are personal and do not necessarily represent the views and/or official position of the Hellenic Competition Commission.

[1]In the context of the financial and economic crisis, several EU Member States have undertaken a similar reform effort, aimed at unleashing the growth potential of their economies. Many of these reforms have been implemented under the so-called Memoranda of Understanding, in the context of Economic Adjustment Programmes, in countries such as Portugal, Greece and Cyprus, but reforms are also being promoted and monitored in countries such as Italy and Spain.

[2]Greece has been receiving financial support from Euro area countries and the International Monetary Fund (IMF) to cope with its financial difficulties and economic challenges, since May 2010 (after effectively losing access to the sovereign debt markets). In August 2015, a third assistance programme was launched under the European Stability Mechanism (ESM) framework. Greece's stability support programme aims to support the Greek government's efforts to: (a) address economic imbalances, (b) tackle ensuing social challenges, and (c) pave the way for sustainable economic growth and job creation.

D. Loukas
Hellenic Competition Commission, Athens, Greece



B. Begović, D. V. Popović (eds.), *Competition Authorities in South Eastern Europe*, Contributions to Economics, https://doi.org/10.1007/978-3-319-76644-7_6

2009 financial crisis exposed the structural rigidities and inefficiencies of the Greek economy. Greece's Adjustment Programme thus entailed structural components aimed at reforming and further liberalising the product and services markets.[3] This in turn triggered the most intense and sustained reform pursued by the Greek authorities in this field—a reform in which the HCC, as an independent authority,[4] has played a crucial role. However, aside from the pertinent conditionalities of the Adjustment Programme, the HCC also has taken additional advocacy initiatives, thereby complementing both the reforms detailed in that Programme and its own enforcement action.

A variety of instruments have been used by the Authority for the purposes of diversifying and expanding its advocacy role, including: (a) formal opinions—recommendations for legislative change, addressed to the government (upon request by the competent line ministries or at its own initiative); (b) targeted screening and regulatory impact assessment initiatives in cooperation with the OECD; and (c) publication of compliance and awareness guides. Each of these activities is described below (see Sects. 4–7).

## 2 State-of-Play Before the Adjustment Programme

International reports have consistently painted a grim picture of the progress made by Greece prior to 2010 in promoting structural reforms in the product and services markets, and in particular in the area of professional services. By way of example, the European Commission's 2005 Communication on Professional Services found that Greece had the highest level of regulation with regard to a number of key professional services, compared to other Member States (see Fig. 1).

[3]Several economic and empirical studies, e.g. Nickell (1996), Ahn (2002), Nicoletti and Scarpetta (2003), Voigt (2009), Forlani (2010), Bourlès et al. (2013), Buccirossi et al. (2013), substantiate the positive effect of competition and competition policy on macro-economic outcomes, such as productivity, growth and innovation. Fewer studies, e.g. Mitsopoulos and Pelagidis (2009), Ioannides et al. (2014), Kourandi (2014), Zonzilos (2014), Kotsi et al. (2015), (2016), have recently attempted to address the impact of business environment reforms in the Greek context, albeit most pertinent evidence can be found in regular reports of international organisations, e.g. European Commission, IMF, OECD, World Bank and Bank of Greece, on the occasion of Greece's ongoing economic adjustment programme.

[4]The HCC has the status of an independent administrative authority, in accordance with Greek law. In particular, the HCC enjoys both administrative independence (notably in the sense that there is no oversight or involvement of ministries or other members of the executive in its decision-making process, nor in the selection of staff for management posts within its services or with regard to other administrative decisions usually associated with internal organization and enforcement operations; its Board members are appointed through special parliamentary procedure, while the Authority reports annually to Parliament) and financial independence (in the sense that it has its own financial resources in the form of a contributory fee paid by enterprises and it is not financed through the State budget).

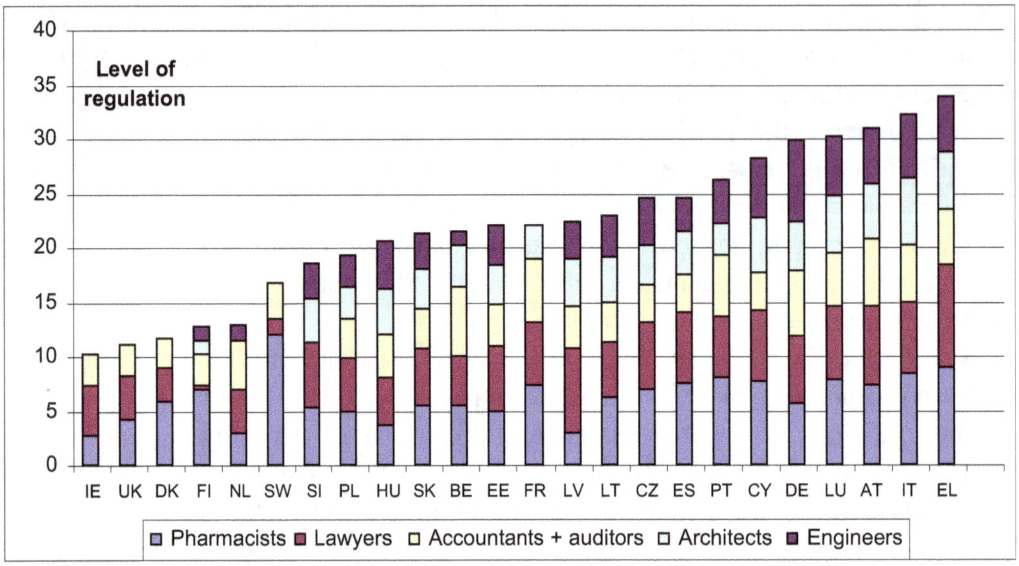


**Fig. 1** Level of regulation in Member States (2005). Source: EUR-Lex database (2005)

According to the EU Commission's findings, Greece did not avail itself of the opportunity to promote structural reforms in professional services in 2004–2005,[5] thereby lagging significantly behind other Member States, based on a comparison of Greece's reform activity against its level of then existing regulation in the professional services sector.

Similarly, the OECD has consistently recorded a high and intense level of regulation in product and services markets in Greece relative to most other OECD Members (see Figs. 2, 3, 4, and 5).

## 3 Increased Focus on Advocacy: Realigned Strategy

Against this backdrop, the Adjustment Programme entailed several milestones pertaining to structural reforms, which in turn prompted the HCC's enhanced focus in advocacy. From the point of view of the Authority, three main pillars

[5]After a series of fact-finding and comparative studies between 2001 and 2003, in the context of the Lisbon Agenda, followed by a structured dialogue with professional associations during 2003–2004, the Commission published a Report on Competition in Professional Services, in February 2004. This Report was supplemented by the Stocktaking Exercise on Regulation of Professional Services in the new EU Member States, published in November 2004. Finally, in September 2005, the Commission issued a follow-up to the 2004 Report, the Professional Services—Scope for More Reform Communication. Overall, national governments were essentially called upon to review the compatibility of their national legislations with EU law and to liberalize professional services in an attempt to promote further internal market integration. However, not all Member States corresponded accordingly.

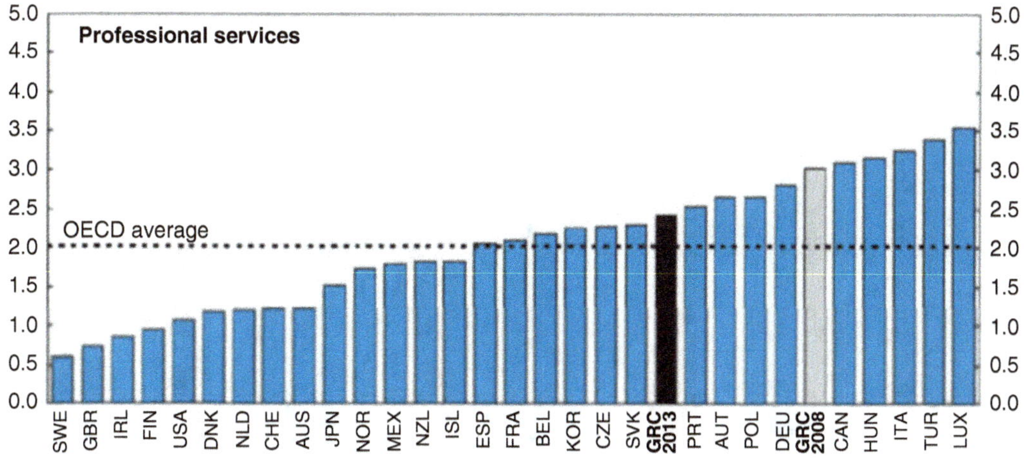


**Fig. 2** Regulatory barriers in professional services. Progress made by Greece—OECD PMR (2013a). Source: OECD (2013b), Regulatory barriers in professional services: Index scale from 0 (least restrictive) to 6 (most restrictive), in OECD Economic Surveys: Greece 2013, OECD Publishing, Paris. https://doi.org/10.1787/eco_surveys-grc-2013-graph-46-en

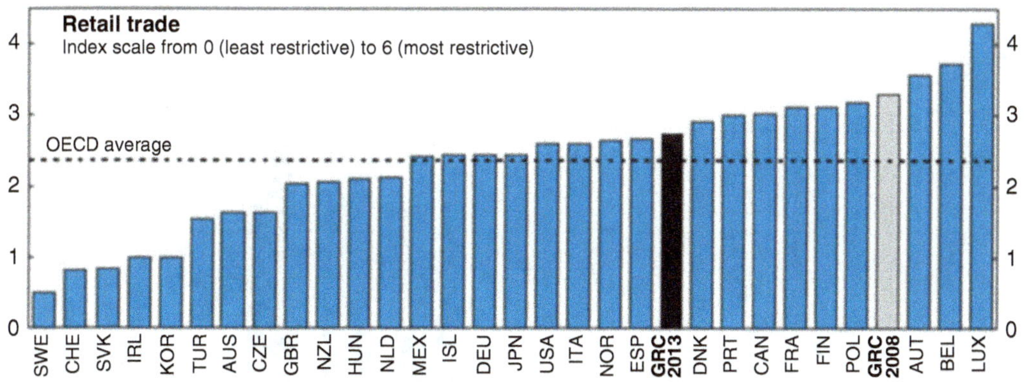


**Fig. 3** Regulatory barriers in retail services. Progress made by Greece—OECD PMR (2013a). Source: OECD (2013b), *OECD Economic Surveys: Greece 2013*, OECD Publishing, Paris. https://doi.org/10.1787/eco_surveys-grc-2013-en

underpinned its priorities in coping with the severe economic crisis, while also contributing to the implementation of the Adjustment Programme:

- maintaining a consistent level of competition enforcement regardless of the crisis, while adapting case allocation and focus;
- strengthening market monitoring activities; and
- considerably diversifying and expanding competition advocacy and outreach efforts, in order to promote structural reforms (pledged in the context of Greece's Economic Adjustment Programme), and increase overall competition awareness.

**Fig. 4** Regulatory barriers in retail services. Comparison Greece v. OECD Average—OECD PMR (2013a). Source: Prepared by the author based on the OECD Indicators of Product Market Regulation database, http://www.oecd.org/eco/growth/indicatorsofproductmarketregulationhomepage.htm#indicators

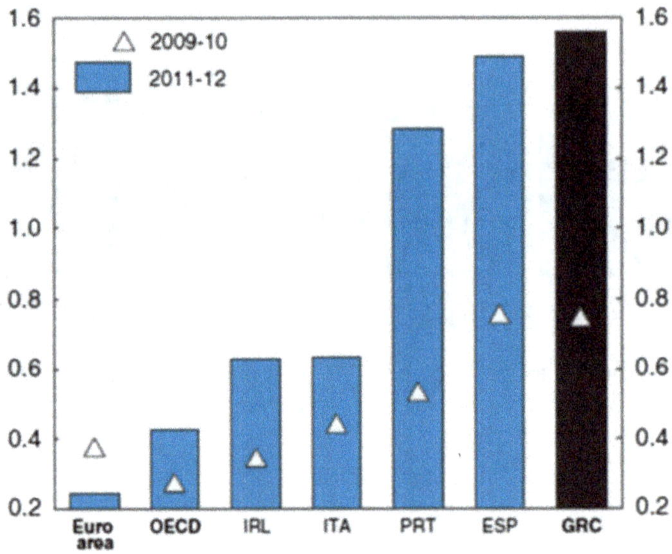


**Fig. 5** Responsiveness to structural reforms recommended by the OECD. Adjusted for the difficulty of undertaking reform (2013). Source: OECD (2013b), Responsiveness to OECD structural reforms recommended in Going for Growth: Adjusted for the difficulty of undertaking reform, in OECD Economic Surveys: Greece 2013, OECD Publishing, Paris. https://doi.org/10.1787/eco_surveys-grc-2013-graph9-en

In particular, the HCC allocated a significant part of its resources to advocacy functions, focused primarily on identifying and removing regulatory obstacles to competition and promoting a genuine competition culture, through outreach activities. During the 2011–2014 period, advocacy work accounted for up to 25% of the

HCC's total output.[6] Furthermore, it amounted to 15% of total output during 2013, thus maintaining record levels compared with the OECD average.

As mentioned, the main reason that prompted the Authority's increased focus on competition advocacy had to do with the Adjustment Programme, in response to the unprecedented economic crisis, which had exposed the structural rigidities and inefficiencies of the Greek economy. In this context, the HCC realigned its strategy, so as to increase the exercise of its advisory powers in the field of identifying and removing regulatory obstacles to competition—the objective being to complement the core enforcement work with initiatives promoting structural reforms—while further promoting competition awareness in areas exhibiting a high risk of anticompetitive conduct (as indicated by recent enforcement action and ensuing patterns in terms of likely and/or repetitive types of infringers). Two factors contributed to this strategic re-alignment:

- the revision of the Greek Competition Act (Law 3959/2011), which gave the HCC the power to issue formal opinions/recommendations for draft legislation potentially affecting competition[7]; and
- specific provisions in the context of Greece's Adjustment Programme, agreed between the EU-ECB-IMF and the Greek government, which gave the Authority a special role in promoting certain reforms (notably, in the area of professional services).

Since 2011, the HCC's advocacy and outreach agenda has revolved around four key themes:

- liberalization of professional services (liberal professions),
- Greece's Competition Assessment Projects—ex post competition assessment of laws and regulations (an OECD-managed project, in partnership with the HCC, which applied the OECD's Competition Assessment Toolkit[8] in designated sectors of the Greek economy), and
- addressing legislative distortions mostly affecting retail and food supply chains,

[6] Measured by the total number of formal decisions and recommendations issued by the HCC in that time frame.

[7] The revision of the Greek Competition Act was a condition of the first Adjustment Programme. In particular, the commitment agreed upon by the Greek government in the context of the Adjustment Programme included the abolition of the notification system for anti-competitive agreements that would allow a full-fledged pass-on to the "legal exemption" regime (as established by EU Regulation 1/2003), the introduction of a prioritisation system regarding complaints that would enhance the HCC's competence to reject complaints, the strengthening of the HCC's members independence and the establishment of a more reasonable time-frame for the resolution of cases.

[8] The OECD's Competition Assessment Toolkit helps governments to eliminate barriers to competition by providing a method for identifying unnecessary restraints on market activities and developing alternative, less restrictive measures that still achieve government policy objectives. The full text of the OECD's Competition Assessment Toolkit, including principles and guidelines for applying the methodology set out therein, can be found at: http://www.oecd.org/daf/competition/assessment-toolkit.htm. The Toolkit was first published in 2007 and then updated in 2010 and 2015. The updated version provides additional examples of the benefits of competition and is

– the publication of competition compliance and awareness guides, primarily addressing trade associations, as well as procurement/contract awarding public authorities.

Each of these advocacy initiatives is further explained below.

## 4 Liberalization of Professional Services

In the context of Greece's Adjustment Programme, the HCC (as an independent authority) was called upon to issue formal opinions/recommendations aimed at liberalising several professions. This was an exercise that essentially consisted of an extensive review of existing laws and regulations from the point of view of competition, focusing on the entry and exercise of a number of regulated professions.

This prompted the most far-reaching intervention by the HCC in the area of liberal professions (and the most far-reaching intervention ever in terms of regulatory obstacles to competition). During 2011–2012 alone, the HCC's task force on liberal professions reviewed laws and regulations affecting more than 55 regulated professions (ultimately issuing 17 formal opinions). The following year (2013), the HCC issued three new formal opinions aimed at identifying and removing regulatory obstacles pertaining to the access and exercise of a number of professional services.

Overall, the professional services reviewed by the HCC in this context fell within two broad categories. The first category included some key regulated professions, such as lawyers, accountants, and engineers, which were addressed specifically by Law 3919/2011. In particular, this legislation, which was a significant component of Greece's action plan on structural reforms: (1) provided for the across-the-board abolition of a number of restrictions affecting all liberal professions, including fixing of fees,[9] entry requirements, and reserved rights/activities[10] (e.g. quantitative and/or qualitative admission requirements to a profession, fixed number of professionals

further supplemented by a companion volume with detailed technical guidance on key issues to be considered when performing competition assessment.

[9]This restriction, notably in the form of fixed or minimum fees/prices/charges for professional services provided, is perceived to have the most detrimental effects on competition. Recommended prices may also potentially have a negative effect on competition, as it may facilitate the coordination of prices between service providers and/or mislead consumers about reasonable price levels.

[10]Excessive licensing regulation is also perceived as reducing the supply of service providers, with negative consequences for competition and quality of service. According to the EU Commission's findings, several professions are subject to qualitative entry restrictions in most Member States. Furthermore, in many cases, entry restrictions are coupled with reserved rights to provide certain services (e.g. in some Member States the pharmacist and notary professions are even subject to quantitative entry restrictions based on demographic criteria). Unjustified entry restrictions of that sort, combined with reserved rights, may restrict new entries and increase of output to the detriment of competition and economic efficiency.

allowed to exercise a profession, territorial restrictions in the exercise of a profession[11]), restrictions on advertising,[12] etc.; (2) replaced the previous administrative license system (where applicable) with a simple notification and ex-post review system; and (3) included specific provisions for the liberalization of certain key regulated professions, such as lawyers, notaries, chartered accountants, and engineers. For the latter selected professional activities, the HCC issued a number of recommendations, including for example:

- for lawyers: the removal of fixed minimum fees, advertising restrictions, and also territorial restrictions on where lawyers can practice in Greece;
- for notaries: the relaxing of rules on fixed fees and the maximum number of notaries allowed to operate per prefecture;
- for architects/engineers: the removal of fixed minimum fees; and
- for chartered accountants: the removal of fixed minimum fees.

The second category included all other liberal professions, where a horizontal approach was opted for by Law 3919/2011. As indicated above, for all other professional activities, the legislation just provided, in a general manner, for the abolition of certain regulatory restrictions (e.g. fixing of fees, quantitative entry requirements and territorial restrictions, etc.) and for the abolition of the previous administrative license system for the entry into and exercising of each profession.

However, it also provided the opportunity to obtain exemption from full liberalization by profession, on the basis of overriding public policy considerations and being subject to the principle of proportionality. In this context, the government entrusted the HCC with the task of reviewing all such exemption requests pertaining to Law 3919/2011, i.e. requests to maintain and/or re-instate prior authorization requirements and other restrictions regarding the exercising and access to those liberal professions where the across-the-board liberalization approach had been applied. In this regard, the HCC applied the key methodology of the OECD Competition Toolkit and/or similar competition impact assessment techniques, notably by assessing and weighing public policy considerations in light of the principle of proportionality. By way of example, the HCC reviewed exemption requests pertaining to the following professions: chartered (sworn-in) appraisers/valuers; actuaries; accountants; tax consultants; geotechnicians (including the production and marketing of propagating material and fertilizers); licensed providers of services relating to public security and public safety; tourist guides; licensed providers of educational services; licensed providers of health-related services; and licensed sellers of tobacco products.

---

[11]Usually, requirements that licensed professionals exercise the profession within a particular geographic area of Greece or restrictions on their ability to open and/or operate from a secondary/subsidiary establishment (outside the primary geographic area of their activities).

[12]Advertising may similarly facilitate competition by informing consumers about different products and allowing them to make better-informed purchasing decisions. It is also widely recognized that advertising, and in particular comparative advertising, can be a crucial competitive tool for new firms that are entering the market and for existing firms that want to launch new products.

The intensity of the HCC's review varied according to the conditions prevailing in each profession. In certain cases, the Authority's recommendations were tailored-made as to correspond to the specific exemption request made, while in other cases the HCC opted for issuing wide-ranging recommendations (essentially comprising an overhaul of the way a certain profession is organised and performed).

The opinion concerning chartered (sworn in) appraisers/valuers (HCC Opinion No. 16/VI/2012) is an example of the latter approach. In their request for exemption, chartered appraisers asked to maintain: (i) the limited access to the profession (*numerus clausus*), (ii) the exclusive rights to provide certain valuation services, (iii) the prohibition in the exercise of the profession by legal entities or other EU nationals, and (iv) their fixed remuneration. In doing so, they claimed overriding public policy considerations, such as the protection of consumers and the effectiveness of the tax collection system. However, in its opinion/recommendations addressed to the government, the HCC found that the stated public considerations were not substantiated and, in any event, did not comply with the principle of proportionality. The HCC, therefore, recommended that all such restrictions should be lifted. Furthermore, after reviewing the conditions of entry into, and exercise of, this profession, the HCC further proposed, *inter alia*, that the membership of the appraisers' organization be substantially broadened based on transparent and objective criteria, either through the admission of all natural and legal entities having equivalent vocational qualifications or, alternatively, by accrediting additional (and competing) professional associations. The HCC also recommended that a registry of certified appraisers be created (by specialty).

Following the conclusion of the exemption review exercise, the Greek government proceeded with the adoption of the secondary legislation necessary to ensure the proper implementation of the reform. To that effect, the Ministry of Finance, in cooperation with the respective competent line ministries by profession, issued a large number of decrees, administrative orders, and mostly circulars addressed to the administration, thereby clarifying the applicable (new) rules by profession, as well the conditions for entry and exercise of each profession.

Overall, according to OECD estimates included in Greece's Economic Survey (Nov. 2013), around 75% of nearly 350 regulated professions were opened to competition by the beginning of 2013, in line with the Hellenic Competition Commission recommendations.

Moving forward, the HCC participated in several follow-on reviews coordinated by the Ministry of Economy (2014–2016), aimed at reviewing the qualifications and other requirements for entry into a number of regulated professions, with a view to lift unnecessary restrictions and overall simplifying access.

By way of example, the HCC issued Opinion No. 34/2014, following a formal request from the Greek Government, on a draft legislation amending the current national legal framework on professional rights of engineers. To this end, the HCC underlined the need for a general revision of the legal framework for the engineering profession and its consolidation into one piece of legislation, as well as the need to remove, uniformly and systematically, the existing contradictions and ambiguities for all engineering projects, public or private. The HCC proposed that the new legal framework: (a) describe the shared and, where necessary and proportionate in light of overriding public interest, the exclusive professional activities of engineers with different specialties, and (b) identify objective criteria for access to and exercise of those professions, based on the engineer's expertise, aptitudes and experience, without reference solely to specific academic titles. The HCC also proposed integrating the current separate registries related to the construction industry based on objective criteria. Finally, the new legal framework could be supplemented by rules of professional conduct and responsibility, which would enable the development and adoption of self-regulatory rules. As immediate measures, the HCC recommended that the government amend the current legislation on civil engineers, architects and topographers so that access to specific professions is determined by objective criteria of expertise and experience, and not merely by reference to academic titles granted by specific institutions. Additionally, the HCC suggested amending specific provisions of the draft laws to ensure equivalence of professional rights among graduates of universities, whether national or foreign, that award engineer degrees corresponding to the abovementioned professions. Following this Opinion, the HCC acted as chair of a legislative committee assigned the task of drawing up Presidential Decrees regarding the criteria for access to, and exercise of, the engineering profession.

## 5 Greece's OECD Competition Assessment Project

### *5.1 First Competition Assessment Project*

The year 2013 saw the successful completion of the most intense advocacy project in recent years, Greece's OECD Competition Assessment Project. During the course of 10 months, a core project team consisting of competition experts from both the OECD and the HCC carried out an assessment of the costs and benefits of regulations potentially restricting competition in four designated sectors of the Greek economy, namely[13]: retail trade, food processing, building materials, and tourism.

The aim of the project was to evaluate existing regulations and propose alternative (less restrictive) regulations, in order to increase competition and bring about longer-term gains to productivity and economic growth. Using the methodology set out in the OECD's Competition Toolkit, the team of experts reviewed more than 1000 pieces of legislation, ultimately identifying 555 problematic regulations and making more than 320 recommendations for legal provisions that should be amended or repealed. By way of example, recommendations included:

[13]These sectors represented 21% of Greece's GDP output, and had a combined turnover of 44.26 billion euros (2011 data). They also represented 1,103,500 jobs, i.e. 24.8% of the total employment in Greece. Lifting the restrictions to competition in these sectors was therefore likely to have significant positive economic impact, both in the short term and in the long term.

- abolishing requirements to seek price approval or price notifications to the authorities or industry associations;
- removing all third-party levies and fees (including the tax on advertising and the levies on flour and cement);
- fully liberalising Sunday trading;
- lifting the 5-day restriction on the shelf life of fresh milk (and replace with less restrictive labelling arrangements);
- liberalising prices of over-the-counter medicines (OTCs) and dietary supplements, as well as distribution channels;
- relaxing regulations on shop promotions and discounts;
- relaxing regulations on cruises and moorings, while allowing marina operators to compete with nearby commercial or fishing ports on prices;
- abolishing all barriers to entry that have been identified (e.g. licensing requirements in the asphalt sector; minimum requirements for storage, or minimum capital requirements in the building materials sector; numerous barriers to investment in tourism activities, such as geographical restrictions or minimum quality requirements; limits on tourist coach activities; restrictions on offices of travel agents; limits to the trade of blended olive oils); and
- removing horizontal regulations that hamper or thwart the proper functioning of markets.

According to the findings from this project, if the recommendations detailed in the report are implemented, considerable benefits are likely to accrue. The project sought to identify the sources of those benefits and, where possible, provide quantitative estimates, either on the basis of certain experiences of deregulation in other countries, or by relating conservative estimates of efficiency gains to the overall size of the business activity affected. Overall, by referencing 66 recommendations out of 329, the project estimated a positive effect for the Greek economy of around 5.2 billion euros, which represents the total of the estimated resulting positive effects on consumer surplus, increased expenditure and higher turnover in the sectors analysed, as a result of the removal of regulatory barriers to competition. The cumulative long-term impact of the lifting of all the restrictions was considered likely to be greater.

Following the publication of the report, the Greek government announced its intention to adopt approximately 80% of the recommendations made, through legislation. The IMF estimated that 237 of the 329 recommendations were fully implemented by June 2014 (IMF Country Report No.14/151). Most of these implemented recommendations were enacted into law by Act No. L. 4254/2014. However, a number of politically sensitive recommendations (e.g. on liberalising Sunday trading, liberalising prices and distribution channels for OTCs and dietary supplements, and extending the shelf life of fresh milk) were adopted either in a partial or in a pilot manner, with some ultimately abandoned, following strong opposition by the professional/trade associations most affected by them.

## 5.2 Second Competition Assessment Project

The second phase of the project was successfully completed in December 2014, following a 5-month in-depth review of legislation, aimed at identifying potential regulatory obstacles to competition in four additional sectors of the economy:

- manufacture of coke and refined petroleum products;
- manufacture of textiles, wearing apparel, leather and related products;
- manufacture of beverages; and
- manufacture of machinery and equipment.

The team of experts reviewed 482 pieces of legislation, identified 154 potential restrictions, and made 88 recommendations for change. The vast majority of these recommendations were subsequently enacted into law (with less recorded opposition levelled against them by professional and trade associations alike).

## 5.3 Third Competition Assessment Project

Following the successful implementation of the first and the second OECD Competition Assessment Projects, a third phase of the Competition Assessment Project was initiated in 2015 and concluded in 2016. Again, the core project team, consisting of competition experts from both the OECD and the HCC, undertook an assessment of regulations potentially restricting competition in the following designated sectors of the Greek economy:

- e-commerce,
- construction,
- media,
- wholesale trade, and
- select subsectors of manufacturing, such as chemicals and pharmaceuticals.

Using the methodology provided in the Competition Assessment Toolkit, the team examined 1288 sector-relevant pieces of legislation, identified 577 possible restrictions to competition, and made 356 recommendations to correct them by less restrictive policies. Similarly, the vast majority of these recommendations were subsequently enacted into law (with less recorded opposition levelled against them by both professional and trade associations, particularly in view of their less politically sensitive nature).

Overall, the HCC's partnership with the OECD on these competition assessment projects has been a testament to the Authority's capabilities and commitment to further strengthening its advocacy role.

## 6 Other Initiatives Regarding Regulatory Distortions Mostly Affecting Retail and the Food Supply Chain

In addition to the abovementioned exercising of its consultative powers under the new Competition Act, and in the context of Greece's Economic Adjustment Programme, the HCC has pursued additional initiatives to promote a genuine competition culture. These advocacy initiatives have mostly targeted regulatory distortions affecting retail and the functioning of the food supply chain, but they also have had a broader educational function.

For example, the HCC issued recommendations focusing on:

- the reform of the so-called Product and Market Regulation Code,[14] in particular by (a) abolishing all delegated powers concerning minimum and/or fixed prices, export bans and/or export restrictions, as well as transportation fees, and (b) retaining certain delegated powers to regulate the conditions for the sale and marketing of certain products only to the extent they comply with EU regulations;
- the abolition of the regulation requiring that all types of infant milk (formulas) for infants under the age of 6 months be sold solely through pharmacies;
- the abolition of the obligation imposed on companies to regularly report their wholesale price lists to the competent line ministry; and
- the removal of regulatory obstacles impeding effective competition in the fuel and the cement sectors.

Some of these recommendations were ultimately enacted into law by the Greek government, while others were adopted partially (recommendations in the fuel and cement sectors), or not effectively implemented (lifting of the restriction to sell baby formulas only through pharmacies).[15]

More recently, the HCC participated in two reviews, undertaken by the Ministry of Development and Competiveness, regarding:

- a market study focusing on barriers to entry to the wholesale sector (completed in December 2014),
- a market study focusing on barriers to entry in e-commerce (completed in December 2014), as well as
- preparation of a Code of Conduct for rebates, offers, promotional actions and stock management (the committee set up for this purpose submitted its final proposal in September 2014, and a Ministerial Decision by the Minister of Development and Competitiveness was issued in November 2014).

---

[14]This Code is essentially a consolidated version of all applicable implementing legislation pertaining to the way products are marketed and sold through various distribution channels in Greece (partly transposing EU legislation in that respect).

[15]The Greek Pharmacists Association successfully challenged the Ministerial Decision implementing this liberalization measure before Greece's Supreme Administrative Court. However, subsequently, and following pressure by the creditors in the context of the Adjustment Project, the measure was re-enacted as a law.

## 7 Overall Progress: Indices

Due to the ongoing recession and the transitional phase of the Greek economy, it is still difficult to quantify the benefits to economic growth brought about by such liberalization efforts and/or measure them in terms of e.g. new professionals entering a specific profession or economic activity in specific sectors, expanding the whole. Nonetheless, several comparative assessment reports, notably those carried out regularly by the OECD, clearly capture Greece's advancement in removing regulatory barriers in professional services to the benefit of competition.[16] Figures 2, 3, and 4 are telling in that respect.

The Greek Centre of Planning and Economic Research (KEPE) reported similar findings in two relatively recent impact assessment reports pertaining to the liberalization of professional services in Greece. In particular, Kotsi et al. (2016) recorded significant progress in terms of lowering the scope and intensity of regulation mostly related to the conditions for entry to a number of professions in Greece and, to a lesser extent, the conditions for exercising those professions. Similarly, the report concludes that it is difficult to quantify—given the transitional status of the Greek economy—the concrete benefits brought about by these liberalization efforts or to determine to what extent the observed decrease in prices of certain professional services are attributable to the implementation of the structural reforms under consideration.

Similarly, considerable progress is recorded by the OECD (2013a, b, c) in terms of promoting structural reforms in the retail sector (relative to other OECD member countries), as well as with respect to the level and intensity of product market regulation as a whole:

The perceived responsiveness of the Greek administration to structural reforms, as adjusted for the difficulty in undertaking those reforms (e.g. in view of the continuous economic crisis, their ensuing impact on and/or resistance of vested interests), is also deemed more significant relative to other OECD Members for that same period (see Fig. 5).

As an aside, the Word Bank Doing Business Survey recorded significant progress made by Greece in terms of easing conditions of entry into business during the 2011–2014 period (by the overall cutting red tape, relaxing regulations and reducing costs), notably as compared to Italy, Portugal and Spain, which is consistent with the above OECD findings.

[16]According to the OECD's Economic Survey of Greece (Nov. 2013), significant progress has been achieved overall in promoting market reforms, since the inception of the crisis (2009–2010), albeit from a low starting point. The OECD recommended that product and services reforms be continued unabated, as such regulations were still (as of early 2013) among the most restrictive in the OECD.

## 8 Competition Compliance and Awareness Guides and Other Outreach Activities

During the last 5 years (2011–2016), the HCC also issued a number of compliance and awareness guides promoting competition. The following campaigns are noteworthy.

### *8.1 Trade Associations*

The HCC launched an initiative to publish a new competition compliance guide, specifically addressing trade associations. This initiative was complemented by speeches and workshops, undertaken by the Authority in cooperation with interested professional associations, the aim being to promote awareness of competition law and of the overall benefits of effective competition. The HCC's advocacy focus on trade associations follows a relatively high number of infringement decisions issued in recent years related to collusive practices by trade associations and other professional bodies. This appears to be a Greek particularity as compared to most other EU Member States. However, it comes as a direct result of the disproportionate number of self-employed professionals and of the intra-profession protectionist culture still widespread in the services markets. The Authority's outreach efforts in this regard aim to promote a genuine competition culture and encourage self-regulation that respects competition rules.

### *8.2 Public Procurement and Bid-Rigging*

A new guide specifically addressing public procurement/contract awarding entities was published in 2015, particularly focusing on practical examples and methods to detect and/or avert bid-rigging. The *Guide for Public Procurement Authorities: Detection and Prevention of Collusive Practices in Procurement Tenders* specifically aimed at enhancing the awareness of public officials with regard to bid-rigging practices. It was followed by two competition training sessions for public procurement officials on bid-rigging detection and prevention (partly in cooperation with the OECD). As indicated by recent HCC enforcement activities,[17] this is an area that increasingly exhibits a high risk of anticompetitive conduct, thus the need for the Authority to engage in focused outreach activities.

[17]See e.g. HCC investigations into the construction sector, haemodialysis filters, and waste management.

### 8.3 *Franchising*

Likewise, the HCC issued guidelines (in the form of Q&As) with regard to the application of competition law rules in franchise agreements, in order to help franchisors and franchisees understand the types of conduct that may infringe competition law.

### 8.4 *Regulatory Impact Assessment: Legislative Process*

The HCC is currently cooperating closely with the General Secretariat of the Government in an attempt to promote a coherent Regulatory Impact Assessment (RIA) strategy at the central administration level. In this context, the Authority will be publishing competition-specific guidelines for the assessment of laws and regulation by the competent line ministries—competition being a significant component of the RIA.

## 9 Concluding Remarks

The scope and intensity of the Authority's advocacy agenda in recent years has involved certain risks. The first risk pertains to the over-extension of scarce human resources, often to the detriment of expeditious and effective enforcement. The second risk pertains to the possibility of non-competition policy considerations creeping in to the Authority's decision making process in the area of advocacy, given that its recommendations often entail special weight pursuant to the Adjustment Programme and, as a result, there is increased pressure to give precedence to other policy considerations (incl. Social policy, labour issues, etc.) when carrying out the assessment of laws and regulations.

However, one needs to recall that the HCC's efforts in this regard have taken place against a backdrop of the longest and steepest recession in the history of the European Union, with the Greek economy in 2013 contracting for the sixth consecutive year (a cumulative drop in real GDP of more than 20% since the inception of the crisis, coupled with record levels of unemployment). Several studies suggest that economic recovery in Greece has been partly hampered by the prevailing situation in the products and services markets, which remain among the most strictly regulated markets in the OECD area. Therefore, structural reforms, particularly in the context of professional services, are a necessary precondition for overcoming the constraints imposed by the crisis, for building competitive industries that can withstand international pressure, and, ultimately, for sustaining a new growth model that will realise the economy's productive potential.

It is important to carefully design the timing and manner of publicly presenting the outcomes of the competition assessment review, particularly in cases where there is a trade off in terms of the cost of implementing the proposed recommendations (e.g. a funding gap created by lifting third-party levies on goods or services), so as to mitigate adverse publicity and allow for a substantive debate on the optimal way forward, while anticipating unfounded opposition by professional vested interests.

Most importantly, the HCC's recent experience in advocacy and other outreach efforts speaks plainly about the urgent need to change the legislation production process, the need to pursue efficient outcomes that more accurately reflect the general public interest, and the need to move away from often favouring the interests of certain professional groups and other vested interests. In particular, it speaks towards the need to implement a coherent Regulatory Impact Assessment strategy at the level of the central administration, so as to promote the ex ante control of draft laws and regulations, thereby pre-empting regulatory barriers to competition and safeguarding the previously implemented reforms. This is particularly important, as the conclusion of the Adjustment Programme is most likely to ease the pressure on the central administration to continue promoting structural reforms.

## References


Ahn S (2002) Competition, innovation and productivity growth. OECD economics department working papers, no. 137. https://doi.org/10.1787/182144868160

Bourlès R, Cette G, Lopez J, Mairesse J, Nicoletti G (2013) Do product market regulations in upstream sectors curb productivity growth? Panel data evidence for OECD countries. Rev Econ and Stat 95(5):1750–1768. https://doi.org/10.1162/rest_a_00338

Buccirossi P, Ciari L, Duso T, Spagnolo G, Vitale C (2013) Competition policy and productivity growth: an empirical assessment. Rev Econ Stat 95(4):1324–1336. https://doi.org/10.1162/rest_a_00304

EUR-Lex database (2005) Communication from the commission to the council, the European Parliament, the European economic and social committee and the committee of the regions—professional services—scope for more reform—follow-up to the report on competition in professional services, COM(2004) 83 of 9 February 2004 (SEC(2005) 1064) /* COM/2005/0405 final (hereinafter: 2005 communication). http://eur-lex.europa.eu/legal-content/en/TXT/?uri=CELEX%3A52005DC0405

Forlani E (2010) Competition in the services sector and the performances of manufacturing firms: does liberalization matter? CESifo working paper no. 2942. https://www.cesifo-group.de/DocDL/cesifo1_wp2973.pdf. Accessed 8 Nov 2017

Hellenic Competition Commission (2012–2015) Annual reports 2012, 2013, 2014, 2015. https://www.epant.gr/. Accessed 8 Nov 2017

Hellenic Competition Commission (2012–2015) Annual report on competition policy developments (submissions to the OECD). https://www.epant.gr/. Accessed 8 Nov 2017

IMF (2014, June) IMF country report no. 14/151. http://www.imf.org/external/pubs/ft/scr/2014/cr14151.pdf. Accessed 8 Nov 2017

Ioannides S, Danchev S, Giotopoulos I, Paratsiokas N, Pavlou G, Peppas K, Stavraki S (2014) The microeconomic effects of business environment reforms. http://ketlib.lib.unipi.gr/xmlui/bitstream/handle/ket/671/micro_effects_business_environment_reforms_en.pdf?sequence=2. Accessed 8 Nov 2017

Kotsi A, Athanassiou E, Kanellopoulos NC, Karagiannis R, Papaioannou S, Katselidis I (2015) Liberalization of professions: extent and expected effect. Report no 71, resource document. The Centre of Planning and Economic Research (KEPE). https://www.kepe.gr/index.php/en/research/recent-publications/reports/item/2734-vathmos_apel. Accessed 8 Nov 2017
Kotsi A, Athanassiou E, Kanellopoulos NC, Karagiannis R, Katselidis I (2016) Impact assessment of the liberalization in 20 professions. Report no 73, resource document. The Centre of Planning and Economic Research (KEPE). https://www.kepe.gr/index.php/en/research/recent-publications/reports/item/2830-ek_73_en. Accessed 8 Nov 2017
Kourandi F (2014) Indicators of business performance and progress reform. National and Kapodistrian University of Athens. http://ketlib.lib.unipi.gr/xmlui/bitstream/handle/ket/669/indicators_final_report_en.pdf?sequence=2
Mitsopoulos M, Pelagidis T (2009) Vikings in Greece: kleptocratic interest groups in a closed, rent-seeking economy. Cato J 29(3). http://citeseerx.ist.psu.edu/viewdoc/download?doi=10.1.1.306.6716&rep=rep1&type=pdf. Accessed 8 Nov 2017
Nickell SJ (1996) Competition and corporate performance. J Polit Econ 104(4):724–746. https://doi.org/10.1787/536410876068
Nicoletti G, Scarpetta S (2003) Regulation, productivity and growth: OECD evidence. Econ Pol 18 (36):9–72. https://doi.org/10.1787/078677503357
OECD (2013a) Indicators of product market regulation database. http://www.oecd.org/eco/growth/indicatorsofproductmarketregulationhomepage.htm. Accessed 8 Nov 2017
OECD (2013b) OECD economic surveys: Greece 2013. OECD Publishing, Paris. https://doi.org/10.1787/eco_surveys-grc-2013-en
OECD (2013c) Evaluation of competition enforcement and advocacy activities: the results of an OECD survey, DAF/COMP/WP2(2012)7/FINAL, Official OECD documents database. http://www.oecd.org/general/official-unclassied-documents.htm. Accessed 8 Nov 2017
Voigt S (2009) The effects of competition policy on development—cross-country evidence using four new indicators. J Dev Stud 45(8):1225–1248. https://doi.org/10.1080/00220380902866862
Zonzilos N (2014) Assessing the macroeconomic impact of structural reforms in Greece, resource document. Foundation for Economic & Industrial Research. https://memorandabilia.files.wordpress.com/2016/05/macro_narrative_report_en.pdf. Accessed 8 Nov 2017

# The Role of Competition Advocacy: The Serbian Experience

**Ivana Rakić**

## 1 Introduction

As a young competition authority, the Serbian Commission for the Protection of Competition (hereafter, Commission) is buildings up its capacity with the primary goal to effectively and consistently enforcing competition rules. The use of this broad and undoubtedly important "traditional" tool for promotion of a competitive market and thereby protection of competition and consumer welfare has been the first duty of the Commission since its establishment in 2005.[1]

Although the Commission remains committed to the systematic enforcement of the competition rules, enforcement is not the only way and not always the most effective tool to encourage greater competition. The Commission very early on recognised the need to do more than simply enforce competition law and to take into account the other segments of competition policy for which substantial resources should be allocated. Therefore, competition advocacy was included in Serbian competition policy and the Commission proceeded to perform this additional function, allowing it to influence all the policies that affect competition in the national market.

During a period of only 12 years, competition advocacy became a very important segment of Serbian competition policy and a complement to the Commission's

---

The findings, interpretations, and conclusions expressed in this paper are those of the author and do not necessarily reflect the views of the Commission for the Protection of Competition of Republic of Serbia.

[1]The Law on the Protection of Competition (2009, 2013) regulates the protection of competition in the market of the Republic of Serbia, in order to achieve economic prosperity and social well-being, and especially the benefits of the consumers (Article 1).

I. Rakić
Commission for the Protection of Competition of the Republic of Serbia, Belgrade, Serbia

Institute of Comparative Law, Belgrade, Serbia
e-mail: ivana.rakic@kzk.gov.rs



B. Begović, D. V. Popović (eds.), *Competition Authorities in South Eastern Europe*, Contributions to Economics, https://doi.org/10.1007/978-3-319-76644-7_7

enforcement activities, although it substituted competition enforcement on several occasions.[2] The Commission's proactive activities were focused on the development of a competition culture and promotion of an open, competitive market. Its approach stems from the transformational processes in the Serbian economy, especially its ongoing fundamental changes.

Considering the importance of competition advocacy in developing and transition countries, such as Serbia, the aim of this article is to provide a short review and analysis of the stipulations of the Law on the Protection of Competition related to the competencies of the Commission in the field of advocacy, and to give a *de lege lata* overview of several examples from the Commission's practice.

Section 2 of this paper examines the definition of competition advocacy and the significance of this advocacy in Serbia and other developing and/or transition countries, as well as certain prerequisites for effective advocacy by competition authorities. Section 3 is related to the Serbian legal framework for competition advocacy. Section 4 focuses on the most successful examples and highlights Serbian experience and some realised cases of advocacy initiatives. The material in this section is organised into several parts in order to include the large number of activities that should be classified as forms of competition advocacy (giving opinions, cooperation with other state authorities, i.e. independent sector regulators, the use of market studies, etc.). The Conclusion is the last part of the paper, which includes final remarks and recommendations for the Serbian Commission and policy makers.

## 2 The Definition and Importance of Competition Advocacy

According to the widely accepted definition of competition advocacy advanced by the International Competition Network, competition advocacy refers to "those activities conducted by the competition authority related to the promotion of a competitive environment for economic activities by means of non-enforcement mechanisms, mainly through its relationships with other governmental entities and by increasing public awareness of the benefits of competition" (ICN 2002). By explaining that there are two parts of the definition, the ICN refers to both the ends and the means of competition advocacy.

The first part of this definition defines competition advocacy in terms of what it is not and refers to almost all activities of the competition authority that do not fall under the enforcement category. The second part of the definition identifies the two main branches of competition advocacy: (1) initiatives undertaken by the competition authority towards other public entities in order to influence the regulatory framework and its implementation, and (2) activities by competition authorities

[2]For some examples of competition advocacy as a substitute for competition law enforcement in the Republic of Serbia, see Popovic (2013).

aimed at raising the awareness of economic agents, public authorities and the general public about the benefits of competition to the society as a whole and about the role competition policy can play to promote and protect competition (ICN 2002).

Therefore, the competition authority can use its formal powers to influence actors with rule-making powers (government, legislature, and other public authorities) in order to persuade them not to adopt unnecessarily anticompetitive measures or help them to delineate the boundaries of business regulation by adapting regulations and policies which unnecessarily restrict competition in the market. This means that competition authorities must act proactively to help the government to eliminate barriers to competition and to bring about public policies that lower barriers to entry, promote deregulation and trade liberalisation, and otherwise minimise unnecessary government intervention in the marketplace (Shyam Khemani et al. 1999).

To address the problems of government-created barriers to competition, the competition authorities analyse and advocate for policies that promote and protect competition by providing methods for identifying unnecessary restraints on market activities and by developing alternative, less restrictive regulatory approaches that can achieve the same goals, but at a lower cost than the competitive process. For this reason, competition advocacy becomes a more effective segment of competition policy than legislation enforcement, since the latter is inevitable and very resources consuming, i.e. it inevitably creates a huge administrative burden on the competition authority and other institutions (Begović et al. 2003).

That is why competition advocacy represents a *soft power* in promoting competition and liberalisation measures to improve the performance of market-based economies. Having in mind its objective, "the promotion of a competitive environment for economic activities", replacing (or avoiding) regulations with greater anti-competitive effects by government measures with less adverse consequences appears to be one operational way of interpreting this objective of competition advocacy (Evenett 2006).

Hence, the need for appropriate competition advocacy appears to be quite clear in developing and transition countries as their economic policies are undergoing fundamental market driven changes: markets in these countries are becoming more open; new government and regulatory institutions are being formed; foreign trade is assuming greater influence; and state owned enterprises are being privatised (Clark 2005). Furthermore, it is considered that competition advocacy by competition authorities in the EU candidate countries, like in Serbia, is extremely important.

Some of the existing reports on competition advocacy believe that competition authorities should give priority to advocacy activities over enforcement of competition law in developing and transition countries (Evenett 2006), although these activities unite under a single banner: promoting efficiency (Stucke 2008). ICN Report on Advocacy and Competition Policy pointed out that the rationale for prioritising competition advocacy over enforcement activities in these countries could be explained with three reasons (ICN 2002, 2004).[3] First, in developing and

[3]See also Kovacic (1997) and Rodriguez and Coate (1997).

transition countries, the spread of market reform (caused, for example, by privatisation) has given rise to an intensive rule making process and dialogue between the competition authority and the rule makers at an early stage may ensure that competition provides the foundation for legislation. A second reason is that these countries have undergone a substantial liberalisation which has triggered the activity of interest groups lobbying with public authorities for lost privileges. Therefore, competition authorities are trying to instil competitive values in sector-specific regulation through advocacy, and to reduce the possibility of regulatory capture by interest groups. According to the third reason, competition law enforcement requires sophisticated adjudication, with which young competition authorities and judicial systems have little experience.

All these rationales are important for Serbia, but it appears that the first is particularly important in regulated sectors, since the country is moving from the domination of state-owned enterprises towards a more competitive market structure and advocacy can enhance understanding competitive market forces. Free and undistorted competition and a market without considerable barriers to entry are key remedies for the Serbian economy, which has been plagued for decades by challenges that can arise in a small market economy within a specific political and international relations framework.

In this context, the advocacy efforts of the Commission could promote new ideas of competition protection among businessmen, lawyers, politicians and economic policymakers, and at the same time influence other public policies that create non-competitive market structures and behaviour (for example, foreign trade policies, privatisation and restructuring policies, various public policies that affect barriers to entry for new firms, etc.). Therefore, the accepted meaning in Serbia could be "promoting a competitive environment", which seems to suggest that the government measures are broader than those that promote entry into markets (Evenett 2006).

As many studies based on the best practices of developing and transition countries have already shown, young competition authorities should confine themselves to advocacy during the early implementation stages of competition policy and only gradually introduce enforcement of competition law (ICN 2002). Advocacy is most effective in the phase of the "consolidation" of competition culture, and it is more effective than legislation enforcement under these circumstances. A variety of arguments have been brought up in support of this viewpoint (ICN 2002).

Several other differences that affect competition advocacy exist between developed countries, on one hand, and developing and transition countries on the other. For example, in developing and transition countries market institutions are much weaker and less effective, the transparency of procedures and the accountability of public authorities is usually lower, and there are severe limitations upon the availability of the resources necessary to set up an efficient competition authority, especially in the smaller countries (ICN 2002).

All these circumstances lead to the conclusion that an effective competition advocacy in developing and transition countries requires certain essential conditions, i.e. prerequisites that represent challenges to most young competition authorities. In the first place, the competition authority should have a significant degree of independence from political influence from both inside and outside the government. Furthermore, it should have sufficient resources to support both its enforcement and advocacy functions. It is also important to acquire credibility and extend it throughout the public and private sectors, to policymakers and their constituents—businesses, workers and consumers (Clark 2005).

For Serbia, in this context it is also important to create public awareness which would include dissemination of information on competition law to enterprises, particularly widespread adoption of knowledge about the effects of non-competitive market structures and behaviour. However, the Commission should be aware that it might take a long time for such efforts pay off, thereby it should continue its competition advocacy efforts.

## 3 Competencies of the Serbian Commission

Competition advocacy often targets state-owned enterprises sheltered from the competitive process, including railroads, mail, telecommunications and energy, as well as other state institutions, such as the courts, administrative agencies, and legislatures (Stucke 2008). Serbian targeting activities should be similar and focused on legislation, government policy and regulatory reform in the most significant areas that may benefit from competition advocacy, such as foreign trade liberalisation, economic deregulation, state aid, state-owned enterprises, operation of local authorities, privatisation, building a competition culture, etc.[4]

In brief, the opportunities for competition advocacy in Serbia are numerous but the Commission should stay focused on reviewing inadequate regulatory regimes and existing or proposed regulations enforced by sectoral regulators. However, the variety of advocacy instruments suggests that there is no one best advocacy technique to create a competitive environment and improve the overall quality of legislation.

An important advantage of the Serbian competition advocacy is the possibility to use a wide array of advocacy tools and methods to create a competitive environment and influence policymakers, provided by the Law on the Protection of Competition.

In line with the Article 21 of the Law, the Commission is authorised to:

- take part in the preparation of regulations enacted in the field of protection of competition;
- propose to the Government passing regulations pertaining to the implementation of the Law;
- issue instructions and guidelines for implementation of the Law;
- monitor and analyse competition conditions in individual markets and sectors;

[4]For more information on policy areas in which competition advocacy in developing and transition countries can be most important, see Shyam Khemani et al. (1999) and Clark (2005).

- give opinions to competent authorities on draft regulations, as well as on current regulations that have an impact on market competition;
- give opinions regarding implementation of regulations in the field of protection of competition;
- establish international cooperation in the field of protection of competition, for the purpose fulfilling international obligations in this area, and collect information on the protection of competition in other countries;
- cooperate with national, provincial and local authorities in order to ensure implementation of the Law and other regulations that regulate issues of importance to the protection of competition; and
- undertake activities to raise awareness on the need to protect competition.

Stemming from the Commission's competencies, as stipulated in Article 21 of the Law, the most important tools for implementing advocacy policies in its practice are: providing opinions on the drafts laws and laws proposals and on current regulations affecting competition policy; conducting sectoral inquiries; enabling direct education via conferences, seminars and workshops; participating in roundtables and conferences; publishing brochures and specialised publications; campaigning; issuing public statements and media interviews with Commission, etc.[5]

The Commission can thus exercise competition advocacy through assessment of the compliance of draft legal acts and legal acts in force with the principles of the competitive environment for economic activities, as well as through proposals to competent state authorities to revise their restrictive acts. Opportunities for discovering advocacy are numerous: government and ministries can consult the Commission before issuing laws or regulations (based on prior working relationships or prior considerations of competition issues or particular concerns); the Commission can undertake competition screening of legislation or legislative proposals on its own initiative, as part of conducting enforcement activities or investigating individual markets/sectors, or based on information from third parties, etc.

In general, these competencies are in line with the best comparative practice which shows an expansion of advocacy tools and methods. Competition authorities worldwide are engaged in policy review in many different ways, based on both explicit (statutory) and implied (informal) grounds (Dabbah 2010). In some jurisdictions, competition authorities enjoy a certain mandate to submit their views on specific matters to the relevant ministry or regulatory agency or other public bodies, but in other jurisdictions, there are no explicit rules on the role of the competition authority under such circumstances (Dabbah 2010). Competition authorities should in any case carefully consider the most appropriate action for a particular situation and be actively involved in legislative affairs.

[5]See http://www.kzk.gov.rs/en/medunarodne-i-domace-aktivnosti/domaca-saradnja, last visited 14 August, 2017. For further information on competition policy in Serbia, see Rakić (2009, 2012, 2014).

# 4 Serbian Experience

Since the establishment of the Commission, it has been engaged in a large number of wide-ranging advocacy activities, considered to be particularly necessary for the promotion of a competitive environment for economic activities. The most relevant and demanding task has been addressing laws and regulations in order to eliminate unnecessary restraints on competition, which could be considered as advocacy in the narrow sense of the term.

In the coming years, as the Commission becomes more experienced in competition advocacy activities, it could be expected that the Commission's advocacy practice will increase further, along with the first assessments of its achievements, since it is gradually becoming well-established.

The following examples were selected from the Commission's relatively developed practice of competition assessment of laws and regulations, with aim of pointing out parts of the Serbian competition advocacy program that were successfully carried out and other parts that require a more active approach.

## 4.1 *Non-binding Opinions*

In the area of competition impact assessment, the Commission is authorised to give opinions to competent authorities on draft regulations, as well as on current regulations that have an impact on market competition. It can carry out such assessments at the request of the relevant state authorities, on its own initiative, or based on information from third parties.

According to information on the Commission's website and in the Commission's annual reports, during the 2006–2016 the Commission issued and submitted 55 opinions to the competent public authorities.[6] The assessments mostly focused on mapping administrative authorization proceedings and granting exclusive rights that may result in barriers to entry, as well as evaluating other restrictions with regard to market access.

In Serbia, as well as in other countries, the advocacy opinions are not binding for the competent state authorities, including regulators. Moreover, competent state authorities are not obliged to explain the reasons for their decisions if they diverge from the Commission's opinions, although in practice they usually provide an explanation. The law allows them to decide whether to conform to the Commission's opinions or not, or to conform to it only to a certain extent. The possibility of issuing binding opinions would be an effective way of extending influence, but it would also

[6]See the Commission's opinions at http://www.kzk.gov.rs/misljenja-na-predloge-propisa-i-na-vazece-propise-koji-imaju-uticaj-na-konkurenciju-na-trzistu and http://www.kzk.gov.rs/ostala-misljenja, as well as Commission's annual reports, available at http://www.kzk.gov.rs/izvestaji, last visited 14 August, 2017.

effectively create veto power and introduce distinctive incentives to the Commission and legislator, which could have adverse effects. At the same time, the law does not provide a basis for such binding opinions.

Therefore, the success of this advocacy activity depends on the Commission's ability to influence relevant authorities whether its opinions are considered in the regulation and policy making activity of the authority concerned, or to ensure sufficient political support. At any rate, the Commission should be able to assess legislation before it is introduced because policymakers are then more likely to conform, and ex post assessment, i.e., reviewing existing laws, is less effective than reviewing draft legislation.

In line with certain recommendations, it is necessary to adopt explicit rules governing state authorities, in order to mandate effects on competition, or the opinions of the competition authority, must be taken into account when designing regulations and associated policies. Without such rules some state authorities may argue that the competition authority is requiring them to take into account factors that are not part of their legal mandates. Failure to provide such rules may thus narrow the scope of the competition advocacy function (Evenett 2006).

For this reason, an initiative was sent to the Government of the Republic of Serbia to amend its Rules of Procedure, requiring the submission of proposals to the Commission for assessment. However, there has been no response regarding the issue and the Commission's opinions still have no binding force. Nevertheless, the Commission has continued issuing and publishing opinions on regulations, either upon request, or on its own initiative.[7]

Future reform of the Law on the Protection of Competition could introduce the requirement for government departments to seek the opinion of the Commission when introducing restrictions on access to economic activity, or to consider some of the solutions addressing this issue, as stipulated in comparative law. For example, when Italian competition law was amended and advocacy powers were strengthened, the Italian Competition Authority (ICA) got a new competency (according to Art. 21 *bis* of law 287/1990) to challenge, before the Administrative Courts, legal and administrative acts adopted by public administrations, which have not complied with the Authority's previous (and mandatory) opinions stating that the given administrative act, in the ICA's opinion, is in violation of competition law and principles (Rebecchini 2014; Carpagnano 2016). After this amendment to the law, the effectiveness of such advocacy interventions in Italian practice became significant (Rebecchini 2014).

In the meanwhile, the Serbian Commission has to use persuasion, rather than coercion, to provide political support and convince the government to pursue policies that further competition and enhances consumer welfare and choice. One

[7]See Commission for Protection of Competition (2012), Annual Report for 2011, available at http://www.kzk.gov.rs/kzk/wp-content/uploads/2012/08/Annual-Report_2011.pdf, last visited 14 August, 2017, p. 59.

such situation followed the adoption of the Law on Amendments to the Law on Public Utilities.

The Commission issued the Opinion on the Draft Law on Amendments to the Law on Public Utilities, at the request of the Ministry of Construction, Transport and Infrastructure.[8] The Commission had previously reacted on several occasions, in its written communications addressed to the Ministry, with regard to the Law that was currently in force, as well as the Draft Law. The Commission stressed the importance of providing equal conditions for all participants in the public utilities market, and in this context drew attention to the negative effects of the creation of a statutory monopoly. It expressed concern that the Ministry opted for solutions that would further limit the potential for competition in the public utilities market and noted that only competition between competitors, through quality and price, can lead to economic progress and well-being of society, especially the benefit of consumers.[9]

The Ministry eventually accepted the comments and suggestions of the Commission, expressed in the Opinion and changed the Draft Law. The Opinion pointed out the provisions stipulating that the Chamber of Commerce and Industry of Serbia will be responsible for issuing certificates on compliance with conditions for performing utility services, to public enterprises, companies, entrepreneurs or other business entities. According to the Commission's opinion, this regulation would have presented an additional barrier to the entrance of new, as well as to the continuation of business operations of current market enterprises that are registered for providing utility services. In the final version of the Draft Law, the Ministry also included the Commission's suggestions that certain services that can be performed independently and are related to the utility services, be clearly defined as the commercial services (e.g. burial service) that can be provided by registered enterprises, under equal conditions, and not exclusively by public companies or companies in which the Republic of Serbia or local authorities owns a minimum 51% stakes.[10] In the Commission's view, the Ministry's willingness to fully cooperate is the best example of joint efforts directed toward better quality regulation, which will enable more efficient market competition.[11]

---

[8]See Opinion and press release dated 23 May 2016, available at http://www.kzk.gov.rs/komisija-uputila-misljenje-na-nacrt-zakona-o-izmenama-i-dopunama-zakona-o-komunalnim-delatnostima, last visited 14 August, 2017.

[9]See press release "Commission expressed concern about the proposed amendments to the Law on Public Utilities", dated 2 December 2015, available at http://www.kzk.gov.rs/en/komisija-izrazila-zabrinutost-povodom-predlozenih-izmena-zakona-o-komunalnim-delatnostima, last visited 14 August, 2017.

[10]See press release "The Ministry Accepted Comments and Suggestions of the Commission on the Draft Law on Amendments to the Law on Utility Services", dated 24 July 2016, available at http://www.kzk.gov.rs/en/ministarstvo-usvojilo-primedbe-i-pre, last visited 14 August, 2017.

[11]In the 2016–2017 Competition Advocacy Contest, organised by the International Competition Network and the World Bank Group, the Commission received the Honourable Mention for the report on the implementation of competition advocacy regarding the adoption of the Law on Amendments to the Law on Public Utilities. The Commission's entry is presented in the category "Implementing advocacy strategies at multiple levels (regional, national, subnational, economy

The Commission reviewed the proposal of the Law on Investments, on its own initiative and issued an opinion which was delivered directly to the competent committee of the National Assembly. The Commission expressed concern about the proposed amendments to the Law on Investments, pointing out the possibility that the Commission could be prevented from carrying out its duties which could indirectly have a negative effect on investors in the Serbian market, as well as affect the protection of competition and the legal security of all investors. The National Assembly accepted the Commission's proposal that provided exemption for the Commission from the rules on priority treatment of applications from investors by public authorities. The Commission was again satisfied with the cooperation with the Ministry of Economy and National Assembly.[12]

By initiative of a third party, a company that provides beer-canning services, the Commission successfully influenced the Serbian Ministry of Agriculture, Forestry and Water Management to change, at the Commission's request, the provision of the Draft Law on Beer, which could have been restrictive in terms of competition. The restrictive provision stated that the filling of original packaging in the case of beer imported in bulk, as well as the service charge for the original packaging, can only be done by the producer.[13] The amended rules provided that canning of such beer could be carried out both by producers and enterprises providing beer-canning services.

## 4.2 *Advocacy with Local Authorities*

Promoting effective competition throughout the country is also difficult task for the Commission because achieving this aim requires it to encourage negotiations at the local, i.e. municipal level and to ensure additional political support and knowledge of competition principles.

Furthermore, economic reforms in Serbia, like in other developing and transition countries, result in ownership of communal service facilities by local governments which cause a conflict of interest in this situation. Since the local authorities are the owners of these assets, they are interested in the profitability of its business, which can be enhanced by increasing prices and lowering of quality of services (Shyam Khemani et al. 1999). Under the competition law, the competition authority cannot legally intervene against local authorities and the competition advocacy is thus the only tool that can be used to change such anticompetitive practices.

---

wide and sector specific)". See http://www.worldbank.org/en/events/2016/10/24/the-2016---2017-competition-advocacy-contest#4, last visited 14 August, 2017.

[12]See Opinion and press releases date 19 October 2015 available at http://www.kzk.gov.rs/komisija-uputila-misljenjena-predlog-zakona-o-ulaganjima, and dated 23 October 2015 available at http://www.kzk.gov.rs/usvojeno-misljenje-komisije, last visited 14 August, 2017.

[13]See Press Release available at http://www.kzk.gov.rs/kzk/wp-content/uploads/2016/06/Misljenje-na-clan-9-Predloga-Zakona-o-pivu.pdf, last visited 14 August, 2017.

The Commission nonetheless succeeded in influencing some local authorities to change their policies on providing utility services of burial and cemetery management. Following analysis of the initiative for investigation of possible competition infringement, the Commission sent opinions to the City of Novi Sad and City of Pančevo assemblies on the necessity to amend provisions of the decision regulating burial and cemetery management utility services, in order not to distort competition and provide monopolies for the public utility companies in those cities.

The City of Novi Sad and City of Pančevo assemblies positively reacted and informed the Commission that they had drafted amendment to modify the provisions of the disputed decisions regulating public utility burials and cemetery management services, and would adopt the amendments.[14]

The Commission also sent an opinion to the City of Subotica Assembly regarding a similar issue, where the Commission's position has not been acknowledged nor fully implemented. The Commission expressed its concern due to the City of Subotica Assembly failure to fully act on the Commission's opinion pertaining the disputed provisions of the decision regulating burial and cemetery management utility services in Subotica. Likewise, the Commission also sent an opinion to the line ministry pointing out the need to precisely define the terms of organise the area of burial and cemetery management in future regulations so as to avoid the monopolization of those activities based on different interpretations of the legal stipulations.[15] The reactions of the City of Subotica and the Ministry, as well as the results of these advocacy activities, are still unknown.

Although the Commission was not provided enough political support, nor gained the understanding of the competent authorities, which is the most probable cause of its failure to achieve the advocacy goal, it again took the opportunity to emphasise the significance of the conduct of local authorities.

### 4.3 *Market Studies*

As a common component of the work portfolios of competition authorities, market studies serve two primary purposes: as a prelude or precursor to litigation and as a spearhead or foundation for competition advocacy (OECD 2008). Market studies are typically an instrument for competition advocacy, particularly used when there is no suspicion of violation of competition laws, yet it does not appear that the market is really working well, mostly because of public restrictions on competition. As a

[14]See press releases available at http://www.kzk.gov.rs/en/grad-novi-sad-obavestio-komisiju-da-je-spreman-da-izmenom-odredbi-odluke-koja-ureduje-komunalnu-delatnost-sahranjivanja-i-upravljanja-grobljima-omoguci-obavljanje-pojedinih-pogrebnih-usluga-svim-zaint and http://www.kzk.gov.rs/en/grad-pancevo-ce-izmenom-propisa-omoguciti-obavljanje-pogrebnih-usluga-svim-zainteresovanim-ucesnicima, last visited 14 August, 2017.

[15]See Press Release available at http://www.kzk.gov.rs/en/skupstina-grada-subotice-nije-u-potpu, last visited 14 August, 2017.

result, market studies may lead to proposals to deregulate, decrease barriers to entry, reform market institutions, or improve information dissemination to consumers or suppliers (OECD 2008).

Although the market studies can be costly and time consuming for a competition authority, they need to be used by competition authorities in order to: identify the causes of competition problems in a market—whether structural, government imposed or other; design more effective solutions to remedy a competition problem that can be implemented by government; and provide concrete market information to substantiate claims and recommendations made by a competition authority when engaging in advocacy efforts towards other government entities (OECD 2010).

In conclusion, market studies provide the competition authority with an in-depth understanding of the functioning of the market and its structures (number of players, barriers to entry, substitute markets, etc.). Therefore, it helps carry out more effective advocacy activities, especially when they are carried out in conjunction with regulators and through public consultations.

The Commission also uses market studies as an advocacy tool, with the clear objective of carrying out an effective advocacy program, pursuant to the Law on Protection of Competition. The Commission is authorised to monitor and analyse conditions of competition in individual markets and in individual sectors, as well as to analyse the state of competition in a particular sector of the economy or certain categories of agreements in various industries (sectoral analysis) in cases where the price dynamics or other circumstances suggest the possibility of restriction or distortion of competition.[16]

In 2016, the Commission conducted the Sector Inquiry on Competition Issues in Aftermarkets, based on the decision of the Commission's Council. The inquiry encompassed, inter alia, after sales services, warranties, turnover, and use of spare parts for motor vehicles and top selling home appliances—refrigerators and washing machines. The main goal of this inquiry was to establish the structure and relations between undertakings, their market shares and market power, with the objective of detecting potential market vulnerabilities, that is, existence of conditions leading to the infringement of competition. The added aim of this inquiry, and in particular of its conclusions and recommendations, is to point the competent government institutions to the conditions of the examined markets, while facilitating the proactive operation of the Commission aimed at deterring undertakings from competition infringement related conduct.[17]

The project was conducted in cooperation with the Public Policy Secretariat of the Republic of Serbia, with financial and technical support from the PERFORM Project, i.e. the Swiss Agency for Development and Cooperation. As per the project's ToR, prepared by the Commission, as the contracting authority of the inquiry,

[16]See the Law on Protection of Competition, Art. 21. and 47.

[17]See press releases date 15 November 2016, available at http://www.kzk.gov.rs/en/sektorska-analiza-trzista-postprodajnih-usluga, and dated 9 June 2017, available at http://www.kzk.gov.rs/en/komisija-upozorila-na-moguce-nekonku, last visited 14 August, 2017.

the study was conducted by the Institute of Economic Sciences, as the research partner on the project. After the Sector Inquiry, all undertakings and others in the expert community were invited to submit their comments in accordance with the Report.

The results of the inquiry will be used in the course of preparing the draft regulation on conditions for group exemption of agreements in the motor vehicle sector, transporting the EU Commission Regulation 461/2010 into Serbian legislative system. The Commission is recommended to initiate the procedure of adopting such regulation.

The Commission is also recommended to consider revision of Regulation on Agreements between Undertakings Operating at Different Levels of Production or Distribution Chain Exempted from Prohibition, in order to harmonise the Regulation with EU Commission Regulation 330/2010 on categories of vertical agreements and concerted practices.

The Ministry of Construction, Transport and Infrastructure of the Republic of Serbia is recommended to initiate the adoption of a legal act, adopting EU rules on the obligation of producers of motor vehicles to communicate vehicle repair and maintenance information.

The preparation of the recommended regulations and legal acts is still ongoing, hence it takes time to see the final results of such advocacy activities. The Commission, in the meanwhile, has been intensively involved in additional reviewing of this document, in the context of the existence of potential competition infringements by undertakings operating in these sectors. The Commission formulated the findings and forwarded them to the competent state authorities, business associations, as well as undertakings operating in the motor vehicles and home appliances aftermarkets, in order to notify them of the possibility that they may become the subject of the Commission's proceedings in the event that they failing to amend certain portions of the agreements with their suppliers or dealers.

## 4.4 Cooperation with Sector Regulators

In the coming years, as the sector regulators in Serbia also become experienced in regulating the relevant markets, the success of competition advocacy could depend on the Commission's cooperation with regulators. The Commission should more actively influence regulators to create a competitive environment in the regulated markets, particularly in markets such as telecommunication and energy.

The Commission constantly undertakes activities to ensure continuous dialogue and provide an information exchange system with regulators and other state authorities in order to develop competition in the market. This cooperation with the regulators is covered by signed protocols of cooperation during previous years (National Bank of Serbia, Energy Agency of the Republic of Serbia, Regulatory Agency for Electronic Communications and Postal Services of the Republic of Serbia, Regulatory Authority for Electronic Media of the Republic of Serbia). It is, in Commission's view, assessed as useful, primarily in the case of data exchange, but also in exchanging opinions on all current topics and proceedings conducted before the Commission or other authorities and institutions. It provides the possibility to use market analyses and other studies and findings by regulators, to obtain new sources of information and new initiatives, exchange information, etc.[18]

Such cooperation, with the main aim of information exchange, could be an issue in achieving the objectives of the advocacy program in Serbia, because there is no open and active dialogue about anticompetitive measures, regulations and policies that are needlessly restricting competition in the market. Cooperation with sector regulators is two-way: the Commission requests data, in order to conduct proceedings and to carry out sectoral analyses of the markets or to act on received initiatives and petitions; and the Commission also acts on requests for opinions, data, information, etc. Even the Commission's opinions on regulators' reports are provided with the aim of determining compliance of these reports with competition rules. Moreover, this cooperation needs to be improved because it appears that comments to regulators tend to have greater success than those to state legislators (Cooper et al. 2005). Even closer cooperation should be established with regulators, but with substantial advocacy objectives.

### *4.5 Building Public Awareness of Competition Policy*

In the context of using different tools for implementing competition advocacy activities with regard to the different groups of stakeholders, it is also important to create public awareness about competition law and explain the benefits of open competitive markets to the public (Sofia Competition Forum).

The Serbian Commission conducts advocacy activities also through select communication means (seminars, working groups, business meetings, articles in magazines), through the media (e.g. radio and TV broadcasts, newsletters, electronic media), publication of guidelines and reports, on its website, and other tools—video, social networks, etc.

Guidelines and reports are published on-line, such as the Annual Report of Commission (in which there is a part devoted to competition advocacy activities) and the Commission's opinions on drafts and current regulations affecting competition in the market.[19] All decisions enacted by the Commission in the proceedings instituted on submitted notifications or ex officio, are also available to experts and the general public, via the website.

[18]See Annual Reports of the Commission.

[19]See http://www.kzk.gov.rs/misljenja-na-predloge-propisa-i-na-vazece-propise-koji-imaju-uticaj-na-konkurenciju-na-trzistu, last visited 14 August, 2017.

In addition to the Commission's website, some videos are uploaded to the YouTube.com website, which is interesting, considering that is an advocacy activity. These short films are about competition law awareness.[20]

The Commission published a booklet/glossary *Essential for Competition*, which contains explanations of the most frequent Serbian-English terms related to competition policy. During the preparation, particular attention was placed on the design and visual identity of the booklet so that the material would be attractive to the widest audience. The glossary is primarily designed for the media, the general public, as well as the expert audience. Over 400 copies were distributed to all news editors and journalists from electronic and print media outlets, public authorities, independent regulatory and supervisory agencies and most influential business associations. A particular goal of the publication is to establish a cooperative communication channel and improve levels of information dissemination.[21]

## 5 Lessons Learnt

Bearing in mind the Serbian experience, it can be concluded that competition advocacy is a complex and difficult task for competition authorities and outright success is relatively rare. Constant and continuing efforts are necessary because competition authorities will always be in a position to seek political support and at the same time be under the pressures from the private sector. The role of competition advocacy thus appears to be especially critical in developing countries, such as Serbia, because of their ongoing market and economic policy changes. Its fundamental role in such transition processes is very challenging for the Commission, as a relatively new competition authority, because it has to acquire the influence and skills necessary for this purpose.

The Serbian experience provides examples of competition advocacy work from which developing and transition countries could learn valuable lessons, in order to better understand how competition advocacy activities should be carried out and how competition authorities actually act.

Competition advocacy is a process that can mostly benefit from greater resources (both financial and human) and expertise, in order to enable the competition authority to provide high quality advice. In developing countries where resources will always be insufficient and unequally distributed, competition advocacy has somewhat limited value because limited resources limit the effectiveness of advocacy. Therefore, the most common pitfall of the competition work of young competition authorities is not to have the right resources or not to allocate them effectively.

[20] See https://www.youtube.com/channel/UC4r4DQ1UM8t339x9EaGCl_w, last visited 14 August, 2017.

[21] See http://www.kzk.gov.rs/en/medunarodne-i-domace-aktivnosti/domaca-saradnja, last visited 14 August, 2017.

Competition authorities do not effectively allocate their resources mostly because advocacy is not enforcement and politicians thus do not pay attention to such work, although it is legitimate effort against anticompetitive harms. Furthermore, competition authorities are constrained because of the potential political backlash (Sokol 2009).

It is also important to point out that young competition authorities need to recruit and retain high quality staff and, if possible, create a special advocacy team that would be in charge of carrying out competition advocacy activities. It is recommended to simultaneously train the team and consult international organizations or engage external experts to scrutinise specific activities, which would be crucial for the competition authority to demonstrate an in-depth understanding of its competencies. Providing such an advocacy team with the power to undertake advocacy activities at their own initiative can be helpful in increasing the engagement of the competition authorities in the "promotion of a competitive environment". It should perform continuous research of drafts and existing laws and, for that purpose, use Internet, databases, journals, ministries and state agencies, non-governmental organisations, international organisations and companies, and also at the request of relevant state authorities, because the competition authority cannot be isolated or uninformed.

The competition authorities also need to gain credibility as an effective and impartial advocate for competition, because it is important to provide political support and understanding throughout the public and private sectors. Additionally, the competition authority should conduct competition advocacy activities in an open, transparent manner in order to safeguard its integrity and credibility, and free of political influence.

Its reputation must build relationships with government and ministries, and sector regulators, which must also be developed, and should extend to create public awareness of competition policy. Communication with different groups of stakeholders thus must be based on mutual respect, recognition of professional expertise and appreciation of the respective responsibilities (Shyam Khemani et al. 1999). At the same time, competition authorities need not be confrontational, since opposition to other state authorities could be risky, difficult and counterproductive (Shyam Khemani et al. 1999).

Further, it is important for the competition authority to continue the process of building suitable competition cultures, because most developing countries lack such awareness of the benefits of competition law and its effects. Building public awareness of competition policy can be achieved by using a variety of communication channels, but it is especially important to maintain face-to-face communication despite it being more resource consuming. Additionally, in order to explain the role of competition policy and competitive environment, the competition authorities need to establish good media relations (Shyam Khemani et al. 1999), which was crucial for the Serbian Commission in case of adopting of the Law on the Amendments to the Law on Public Utilities.

The competition authorities should include criteria for selecting and prioritising advocacy activities in order to identify proposed or existing policies (sector) that may restrict competition and carry out their competition assessment, such as economic importance of the policy, barriers to entry and the existence of public interest. Nonetheless, they should focus on competition matters that have the greatest impact on consumers, that are economically important, politically visible, that will not occupy too many resources, and in which the competition authority has a reasonable chance of success (Clark 2005).

Developing and transition countries should consider introduction a system requiring all state authorities to assess the impact on competition of legislative acts that they propose, since competition advocacy is not legally binding and policy-makers are not legally required to adopt the competition authority's opinions. Moreover, competition authorities should be allowed to offer their opinion on secondary legislation or legislation at regional and local level, as well as at the legislation on national government level.

It is also recommended to adopt explicit rules (e.g. provisions in the law, rules of procedure) on the relationship between the competition authority and the sector regulators, to ensure that the competition authority's opinions are provided in the early stages of legislative reform, i.e. before the legislative is adopted, as well as provisions on mandatory publishing of such opinions. Such ex ante competition assessment of laws and regulations would be in line with comparative best practices and state authorities should be required to state their reasons in case of noncompliance with competition authority's opinions.

Also, in the process of transition, developing and transition countries tend to promote policies aimed at protecting or supporting competitors rather than promoting competition itself. Moreover, young competition authorities should follow practices that include a pro-active approach to competition advocacy whereby opinions are issued not only to eliminate unnecessary restraints, i.e. anticompetitive practice, but also to influence the state authorities to liberalise and open the market to competition. They should act affirmatively and try to change rules because it is procompetitive to do so and it is good for competition. In that way, the competition authorities could at the same time achieve direct influence on government policies and policy proposals as an intermediate step towards achieving broader consumer and market benefits.

However, competition authorities should bear in mind one important limit to the benefits that providing opinions can yield: the competition authority is not a legislator and it only provides legislators and sector regulators with information concerning likely anticompetitive rules.

It is further recommended that competition authorities both enforce and advocate competition law in order to effectively complement and reinforce each other. Competition enforcement and advocacy are complementary and competition authorities should not identify these tasks or mutually substitute them, although competition advocacy is a more cost-effective means than enforcement, compared to fighting state-imposed barriers to competition. Competition advocacy should not replace enforcement even in part, and vice versa—the full implementation of competition rules and their enforcement cannot be achieved without successful advocacy. In many ways these activities are interdependent and complementary, and only a competition authority with both functions can be described as being consistently pro-competition.

In the context of the cooperation with sector regulators, it should be pointed out that sector regulators could at times avoid such cooperation with competition authorities because of the absence of rules on competition authorities' participating in the legislative process. This problem could be resolved simply through the introduction of an institutional measure (a statutory basis for regulatory intervention) but the question remains whether such rules would effectively be applied in practice, and whether competition authorities would come into conflict with certain regulators, due to the legacy of sector-specific policies. The efficacy of advocacy again will be dependent on the ability of the competition authority to provide direct political support for its activities and for establishing a proper relationship with these state authorities.

In this respect, the competition authorities could initiate cooperation with sector regulators, but it would be auspicious if sector regulators also would initiate cooperation, bearing in mind that advocacy activities are more effective when they are carried out in conjunction with the relevant sector regulators and through public hearings or consultations.

Therefore, it is so important to continue the practice of using market studies to improve in-depth understanding of the functioning of the specific sector and its market.

Finally, it should be noted that it is difficult to make the promotion of competition policy consistent due to the fact that competition advocacy faces a number of challenges and changes caused by political and economic developments. Competition advocacy is therefore controversial and not as straightforward. The nature of the competition advocacy of young authorities has changed over time, as in case of Serbia, shifting from advocating general competition issues and increasing public awareness of the benefits of competition, towards playing an increasingly important role in special sector industries.

The Commission followed the same direction, since during its formative stage advocacy activities were used to inform stakeholders of the existence of the competition law and policy and to provide opinions in the domain of privatisation. As time passed, advocacy evolved further, towards carrying out activities related to sector regulation and other policies, and being more active in competition advocacy and strengthening its role in building public confidence in competitive markets.

It appears that the Commission has became much more transparent, especially since 2015, exposed to publicity, open to competition advocacy activities and more aware of significance of competition advocacy, compared to the previous period when such practice was undeveloped. Based on the available information of Commission's practice, it is apparent that it pays more attention to raising awareness of the importance of competition by carrying out numerous activities aimed at advancing the regulatory framework, promoting competition policy and a competitive business environment.

For example, the Commission was particularly active in presenting the business and expert public communities in Serbia with all the aspects of its operations, derived from the competences vested in the Commission by the Law. In that sense, the Commission dedicated 2016, which also marked a decade of its operation, to implementing numerous competition policy advocacy activities. The Commission took part in many more conferences, as well as events organised by different associations, and it also organised and hosted several events that represented a basis for communicating with representatives of the media, aimed at promoting its activities. Among these, important to mention are the Competition Day, celebrating 10 years of operations in Serbia, and international conference Institution Building of the Competition Authorities in the South-East Europe.

Furthermore, the Commission carried out additional sector inquires (Sector Inquiry on Competition Issues in Aftermarkets and Insurance Market Competition Inquiry), in addition to annual inquires on the milk and oil-derivative industries. Moreover, it has been announced that Commission will carry out a retail market sector inquiry, which was the reason for holding the roundtable titled Significance and Challenges of the Retail Trade Sector in Serbia in Terms of Competition Policy.

Communication with the media during 2016 was intensified by utilising various communication channels (press releases, interviews, thematic events, conferences, Q&As, promoting topics and public statements in the media, preparation and distribution of booklets). As a first step in the strategic utilization of the media potentials as communication tools, activities aimed at creating a detailed database relevant for the media relations was initiated during 2016, particularly concerning those specialised in the field of economics, law, markets or specifically the area of the Commission's particular concern—competition.

The Commission also improved its website (including the English version) and started publishing opinions on draft and current regulations, related to competition in the market on a special page, as well as many more press releases on daily and annual activities. Such practice contributed to the considerable increase traffic on the official website, up 31% against the previous year. Consequently, domestic and international media interest in the Commission's activities has increased. Print and e-media journalists have sent a significant number of inquiries concerning the Commission's area of expertise.[22]

To conclude, young competition authorities should continue expanding their role in promoting competition and achievements in order to develop competition law and a competitive market. In this sense, Serbian competition advocacy could be regarded as a positive example for countries experiencing difficulties in promoting economic development during the economic transition process.

Serbian practice has been recognised as a successful example of competition advocacy in the community of developing countries and the business community in Serbia. As mentioned, competition advocacy in Serbia has received a positive evaluation internationally (in 2016–2017 Competition Advocacy Contest, organised by the International Competition Network and the World Bank Group).

[22]See http://www.kzk.gov.rs/en/medunarodne-i-domace-aktivnosti/domaca-saradnja, 14 August, 2017.

Additionally, the traditional review of the business climate in Serbia (*White Book*), published by the Foreign Investors Council in Serbia, reports that significant improvements have been achieved to the Commission's advocacy activities. As per evaluation of the Foreign Investors Council, the progress in the field of protection of competition was propelled, among other, by the Commission's strong advocacy activities.

In the opinion of Foreign Investors Council, an extremely positive development is the public invitation that the Commission sent to all relevant stakeholders, to submit comments to the draft Regulation on Notification of Concentration, whose revision it has initiated.[23]

The advocacy program in Serbia originated from the rigorous enforcement programs in Serbia, although Serbia lacked a competition culture and expertise in competitive analysis, as is the case in most developing countries. With the straightforward aim to promote competition, the Commission engaged in competition advocacy despite the facts that it was a new state authority with limited resources, without highly trained staff, expertise, empirical evidence on how advocacy actually works, reputation, or culture of competition on which to rely.

Serbia did not have a political culture that fully embraced competition and the free market, nor the political and legal institutions that provide greater protection for contract and property rights (including efficient courts and independent media), which made this success even greater. For these reasons, the Commission may be sometimes reluctant to seek legislative changes because it may fear that its powers may be eroded when competition matters come before the legislature. Moreover, it seems that during legislative procedures the Commission's opinions are not sufficiently appreciated in practice. Still, numerous rules have been adopted based on the Commission's opinions.

Hence, the effectiveness of competition advocacy depends not only on the strength and characteristics of the competition authority, but also on the framework within which it operates. Consequently, the Commission could carry out a more systematic approach to competition advocacy and engage more actively in such activities in order to successful implement advocacy program.

## 6 Conclusion

The overview in this article presents how the Serbian Commission is promoting competition and a competitive environment for economic activities. In this regard, competition advocacy should probably become the "essential facility" for the competitiveness of the Serbian market, because the Commission should play an

[23]See press release http://www.kzk.gov.rs/en/komisija-znacajno-napredovala-ocen, http://www.kzk.gov.rs/en/komisija-ucinila-znacajan-pomak-u-svom-radu-po-oceni-saveta-stranih-investitora, 14 August, 2017.

important role in reducing government restraints on competition. The main goal of the advocacy program needs to be the elimination of barriers to competition and barriers to entry into the market, and otherwise minimising unnecessary government intervention in the market, which is considered to be the greatest threat to competition in the Serbian market.

Competition advocacy is still a real challenge in Serbia and it takes time for the Commission to become effective in these activities. The level of success of the advocacy program in Serbia appears to still rely on the extent of the political support enjoyed by the Commission. Moreover, the Commission advocacy activities are not fully recognised by policy makers and it needs to acquire more credibility and resources, as an effective and impartial advocate for competition. The Commission must therefore give ongoing attention to building a competition culture through aggressive public relations and dissemination of information.

Finally, the Commission should collect data on competition advocacy "success" and consider the first results of advocacy program. Since there is no systematic evidence on implementation experience or formal attempts to assess the effectiveness of competition advocacy in Serbia; the collected data would be a basis for such evaluation. The Commission should consider carrying out this evaluation because it is a way to determine what types of advocacy activities are most effective, and in which sectors.[24]

For these reasons, competition advocacy in Serbia should be more actively engaged in order to fully promote the competitive market, and consequently protection of competition and consumer welfare.

## References

Begović B et al. (2003) New competition policy: a policy paper. Center for Liberal-Democratic Studies, Belgrade

Carpagnano M (2016) The effects of competition advocacy on the pro-competitive regulation of the markets. Ital Antitrust Rev 1:109–113

Clark J (2005) Competition advocacy: challenges for developing countries. OECD J Compet Law Policy 6:69–80

Commission for Protection of Competition (2012) Annual report for 2011. http://www.kzk.gov.rs/kzk/wp-content/uploads/2012/08/Annual-Report_2011.pdf

Cooper JC, Pautler PA, Zywicki TJ (2005) Theory and practice of competition advocacy at the FTC. Antitrust Law J 72:1091–1112

[24]It has been pointed out that the evaluation of competition advocacy is important for several reasons: competition authorities are accountable to representatives for their use of state resources and the powers entrusted to them, and the latter may want evidence of the effectiveness of the former's activities; competition authorities want to know what best practices can be established for competition advocacy; competition authorities have to decide how to allocate scarce budgetary resources, personnel time, media exposure, and other inputs across the enforcement and advocacy functions; competition authorities may want to establish priorities over the different types of competition advocacy that they can perform (Evenett 2006).

Dabbah MM (2010) International and comparative competition law. Cambridge University Press, New York

Evenett SJ (2006) Competition advocacy: time for a rethink. Northwest J Int Law Bus 26:495–514

International Competition Network (2002) Advocacy and competition policy: report prepared by the Advocacy working group. ICN's conference Naples, Italy. http://www.internationalcompetitionnetwork.org/uploads/library/doc358.pdf

International Competition Network (2004, April) Competition advocacy in regulated sectors: examples of success. http://www.internationalcompetitionnetwork.org/uploads/library/doc370.pdf

Kovacic W (1997) Getting started: creating new competition policy institutions in transition economies. Brooklyn J Int Law 23:403–453

Law on Protection of Competition. Official gazette of the RS 51/2009, 95/2013

OECD (2008) Market studies – competition policy roundtables 2008. DAF/COMP (2008) 34. http://www.oecd.org/regreform/sectors/41721965.pdf

OECD (2010) Strategies for competition advocacy: background paper by the OECD secretariat. Latin American competition forum – session III: strategies for competition advocacy. DAF/COMP/LACF (2010) 4. http://www.oecd.org/competition/latinamerica/2010LACF-Strategies-for-competition-advocacy.pdf

Popovic D (2013) Competition law enforcement in times of crisis: the case of Serbia. Yearb Antitrust Reg Stud 6:35–51

Rakić I (2009) Control of concentrations in the Republic of Serbia. In: Milošević M (ed) Serbian law in transition. Institute of Comparative Law, Belgrade, pp 101–128

Rakić I (2012) Utvrđivanje relevantnog tržišta – osvrt na zabludu iz slučaja Cellophane. Anali Pravnog fakulteta u Beogradu 60:416–430

Rakić I (2014) Pokajnički program i odgovornost za štetu zbog povrede prava konkurencije. Anali Pravnog fakulteta u Beogradu 62:244–260

Rebecchini S (2014) Competition advocacy: the Italian experience. Ital Antitrust Rev 2:13–24

Rodriguez AE, Coate MB (1997) Competition policy in transition economies. The role of competition advocacy. Brooklyn J Int Law 23:367–401

Shyam Khemani R, Clark J, Fornalczy A (1999) Competition advocacy. In: Shyam Khemani R (ed) A framework for the design and implementation of competition law and policy. World Bank/OECD, Washington, DC/Paris, pp 93–100

Sofia Competition Forum. Guidelines for implementing competition advocacy, Bulgarian Commission on Protection of Competition/United Nations Conference on Trade and Development. http://unctad.org/meetings/en/Contribution/ccpb_SCF_AdvocacyGuidelines_en.pdf

Sokol DD (2009) Limiting anticompetitive government interventions that benefit special interests. Georg Mason Law Rev 17:119–189

Stucke ME (2008) Better competition advocacy. St Johns Law Rev 82:951–1036

# Considerations Determining the Extent of Economic Analysis and the Choice of Legal Standards in Competition Law Enforcement

**Yannis Katsoulacos**

## 1 Introduction

The extent to which economic analysis and evidence is relied upon by competition authorities (CAs) and courts, in assessing whether specific conducts violate competition law (CL), depends crucially on the adopted *legal standards*, i.e. on the *decision rules* that provide the basis for assessment of the conducts. Broadly speaking, there are two types of decision rules that can be used: those that are *effects-based* and those that are *object-based* (to use the terminology common in the EU), which in US are referred to as *rule of reason* and per se rules, respectively, though the terms are not, strictly speaking, exactly equivalent.[1]

Of course, a question that immediately emerges when considering the choice of legal standards, is related to the *substantive (or liability) standard* of the CA—the criterion on the basis of which the CA will make its decision about whether or not specific conduct violates the law.[2] In academic literature, to a large extent, the

[1]Sometimes, a distinction is drawn by legal scholars between *rules* (a term they reserve for per se) and *standards* (e.g. the "rule of reason")—see for example, Blair and Sokol (2012). Below we neglect this distinction.

[2]The notion of *substantive standard* seems to be sometimes confused with that of *legal standard*. The two notions are clearly distinct: the *substantive or liability standard* is the *criterion* used (e.g. impact on consumer welfare) in order to decide whether or not a conduct violates the law; The *legal standards* refer to *how* decisions are reached. Per se rules (or standards, such as the one applied in hard-core cartel cases) are perfectly consistent with welfare-based substantive standards (such as consumer surplus and total welfare), The term *effects-based standard* can, at least in principle, be used when the substantive standard is *not* welfarist—as is used by Wils (2014) in discussing the legal standard adopted by the European Commission and Court on the case of Intel. This is notwithstanding the fact that most people tend to associate the use of the term *effects-based*

Y. Katsoulacos
Athens University of Economics and Business, Athens, Greece
e-mail: ysk@hol.gr



B. Begović, D. V. Popović (eds.), *Competition Authorities in South Eastern Europe*, Contributions to Economics, https://doi.org/10.1007/978-3-319-76644-7_8

alternative substantive standards discussed are *welfarist*—that is, the debate relates to whether a consumer surplus or a total welfare substantive standard should be used.[3] However, in practice, a number of *non-welfarist standards* are common. In Europe, for example, it is often the case that the CA objective is just to "protect the economic freedom of market participants"—which would imply that any conduct that puts one or more competitors at a disadvantage would be considered unlawful, regardless of whether or not there are strong a priori grounds for making a judgement that such conduct has ultimately negative consequences/effects on consumer or total welfare. More generally, there has always been and there is still a lively debate revolving about the issue of *public interest objectives* especially—but not exclusively—related to the jurisdictions in BRICS and other developing countries.[4]

The substantive standard adopted by a CA (or Court) will also have a significant influence on the extent to which economic analysis and evidence is relied upon by CAs in assessing whether there is liability *when an effects-based legal standard is adopted*. Under a welfarist substantive standard, the adoption of an effects-based legal standard will require the utilisation of a significantly greater amount of economic analysis and evidence than an effects-based legal standard would require if the substantive standard is not welfarist[5] (for details see below). This is illustrated by the exchange between Wils[6] and Rey & Venit[7] concerning the low legal standard adopted by the EU Court in the now famous Intel decision; the former commends this decision while the latter criticise it. Wils commends the decision for focusing on the *effect* of the conduct on "the preservation of undistorted competition".[8] The meaning of "preserving undistorted competition" was actually made clear by the Court which, upholding the Commission's decision in its entirety, argued that

---

*legal standard* with the case where the substantive standard is welfarist. Indeed it must be recognized that, neglecting objectives related to public interest concerns, it would make sense to use a "*full effects-based*" *legal standard* or "rule of reason" only if the substantive standard is welfarist. See also discussion below for the role of substantive standards in the choice of legal standards.

[3]In this paper we will not examine the pros and cons of using *consumer welfare* or *total welfare/efficiency* as the right substantive standard. Some CAs are already using a total welfare standard (e.g. in Canada, Australia and New Zealand), although in the EU and the US the CAs lean towards the *consumer welfare* standard (and in EU, as noted below, often a weaker standard is used, such as that concerning the *competitive process*). There is currently quite an intense debate on this issue, with some eminent economists arguing in favor of a total welfare standard, e.g. D. Carlton (2007). For a recent contributions, as well as an extensive review of the recent debate, see Katsoulacos et al. (2016a, b).

[4]These objectives may relate to issues of equality, employment, international competitiveness, growth, and protection of SMEs. See also Fox and Sullivan (1987), and Baker and Salop (2015).

[5]But has a more restricted objective such as protecting the economic freedom of market participants (see also below).

[6]Wils (2014).

[7]Rey and Venit (2015).

[8]Wils (2014) considers that an effects-based standard was used but the effect assessed was not (rightly, according to Wils) related to a welfarist objective.

making it more difficult for a rival to compete "in itself suffices for a finding of infringement". As we shall show below, such positions can be used in order to justify the use of a more object-based assessment for retroactive discounting by a dominant firm—which is exactly what Rey and Venit[9] consider to be the legal standard de facto adopted by the Commission and the Court.

Given these introductory remarks, we can now provide the following definitions of the two broad categories of legal standards.[10] These definitions aim to also clarify their relations to the concept of substantive standards.

*Per se Legal Standard* Decisions about whether or not there is liability in the case of a specific conduct, undertaken by a firm or group of firms, are reached on the basis of a *presumption* about the general class (or a subclass) of conducts, within which the specific conduct falls,[11] without pursuing any investigation concerning the *effects of the specific conduct*, based on whatever criterion for liability[12] has been adopted by the CA—based on which criterion the "*effects*" are established.[13]

*Effects-Based Standards* Decisions about whether or not there is liability in the case of a specific action, undertaken by a firm, are reached after pursuing an *investigation into the effects of the specific conduct*, on whatever criterion for liability is adopted by the CA—on which criterion the "*effects*" are established. Based on what we know about the potential effects of the general class of conducts to which the conduct under investigation belongs, we do not consider that valid inferences (satisfying a sufficiently high standard of proof) can be made for the effects of the specific conduct.

Obviously, in practice there are variations in the legal standards adopted and it is probably best to think of legal standards as forming a *continuum*, the extremes of which are the (strict) per se (or object-based) and the ("full") rule of reason (or full effects-based) standards (these variants are discussed in more detail below).[14] Alternatively, an effects-based standard can be thought of as a series of per se

---

[9] *Ibid.*

[10] Below we will use the American term *per se* and the European term *effects-based* to refer to these two broad categories of legal standards.

[11] Thus, under (strict) per se, the anticompetitive effects are *inferred* from the conduct itself. See also below for the case of modified per se standards.

[12] There will of course be an investigation for establishing the specific characteristics/type of the conduct itself beyond reasonable doubt, e.g. an investigation relating to the evidence for establishing that a collusive agreement existed between a group of firms.

[13] This defines the CA's substantive standard.

[14] See Gavil (2008), and Italianer (2013), referring to Justice Stevens, who was probably the first to point out that one should think of legal standards (for dealing with restraints under US Section 1) as forming a *continuum* with per se and rule of reason being at the opposite ends of this *continuum*. As Italianer /2013) notes, the US Supreme Court has explicitly recognized that "the categories of analysis cannot pigeonholed into terms like 'per se' or .... 'rule of reason'. No categorical line can be drawn between them. Instead, what is required is a situational analysis moving along what the Court referred to as a '*sliding scale*'". See also below.

standards, each one of which is applied to a successively more restricted class of conducts[15]: in this sense, a strict per se standard, in order to establish liability or not, relies on a *presumption about the most general class of conducts* of the type considered, without any investigation concerning the specific conduct or more restricted subclasses to which the specific conduct belongs. Successive per se rules can be applied, relying on presumptions with respect to successively more restricted subclasses of conducts, with specific characteristics. A full effects-based standard can be thought of as a per se standard that relies on the presumption, on the specific conduct, established by a full investigation, taking into account the exact nature of the conduct and the specific market characteristics of the case under investigation.[16]

Given the remarks above, we can consider of the difference between these two broad types of standards as follows. While for certain conducts a sufficiently high *standard of proof* can be achieved by applying a strict per se standard to the widest class of conducts to which the specific conduct belongs, under a wide range of market conditions,[17] for many other conducts this will not be the case. For these other conducts, the presumption of illegality that can be applied to the general class of conducts of this type is not very strong, therefore one needs to rely on presumptions that can be applied to subclasses of conducts and market conditions, to which the specific conduct belongs, with a more restricted set of characteristics, similar to the one under investigation,[18] in order to reach a sufficiently high standard of proof, as needed for the authority to reach the threshold for discharging its burden of proof and establishing its ultimate contention. A full effects-based legal standard must be applied in such cases, in order for the authority to reach the threshold for discharging its burden of proof and establishing its ultimate contention; a full investigation of the effects of the *specific* conduct must be carried out undertaken—no sufficiently strong presumption can be established by just considering the effects of a wider class of conduct similar to the specific one under investigation.

[15]This concern restricts sets of characteristics that converge to the specific characteristics of the case under investigation—in terms of the exact characteristics of the conduct and the characteristics of the specific firm(s) and market.

[16]Note that, while in the US a per se offence concerns conduct that is necessarily and irretrievably unlawful, this is not necessarily the case in the EU, where the object-based standard may refer to a "rebuttable per se" rule; an effects-based standard is usually thought of as falling short of the full-blown rule of reason, in terms of the extent of discretion of the authority's case-by-case decision-making approach. See Katsoulacos and Ulph (2009). Also, Gavil (2008), ibid. p.141. We will return to some of these distinctions below. For all intents and purposes we will treat per se as equivalent to object-based and rule of reason as equivalent to effects-based. In the EU, agreements under Art. 101 are rebuttable. However, there are cases in EU competition law that are strictly prohibited as such: RPM, parallel trade restrictions, and restrictions on cross-sales in vertical contracts.

[17]For example, for explicit horizontal price fixing agreements. The presumption of illegality is extremely strong for this wide class of conducts and therefore it is enough to know that the conduct belongs to this class, to infer with more or less certainty that its effects will be detrimental.

[18]This implies that the CA will have to carry out additional investigation, compared to when a strict per se rule is used, in order to identify the exact subclass of conducts to which the specific conduct belongs.

While this implies that the extent and sophistication of the economic analysis and evidence utilised under a full effects-based standard is greater than under object-based rules, the extent to which economic analysis must be applied will depend on the exact variant of per se/object-based or effects-based rule that is being used.

In the literature we find references to: *modified per se (or modified object-based)* standards, where the application of the object rules requires the conducting of a (contextual) analysis of market and firm characteristics before it can be determined whether the specific conduct belongs to a subclass of conducts for which there is a strong presumption of illegality; *structured rule of reason*[19] where the conduct is assessed through a specific series of screens, to distinguish lawful from unlawful cases; in contrast to the (unstructured or) *full* or *open rule of reason* where all potentially anti-competitive and pro-competitive effects of the specific conduct are assessed and compared.[20]

## 2 Considerations that Influence the Choice of Legal Standards and the Extent of Economic Analysis in CL Enforcement

Three sets of considerations that can influence the choice of legal standards, and hence the extent of economic analysis and evidence in CL enforcement, may be distinguished:

(i) considerations that determine which legal standards are optimal, given the adopted substantive standard; literature generally examines these considerations assuming welfarist substantive standards, so below we refer to them as welfare-related considerations;
(ii) hat is the substantive standard; and
(iii) considerations that affect the reputation/public image of CAs.

[19]For example, a structured rule of reason was proposed recently in the US (Supreme Court of California, In re Cipro Cases I and II, No. S198616 (Cal. May 7, 2015) for "pay-for-delay" settlements between the patent holder and generic manufacturers. Also a structured rule for reason was proposed by the US Supreme Court in dealing with RPM (in Leegin Creative Leather Products Inc. v. PSKS Inc.), 2007. and, different types of structured rules of reason have been proposed for dealing with predatory practices—see De la Mano and Durand (2005).

[20]See Alese (2008, p. 129); O'Donohue and Padilla (2008); Huschelrath (2009). The term "quick look" is also sometimes used as an alternative truncated effects standard, falling short of the "full" rule of reason—see Italianer (ibid., 2013) and Gavil (ibid., 2008).

## 2.1 Welfare-Related Considerations

We can categorise the first set of considerations into four distinct subsets[21] related, respectively, to the:

- costs of decision errors;
- deterrence (i.e. indirect or incentive) effects of legal standards;
- effects on predictability/legal certainty; and
- administrative costs of enforcement.

These are the factors that have received the greatest attention in the literature. In a series of papers, Katsoulacos and Ulph (2009, 2011, 2015 and 2016a, b) used a maximization-of-welfare framework, extending the traditional error-cost-minimization approach, in an attempt to provide answers to how the considerations above affect the choice of the (optimal) legal standard.[22]

According to the decision theoretic approach, the legal standard should minimise the cost of decision errors (of Type I and Type II). A formal analysis of decision errors under alternative legal standards[23] suggests that this involves a comparison of the quality of the models/analysis available to the CA, when undertaking an effects-based investigation of a specific conduct type, in terms of the *ability of the models to discriminate harmful from benign conducts*, with the *strength of the presumption of legality/illegality* of that conduct type.[24] Katsoulacos and Ulph[25] derive an explicit test for deciding whether the effects-based investigation will reduce decision errors: as expected, the discriminatory quality of the investigation must exceed the strength of presumption of illegality (or legality) of the conduct under investigation.

It is clear from this condition that it is certainly not generally true that under effects-based legal standards the welfare costs of decision errors will be lower than under per se legal standards. However, this is likely to be true in a large number of cases. Specifically, there will be an improvement in the overall welfare effect, through the lowering the costs of decision errors of enforcement, whenever a type of conduct potentially violating the law cannot be a priori considered as

---

[21] All of these have been examined in detail in the following articles (which also provide further references): Katsoulacos and Ulph (JIE 2009; ECJ 2011; EJLE 2015; IJIO 2016).

[22] Extensive references and reviews of the literature related to these issues are contained in these papers. See also Padilla (2011, p. 435). Of course, in principle, issues related to decision errors, deterrence and legal uncertainty could also be considered under non-welfarist substantive standards. However, in these cases it is not clear how one would measure the "costs" of errors, over- or under-deterrence, and legal uncertainty, which in the case of welfarist substantive standards are measured in terms of harm (welfare).

[23] Katsoulacos and Ulph (2009).

[24] A measure of how far the conduct is from the borderline of being legal/illegal—Katsoulacos and Ulph (2009).

[25] *Ibid.*

overwhelmingly harmful[26] or overwhelmingly benign[27] to the welfare of those affected (so the presumption of illegality or legality is not very high) and assessment on the basis of economic evidence and economic modelling, related to the specific case, can discriminate between benign and harmful conducts with reasonable accuracy.

Most economists would argue that advances in theoretical, empirical and experimental economics in the last 25 years:

- point quite strongly towards considering as less presumptively illegal many forms of conduct that in the past were considered as strongly presumptively illegal, including a wide class of potentially exclusionary conducts (related to bundling, rebates and exclusive contracts) and vertical restraints;
- allow us to discriminate more accurately between harmful and benign conducts.

Both of these developments suggest that in the case of many conducts that were considered object-restrictions in the past, a move towards adopting effects-based standards would reduce decision errors, and is therefore justified.

Decision errors affect only the welfare consequences of legal standards for the cases that come to the attention of the CAs and are investigated. However, the choice of legal standards could also affect firms whose actions do not come to the attention of CAs, for example by influencing the decision of a firm to engage in potentially efficiency enhancing or anticompetitive conduct. The effects of deterrence (or incentives) on the behaviour of firms, when deciding whether or not to adopt a particular conduct, have been recognised for a long time, as probably the most important factor in legal rulemaking.[28] As Katsoulacos and Ulph[29] demonstrate, effects-based rules generate, relative to per se standards:

- absolute deterrence effects, which are too weak (too strong) when the conduct is presumptively illegal (legal), thus lowering welfare. For example, for the case of presumptively illegal conducts, all these conducts will be deemed illegal under a per se illegality rule, but some conducts will not be deemed illegal (even though

[26]Such as explicit horizontal price fixing agreements. For this type of actions, a per se illegality standard should be (and, indeed, it is) used.

[27]Such as certain information exchanges between firms which by their very nature and characteristics are highly unlikely to have adverse effects and hence a per se legality standard should be used—that is, a standard according to which all such exchanges are deemed as per se legal, without examining the welfare implications of each case, using economic analysis. Note that in the EU a conduct regarded as per se legal can still be rebutted by the authority. The relevant expression for presumptively Legal conducts can be found in Katsoulacos and Ulph (2009).

[28]Joskow (2002) argues that deterrence effects are more important than the costs of decision errors, as they include the (cost of) responses and adaptations that targeted firms, as well as other firms and markets in general make to antitrust rules. Kai-Uwe Kuhn (Kühn 2011) stresses the importance of deterrence effects (which he terms *incentive effects*) in the context of the debate on optimal standards for information exchanges between firms. See in particular page 416 of his contribution to the OECD (2011) report.

[29]Katsoulacos and Ulph (2009).

they are genuinely harmful) and will be allowed under effects-based standards. This implies that absolute deterrence will be stronger under per se rules.
- differential deterrence effects, whereby harmful actions are more heavily deterred than benign actions, thus increasing welfare. This will be so for as long as with effects-based standards the likelihood of condemning harmful conducts is greater than the likelihood of condemning benign conducts.

When a conduct is not very strongly presumptively illegal (or legal), this is sufficient for the differential deterrence effects to dominate, implying that then, in terms of deterrence effects, effects-based standards are superior. This reinforces the argument for using such rules for lowering costs of decision errors.[30]

Finally, the argument that economics or effects-based standards are inferior because they generate legal uncertainty (LU)[31] does not seem to stand-up well to analytical scrutiny for several reasons. Katsoulacos and Ulph[32] show that there is no monotonic link between LU and welfare. Effects-based standards do not necessarily imply legal uncertainty,[33] per se standards do not always guarantee legal certainty[34] and, especially when the CA can adjust its penalty policy under alternative information structures, the superior deterrence effects of effects-based standards will make them the optimal choice even if they involve LU, while per se standards do not. When effects-based do generate LU they may still be superior to per se because of the superior deterrence effects that the uncertainty generates. Indeed, under some circumstances having some degree of LU (partial legal uncertainty) may be welfare-superior to having no LU.

Concerning administrative costs, it is clear that increasing the standard towards more effects-based rules will involve higher administrative costs.[35] Therefore, adopting higher standards needs to be justified by quite strong potential benefits, to compensate for the higher administrative costs.

As noted above, it is likely that for a range of conducts, now understood not to be strongly presumptively illegal (or legal), moving to effects-based standards would

[30]The importance of deterrence and procedural factors is shown in Katsoulacos (2009) where the above framework is applied to the analysis of legal standards for refusals to license intellectual property rights. Katsoulacos and Ulph (2011) also show that it is important to take into account other certain procedural features of a CA's operations: the coverage rate (i.e. the fraction of actions investigated by the CA), delays in decision-making, and the penalty regime. These procedural factors enter explicitly into the welfare comparison of different legal standards.

[31]Katsoulacos and Ulph (2016) make the important distinction between uncertainty generated by decision errors, which always reduces welfare, and uncertainty because firms do not know the assessment that the CA will make were their actions to be investigated. The latter is what is usually considered to be the legal uncertainty associated with effects-based standards.

[32]Katsoulacos and Ulph (2015, 2016).

[33]Katsoulacos and Ulph (2015).

[34]Rey and Venit (2015).

[35]Though it should be recognized that the increase need not be substantial especially given the advances in information technology in recent years and the enhanced ability to gather and process big data sets.

improve welfare due to a reduction in the costs of decision errors and an improvement in deterrence effects. Furthermore, we noted that the (potentially negative) implications of legal certainty may have been exaggerated. These factors suggest that the welfare gains from adopting effects-based standards could well compensate their higher administrative costs and that, therefore, adopting effects-based standards can be justified for conducts that were previously treated by per se rules.

## 2.2 *The Role of the Substantive Standard (SS)*

Where do the considerations examined above and the conclusions reached leave us? Although the above considerations suggest, assuming a welfarist substantive standard, that adopting effects-based standards would be justified, on the grounds of improving welfare, for many conducts that have traditionally been treated as object restrictions, the standards actually adopted remain close to per se and the extent of economic analysis applied by the vast majority of CAs today remains very low.[36] This implies that the arguments concerning decision errors, deterrence effects, legal uncertainty and administrative costs, may not be the only, or even the most important, influences in choosing legal standards and the extent of economic analysis in CL enforcement. In practice, other factors may be very important. One is the substantive standard of the authority or the court.[37]

As noted in some detail in the Introduction, the SS adopted may not be that of consumer or total welfare, and this of course influences the extent of economic analysis and evidence in the assessment of potentially anticompetitive conducts. As explained, even if effects-based legal standards are adopted, the extent of economic analysis used, when the substantive standard is not welfarist,[38] would be limited or very limited. To clarify this further we need to take the following into account.

Non-welfarist SS, or non-welfarist liability criteria, can differ from welfarist SS in two ways:

(a) A non-welfarist SS can be one of a continuum of criteria that need to be examined in order to form a judgement about the ultimate welfare criterion. Hence, for example, the criterion of "preservation of competition" or whether the type of conducts/market conditions under consideration have an "exclusionary effects", becomes part of the process of reaching a judgement based on the welfare criterion. However, in the case of the latter, it is necessary to additionally examine whether the conducts could have substantial efficiency effects that in

---

[36]There are exceptions to this, such as the US and Canada, but the statement does in fact reflect the reality in the vast majority of other jurisdictions.

[37]Generally, the CA will recognize, from case law, and adopt the substantive standard that is used by the Courts.

[38]Such as the preservation of undistorted competition which require that conducts do not make it more difficult for a rival to compete).

many cases might outweigh the potential exclusionary effects and thus increase consumer surplus and efficiency. We believe that the main difference in the liability standard applied in the EU and the US in recent years is of this type.

(b) A non-welfarist SS may be one related to "public interest concerns", which, as mentioned above, have been popular (perhaps increasingly so) in BRICS and developing countries. For example, the SS may focus on non-welfarist criteria such as inequality, employment or international competitiveness. These are not criteria that need to be examined when forming a judgement about the welfare criterion, i.e. they are distinct from the latter. CAs using these non-welfarist liability criteria can adopt per se or effects-based legal standards, in the sense we defined above,[39] in order to reach a decision concerning how the examined conducts/market conditions affect the selected criterion. When a CA emphasises a non-welfarist SS of this type then, of course, the extent to which it will rely on competition-related economic analysis and evidence will be very limited.

Focusing below on the case of a type-A non-welfarist SS (N-WSS), this is expected to lead to a limited application of economic analysis and evidence, for two reasons: first, as already mentioned, even if effects-based legal standards are used, under a N-WSS the extent of economic analysis will be limited, compared to the case where a welfarist SS (WSS) is used; second, with a N-WSS the likelihood of the CA adopting a per se standard[40] is higher than when the SS is welfarist. Below we explain why these statements are true. We assume that the N-WSS is that of "preserving competition" or whether the specific conduct "is likely to have exclusionary effects[41]".

To start with, provided allegations that a specific conduct violates the law, we need to start by specifying the general population of conducts to which the specific conduct belongs and, in many cases, the market conditions that are relevant for this type of conducts, according to competition law and precedents[42]—e.g. the conditions under which dominance exists. Given this population of conducts/market conditions[43] we can consider and compare the following alternatives:

---

[39]Meaning that with per se standards we rely on making inferences about the effects of a specific conduct from what we already know about the effects of populations of similar conducts; with effects-based standards we do not rely on making such inferences and try to identify the effects by investigating the specific conduct in detail.

[40]With very limited use of economics.

[41]Here we interpret the term *exclusionary effects* as making it more difficult for rivals to compete.

[42]Strictly speaking, in the case of conducts for which a contextual analysis of market conditions is important, the per se rule is not a "strict per se" rule—the latter being based purely on a presumption about the characteristics of the conduct. "Modified per se" is a more appropriate term for the case where market conditions are taken into account and it entails the population of conducts/market conditions where a presumption of illegality has to be made. Below we will refer simply to per se rules when considering either "strict per se" or "modified per se" rules.

[43]Tying-related conduct would be a good example. A number of alternative legal standards have been proposed for their assessment, ranging from per se (illegality) to full effects-based; see, Ahlborn et al. (2004) who favour an intermediate legal standard (structured rule of reason).

- *A.1: WSS—per se*: in this case the CA makes inferences, for example, about the effect of the specific conduct on consumer surplus (CS),[44] from the presumed effect of the population of conducts/market conditions on CS.
- *A.2: N-WSS—per se*: in this case the CA makes inferences about the exclusionary effect of the specific conduct from the presumed exclusionary effect of the population of conducts/market conditions.
- *A.3: WSS—truncated effects-based ($WSS_{TEB}$)*: in this case the CA establishes whether the specific conduct has exclusionary effects and makes inferences about the effect of the specific conduct on CS, from the presumed effect on CS of the population of conducts/market conditions that have exclusionary effects.
- *A.4: N-WSS—effects-based (N-$WSS_{EB}$)*: in this case the CA decides on the basis of whether the specific conduct has an exclusionary effect or not, following an investigation into it.
- *A.5: WSS—Effects-Based ($WSS_{EB}$)*: in this case the CA decides on the basis of whether the specific conduct has a negative effect on CS or not, following an investigation into it.

From the descriptions above, we first note that if the CA adopts a N-WSS, even if it chooses an effects-based standard (i.e. the above-mentioned alternative N-$WSS_{EB}$) the extent of the economics applied would be limited relative to using an effects-based standard under a WSS (i.e. alternative $WSS_{EB}$). Since, with $WSS_{EB}$, additional economic analysis will have to be applied, on top of that applied under N-$WSS_{EB}$, in order to show that the specific conduct does not just have an exclusionary effect, but also reduces CS.

Second, we note that since for the general population of conducts/market conditions the probability of a negative presumed effect on exclusion is higher than that of a negative presumed effect on CS (because the former is a necessary but not a sufficient condition for the latter), we can say that the *presumption of illegality* is higher under the alternative A.2 (N-WSS—per se) than under the alternative A.1 (WSS—per se), so ceteris paribus, per se is more likely to be favoured under N-WSS. However, we need to examine this in more detail.

Note that under a WSS the CA may prefer $WSS_{TEB}$ to per se (alternative A.3 to A.1), because under the former the presumption of illegality is much greater (presumption of negative effect on CS is stronger for conducts that have exclusionary effects than for all conducts), *given the quality* (in terms of decision errors) of economic thinking and of models for establishing exclusionary effects under $WSS_{TEB}$. Let us assume that this is the case.

However, under a N-WSS the CA may well prefer per se to N-$WSS_{EB}$ (i.e. alternative A.2–A.4) because under a per se legal standard the presumption of illegality is stronger with a N-WSS (than under WSS—per se), and the discriminatory quality of economic thinking and models for establishing exclusionary effects is the same under N-$WSS_{EB}$ (alternative A.4) as under $WSS_{TEB}$ (alternative A.3), as

[44]The alternative SS could be total welfare.

indicated above. *Thus, under N-WSS the CA is more likely to choose per se than under WSS*. Of course, this would tend to limit the extent of economic and evidence applied in enforcement when the CA uses N-WSS. Indeed, if under a WSS the CA were to prefer to adopt a $WSS_{EB}$ to a $WSS_{TEB}$ (as Rey and Venit (2015), believed should have been the case in the Intel case) then the reduction of the economics applied under a N-WSS (as that adopted in that case by the EU Court and the Commission DG COMP Legal Service) could be substantial.

## 2.3 The Effect of Reputation on the Choice of Standards

Competition authorities are government or independent organisations that typically have a certain degree of freedom to choose among different possible courses of action. While they are concerned with the welfare benefits that their activities bring to society, they are concerned with how their activities affect their public image and reputation. This is consistent with the widely recognised fact that, in many cases, CAs operate under performance criteria that are not always related to the welfare effects of their enforcement activities.[45]

Recent work, by Katsoulacos (2017) and by Katsoulacos et al. (2016a, b) influenced by the work of Harrington (2011) and Schinkel et al. (2015), assumes that CAs maximise a utility function that depends both on a composite indicator of enforcement success and the welfare impact of the CA's decisions, given the legal standards on the basis of which these decisions are made. The enforcement success (and thus the utility) of a CA is affected negatively by the decrease in the number of cases that the CA opens and concludes (independently of whether the decisions concern infringements) and by the increase in the number of reversals of its infringement decisions by the courts of appeal. The CA's utility is affected positively by an increase in the welfare impact of its choices related to legal standards. A reputation-maximising CA, which does not take into account the welfare effect of its choice of legal standards, will not have incentive to adopt effects-based standards, which utilise more economic analysis and evidence, when this can lead to an increase in the likelihood that appealed infringement decisions will be annulled by the courts of appeal. On the other hand, welfare-maximising CAs will choose standards that are more effects-based and will be prepared to apply economic analysis and evidence to a greater extent than reputation-maximising CAs.

[45]The performance criteria used to assess the activities of CAs are extremely heterogeneous. On one side there is the experience of UK's OFT, which is subject to positive impact assessment in order to achieve a target of 5:1 (now 10:1) ratio of benefits to consumers relative to the cost to the taxpayers. On the other side, many authorities still use crude output indicators (e.g. the number of handled cases) or indicators of enforcement success (proportion of decisions supported by the courts) instead of welfare outcome indicators as important performance criteria. At the present, there is still no adequate design for a performance evaluation (Kovacic et al. 2011).

## 3 A Practical Approach to Choosing Legal Standards that Minimise Decision Errors

Consider a CA (and court) that adopts a welfarist SS, which has to decide whether some conduct by a firm or group of firms violates CL. How should it choose the best *legal standard* to apply in assessing the conduct *in order to minimise decision errors*[46]?

We consider the CA deciding in several stages which standard is appropriate.

*Stage 1* Verification and identification of the nature, object (or form) of the conduct; the CA undertakes an investigation that allows it to *characterise fully the nature of the conduct.*

As a result of this investigation the CA can locate the specific conduct, within a subset/subpopulation of conducts, with similar characteristics to the conduct that is alleged to violate the law, within a general category of potential anti-competitive conducts. Further, at this stage the CA is provided with or can obtain some basic information concerning market characteristics and can identify what established economic theory and available empirical evidence and case law suggest *about the specific subpopulation of conducts identified.* Based on what is learned in Stage 1, the CA can determine the frequency of (genuinely) harmful conducts $\widehat{\gamma}$, the loss in welfare (negative harm) from falsely condemning benign conduct ($-\ \widehat{h}_B$), and the loss in welfare from not condemning harmful conduct $\widehat{h}_H$, for the subpopulation of conducts to which the conduct is found to belong, i.e. it can form a prior about the fraction of harmful and benign conducts in this subpopulation and the *average* harm across different potential market characteristics (or environments).

Thus the CA determines the average harm from this subclass of conducts

$$\bar{h} = \widehat{\gamma}\widehat{h}_H + \left(1 - \widehat{\gamma}\right)\widehat{h}_B \quad (1)$$

determining whether the subclass of conducts is *presumptively legal* or it is *presumptively illegal*:

presumptively legal (PL): $\bar{h} < 0$

presumptively illegal (PI): $\bar{h} > 0$

Also it can define indicators of the strength of the presumption of legality, $s_{PL}$ (illegality, $s_{PI}$) as follows[47]:

[46]For the remainder of this section we will assume that the choice is made on the grounds of decision-error minimization; we will also neglect all the other considerations that influence this choice (which were examined above).

[47]See also Katsoulacos and Ulph (2009).

$$s_{PL} = \frac{(1 - \widehat{\gamma})(-\widehat{h}_B)}{\widehat{\gamma}\widehat{h}_h} > 1 \tag{2}$$

$$s_{PI} = \frac{\widehat{\gamma}\widehat{h}_h}{(1 - \widehat{\gamma})(-\widehat{h}_B)} > 1 \tag{3}$$

At the end of Stage 1, the CA can reach a decision on the case without any further investigation, using a per se legality (PSL) standard (thus allowing the conduct), or a per se illegality (PSI) standard (thus disallowing the conduct). This could be appropriate if the strength of the presumption of legality or illegality are very strong, so by using per se the CA can satisfy its standard of proof for establishing its ultimate contention (there is very little risk of substantial decision errors that could justify the use of an effects-based standard that would aim to discriminate whether the conduct in question is benign or harmful). For example, if $\widehat{\gamma}$ is close to unity then this would be sufficient to make the strength of the presumption of illegality in Eq. (3) extremely large, something that would justify the use of a per se illegality standard (for example, this is the rationale for using this standard in the case of explicit horizontal price fixing).

However, assume that the values of $\widehat{\gamma},\ \widehat{h}_H,\ \widehat{h}_B$ are such that the CA does not consider that the strength of the presumption of legality or illegality is sufficiently great to justify (without further analysis) the use of a per se standard—it expects that this could result in too many decision errors. In this case it would need to decide which standard to use by comparing the cost of the decision errors of the alternatives. We can define:

**Costs of Decision Errors** (CDE) = Costs of False Convictions (CFC) + Costs of False Acquittals (CFA).

In the case of per se, the CDE are:

$$CDE^{PSL} = CFA^{PSL} = \widehat{\gamma}\widehat{h}_H \tag{4}$$

with a per se legality standard, and:

$$CDE^{PSI} = CFC^{PSI} = (1 - \widehat{\gamma})(-\ \widehat{h}_B) \tag{5}$$

with a per se illegality standard:

The CA assessment must now move to the second stage.

*Stage 2* Detailed identification of the characteristics of the market environment. At the end of Stage 2 the CA may make a decision using a *modified per se standard subject to a significant market power (SMP) requirement.* This is provided so that the investigation in Stage 2 will allow the CA to revise the values of γ and h. it is assumed that these (revised) values are $\gamma,\ h_H,\ h_B$.

The CA can re-determine the average harm and the strength of the presumption of illegality for these revised values of γ and h, and may decide whether it should use a (modified) per se rule subject to SMP (if for example the revised value of γ is very high, it would be justified in using a per se illegality rule on the basis of the strength of the presumption for the restricted subpopulation of firms with SMP). Using a (modified) per se standard subject to a SMP requirement is consistent with the practice of CAs throughout the world (including the US) prior to the mid-1990s, when dealing with a number of business practices undertaken by dominant firms (bundling, royalty rebates, exclusive contracts with distributors, etc.).

However, even in the presence of SMP the CA could well consider the presumption of illegality not high enough to justify the adoption of per se rules and may consider to use an effects-based standard to make its assessment, although this does not imply that the CA would necessarily move to full-blown rule-of-reason. This is the situation relating to the mentioned practices in the US (and some other countries, e.g. Canada and the UK) in the past two decades.

This suggests a third stage of analysis for choosing the appropriate legal standard.

*Stage 3* Undertaking an effects-based assessment, which implies showing how, given the market environment, the *specific* conduct can generate social harm, on the basis of additional economic analysis, modelling and empirical evidence.[48] The CA can only identify market characteristics and relate them and the characteristics of the conduct to harm by using economic analysis and evidence with certain errors. Whether or not an effects-based standard should be chosen turns on the comparison of the costs of the decision errors with those of staying with per se, and this requires comparing the strength of presumption of illegality (or legality) with the discriminatory quality of an effects-based economic analysis.

Assuming that if the CA adopts an effects-based (EB-type) standard, it considers that the economic models and evidence it can use for assessing the specific type of conduct will lead to the finding of a law violation with probability $\beta$, $0 < \beta < 1$, therefore a finding of no-violation will emerge with probability $1 - \beta$. This compares to the CA deciding that there is violation in *all* cases under a per se illegality standard and deciding that there is violation in *none* of the cases under a per se legality standard. $\beta$ is a probability that is much easier to understand and try to estimate (see below) than probabilities associated with the errors that the CA makes when it adopts an EB standard. Also it is important to introduce this probability to capture the intuition that when the conduct is presumptively illegal then the higher $\beta$ is, the lower the cost will be of decision errors of the EB standard, for any given propensity of this standard to make errors,[49] while oppositely, when the conduct is presumptively legal the lower $\beta$ is, the lower the cost will be of decision errors of the EB standard for any given propensity of this standard to make errors.

Finally, assuming that the CA considers that the following hold, concerning errors in its decisions (to be discussed below):

---

[48]At this point we disregard the fact that the CA may choose a truncated or a structured effects-based standard.

[49]And therefore, the more likely that the CDE of EB will be lower than the CDE of Per Se—see also comparison below.

- Conditional on finding a violation, the probability that the conduct is in fact harmful is $\beta_H$, $0 \leq \beta_H \leq 1$, while the probability that it is truly benign is $(1 - \beta_H)$.
- Conditional on a finding of non-violation, the probability that the conduct is *not* harmful is $\beta_B$, $0 \leq \beta_B \leq 1$, while the probability that the conduct is harmful is $(1 - \beta_B)$.

At a minimum the discriminatory quality of an EB standard must be such that:

$$\beta_H > 1 - \beta_B$$

Although, as we will see below, this is *not* a necessary condition for the CDE of an EB standard to be lower than the CDE of per se standards.

The first thing to note is that the various probabilities are related by the following *consistency constraint*. For harmful cases:

$$\beta\beta_H + (1 - \beta)(1 - \beta_B) = \gamma \tag{6}$$

and for non-harmful cases:

$$(1 - \beta)\beta_B + \beta(1 - \beta_H) = 1 - \gamma \tag{7}$$

These expressions make it clear that if the CA improves its ability to identify correctly harmful conducts, it will have improved its ability to correctly identify benign conducts. They can be used to express the value of $\beta_H(\beta_B)$, which would satisfy the consistency constraint as follows, given β and γ and $\beta_B(\beta_H)$:

$$\beta_H = \frac{\gamma - (1 - \beta_B)(1 - \beta)}{\beta}. \tag{8}$$

$$\beta_B = \frac{(1 - \gamma) - (1 - \beta_H)\beta}{(1 - \beta)}. \tag{9}$$

The CA can infer γ from the investigations it undertook in Stages 1 and 2, of the exact characteristics of the conduct and the characteristics of the market and firm (s) under investigation, and from all the available economic analyses and empirical evidence that is related to this type of conduct.

It can also infer β based on information from its past investigations of this type of conduct (with EB-type standards), and from information of investigations and decisions reached by other authorities worldwide; indeed, the latter is a standard practice used by CAs to examine what other authorities have done in similar cases. Note that given γ and β, the CA has to form judgment about either $\beta_H$ or $\beta_B$, in order to infer the value of the other (given the consistency constraints).

From Eqs. (8) and (9), for $\beta_H \geq 0$ and $\beta_B \geq 0$:

$$(1 - \beta) + \beta\beta_H \geq \gamma \geq (1 - \beta)(1 - \beta_B) \tag{10}$$

Or, given β and γ, for $\beta_H \geq 0$,

$$\beta_B \geq \frac{(1-\beta)-\gamma}{(1-\beta)} \tag{11}$$

and for $\beta_{\mathrm{B}} \geq 0$,

$$\beta_H \geq \frac{\gamma-(1-\beta)}{\beta} \tag{12}$$

**Comparison of Costs of Decision Errors**

The CDE of the EB standard is given by the following expression:

$$CDE^{EB} = CFA^{EB} + CFC^{EB} \tag{13}$$

so:

$$CDE^{EB} = (1-\beta)(1-\beta_{\mathrm{B}})\gamma h_H + \beta(1-\beta_{\mathrm{H}})(1-\gamma)(-h_B) \tag{14}$$

Let

$$m = \frac{h_H}{(-h_B)}$$

(i) By comparing the CDE under EB and per se we come to: for conducts considered to be presumptively legal (PL):

$$CDE^{EB} < CDE^{PSL}$$

iff:

$$q^{EB,PL} + \frac{1}{(1-\beta_H)} > \frac{(1-\gamma)(-h_B)}{\gamma h_H} = \frac{(1-\gamma)}{m\gamma} = s^{PL} \quad q^{EB,PL} = \frac{(1-\beta)\beta_{\mathrm{B}}}{\beta(1-\beta_H)} \tag{15}$$

where $q^{EB,\,PL}$ is an *indicator of the discriminatory quality of the EB standard under PL* (ratio of the probability of not finding to the probability of finding that there is violation of competition law when the conduct is benign);

(ii) for conducts considered to be presumptively illegal (PI):

$$CDE^{EB} < CDE^{PSI}$$

iff:

$$q^{EB,PI} + \frac{1}{(1-\beta_B)} > \frac{\gamma h_H}{(1-\gamma)(-h_B)} = \frac{\gamma m}{(1-\gamma)} = s^{PI} \tag{16}$$

where

$$q^{EB,PI} = \frac{\beta \beta_H}{(1-\beta)(1-\beta_B)} \tag{17}$$

is an *indicator of the discriminatory quality of the EB standard under PI* (ratio of the probability of finding to the probability of not-finding violation when the conduct is harmful).

Results and Observations:

1. The smaller $\gamma$ is and the greater $h_H$ is, relative to $h_B$, the greater the presumption of legality and less likely it is that EB can dominate per se in decision error terms, for presumptively legal conducts.
2. EB is more likely to dominate per se the less (more) likely it is to lead to findings of violation, i.e. the smaller (greater) $\beta$ is, for presumptively legal (illegal) conducts; in fact, for sufficiently small (large) $\beta$, EB will have lower CDE for presumptively legal (illegal) conducts, as long as $\beta_H$ and $\beta_B$ are positive (see also below).
3. When the presumption of legality (illegality) is low (RHS is small) the CDE under EB can be lower than per se, so EB standards will be superior to per se under many potential standards differing in $\beta_H$and in $\beta_B$. That is, EB standards that are low in false convictions or EB standards that are low in false acquittals can be superior to per se standards. However, more importantly, from Eqs. (15) and (16):
4. *For any given $\beta$*, Increasing $\beta_H$ and hence limiting false convictions, is the most efficient way to ensure that EB is superior in CDE terms when the conduct is considered presumptively legal.
5. *For any given $\beta$*, Increasing $\beta_B$ and hence limiting false acquittals is the most efficient way to ensure that EB is superior in CDE terms when the conduct is considered presumptively illegal.
6. Presumptively legal conducts: *If $\beta$ is sufficiently small*, as long as the CA can avoid false acquittals to some extent ($\beta_B > 0$), the CDE of the EB standard will be lower than under per se standard, irrespective of how bad the EB standard is at limiting false convictions (i.e. even with $\beta_H = 0$).
7. Presumptively illegal conducts: *If $\beta$ is sufficiently large*, for as long as the CA can avoid false convictions to some extent ($\beta_H > 0$), the CDE of the EB standard will be lower than under per se standard irrespective of how bad the EB standard is at limiting false acquittals (i.e. even with $\beta_B = 0$).

It is straightforward to produce simulations based on the above expressions, which would allow a CA to use the above formulas in practice, in order to decide which standard minimises decision errors. Here is an example.

Assuming that the CA believes that $\gamma$ is likely to be around 0.6, and that $h_H$ is likely to be twice $-h_B$ (m = 2). The conduct is considered quite strongly presumptively illegal (authors addressing tying arrangements by dominant firms would consider lower values for $\gamma$—see Ahlborn et al. (2004); on the other hand, for RPM a much higher value may be appropriate[50]). The strength of the CA's presumption can be measured by $s^{PI}$, which is $s^{PI} = 3$.

Assume also that given the information available to the CA (as mentioned above), it is believed that $\beta = 0.8$.

From Eq. (8), for $\beta_B = 0$ the value of $\beta_H$ is $\beta_H = 0, 5$. As $\beta_B$ increases the value of $\beta_H$ increases, and $\beta_H = 0, 75$ when $\beta_B = 1$. From Eq. (16), we can see that EB is superior in CDE terms even for the lowest $\beta_B$ and $\beta_H$ values, $\beta_B = 0$ and $\beta_H = 0, 5$, so it is superior for all $\beta_B$ and $\beta_H$ values that are consistent with the "more objectively" identified values of $\beta$ and $\gamma$.

If the strength of the PI is higher, e.g. $\gamma = 0.8$, and $\beta$ is lower, e.g. $\beta = 0.6$, then for $\beta_B = 0$ the value of $\beta_H$ is $\beta_H = 0, 666$ and as $\beta_B$ increases the value of $\beta_H$ increases and $\beta_H = 1$ when $\beta_B = 0, 5$. Now with $\beta_B = 0$ and $\beta_H = 0, 666$, the CDE under EB are less than under per se; it is only when $\beta_B > 0, 2$ and $\beta_H > 0, 8$ that the CDE of EB become lower than those under per se. However, if $\beta = 0.9$ then even with $\beta_B$ and $\beta_H$ values at the lowest end of the relevant ranges, the EB standard will have lower CDE than the per se standards.

The argument here is that if the CA can obtain the information and knowledge required to identify $\beta$, $\gamma$ and m, then it can use these to examine for which ranges of $\beta_B$ and $\beta_H$ values the CDE of EB standards is lower than under per se. If these are "reasonable" in the sense that even at low $\beta_B$ and $\beta_H$ values in the relevant ranges the CDE is lower under EB, then the CA has a very strong case for using EB.

## 4 Concluding Remarks

We have examined the factors influencing the choice of legal standards, and hence determining the extent of economic analysis and evidence applied in competition law enforcement, focusing on recent economic literature. We have emphasised the analytical and practical usefulness of viewing legal standards as a *continuum* between strict per se and rule-of-reason. We have suggested explanations of why the decisions of CAs in relation to the utilization of economic evidence may well diverge from social welfare-maximising decisions. We have emphasised the very significant, but still underexplored, role played by the choice of substantive standards on whether per se or effects-based legal standards are adopted, and on the extent that economic analysis is utilised. We have also proposed a practical methodology that can be used by CAs for identifying which legal standards minimise decision errors in the assessment of specific conducts.

[50] See for example Katsoulacos and Ulph (2009), Section V.

**Acknowledgement** The author is grateful to the participants of the International Conference on Institution Building of the Competition Authorities in South East Europe for many helpful comments and suggestions. The author is also grateful, for the helpful discussions on the subject of this article, to Svetlana Avdasheva, Svetlana Golovaneva, Joe Harrington, Frederic Jenny, Eleni Metsiou and David Ulph.

## References

Ahlborn C, Evans D, Padilla J (2004) The antitrust economics of tying: a farewell to per se illegality. Antitrust Bull 49(1):287–341

Alese F (2008) Federal antitrust and EC competition law analysis. Ashgate Publishing, Farnham, p 129

Baker JB, Salop SC (2015) Antitrust, competition policy and inequality. Georgetown University Law Center, Mimeo

Blair RD, Sokol DD (2012) The rule of reason and the goals of antitrust: an economic approach. Antitrust Law J 78(2):471–504

Carlton DW (2007) Does antitrust need to be modernized? Economic analysis group, discussion paper - EAG 07-03

De la Mano M, Durand B (2005) A three-step structured rule of reason to assess predation under article 82, DG COMP DP. http://ec.europa.eu/dgs/competition/economist/pred_art82.pdf. Accessed 09 Sep 2016

Fox EM, Sullivan L (1987) Antirust-retrospective and prospective: where are we coming from? Where are we going? NYUL Rev 62:936

Gavil AI (2008) Burden of proof in U.S. antitrust law. In: Issues in competition law and policy 1 125, ABA Section of Antitrust Law

Harrington J (2011) When is an antitrust authority not aggressive enough in fighting cartels? Int J Econ Theory 7:39

Huschelrath K (2009) Competition policy analysis: an integrated approach. ZEW Econ Stud 41:241

Italianer A (2013) Competitor agreements under EU competition law. 40th annual conference on international antitrust law and policy, Fordham Competition Law Institute, New York

Joskow PL (2002) Transaction cost economics, antitrust rules, and remedies. J Law Econ Org 18 (1):95–116

Katsoulacos Y (2009) Optimal legal standards for refusals to license intellectual property: a welfare-based analysis. J Compet Law Econ 5:269

Katsoulacos Y (2017) Judicial review, economic evidence and the choice of legal standards by utility maximizing competition authorities, Mimeo. http://www.cresse.info/uploadfiles/Paper%20on%20EB%20vs%20PS%20YK%20New%20Model%2023052017.pdf

Katsoulacos Y, Ulph D (2009) Optimal legal standards for competition policy. J Ind Econ 57 (3):410–437

Katsoulacos Y, Ulph D (2011) Optimal enforcement structures for competition policy: implications of judicial reviews and of internal error correction mechanisms. Eur Compet J 7:71–88

Katsoulacos Y, Ulph D (2015) Legal uncertainty, competition law enforcement procedures and optimal penalties. Eur J Law Econ 41(2):255–282

Katsoulacos Y, Ulph D (2016) Regulatory decision errors, legal uncertainty and welfare: a general treatment. Int J Ind Organ 53:326–352. (Available online 24 May 2016)

Katsoulacos Y, Avdasheva S, Golovaneva S (2016a) Economic analysis and competition law enforcement: lessons for developing countries from the case of Russia. Mimeo, New York (available from authors on request)

Katsoulacos Y, Metsiou E, Ulph D (2016b) Optimal substantive standards for competition authorities. J Ind Compet Trade 16(3):273–295

Kovacic WE, Hollman HM, Grant P (2011) How does your competition agency measure up? Eur Compet J 7:25–45

Kühn K-U (2011) Designing competition policy towards information exchanges – looking beyond the possibility results. In: Information exchanges between competitors under competition law, OECD Competition Committee, 11 July 2011

O'Donohue R, Padilla AJ (2008) The law and economics of art.82 EC. Hart Publishing, New York, pp 183–184

OECD (2011) Information exchanges between competitors under competition law. OECD Competition Committee, 11 July 2011

Padilla J (2011) The elusive challenge of assessing information sharing among competitors under the competition laws. In: Information exchanges between competitors under competition law, OECD Competition Committee, 11 July 2011

Rey P, Venit JS (2015) An effects-based approach to article 102: a response to Wouter Wils. World Compet 38:3–29

Schinkel MP, Tóth L, Tuinstra J (2015) Discretionary authority and prioritizing in government agencies. Amsterdam Center for Law & Economics, working paper no 2014-06. http://papers.ssrn.com/sol3/papers.cfm?abstract_id=2533894. Accessed 9 Sep 2016

Wils W (2014) The judgment of the EU general court in Intel and the so-called more economic approach to abuse of dominance. World Compet 37:405

# Three Economist's Tools for Antitrust Analysis: A Non-technical Introduction

Russell Pittman

## 1 Introduction

The importance of economics to the analysis and enforcement of competition policy and law has increased tremendously in the developed market economies in the past 40 years. In younger and developing market economies, competition law itself has a history of 20–25 years at most—sometimes much less—and economic tools that have proven useful to competition law enforcement in developed market economies in focusing investigations and in assisting decision makers in distinguishing central from secondary issues are inevitably less well understood. While agencies and enforcers face a steep learning curve regarding these tools, companies and their attorneys and economic consultants are already using them to present agencies with sophisticated economic analyses purporting to demonstrate the lack of cause for concern regarding particular deals or practices.

This paper presents a non-technical introduction to three economic tools that have become widespread in competition law enforcement in general and in the analysis of proposed mergers in particular: critical loss analysis, upward pricing pressure, and the vertical arithmetic. The first is used primarily in the context of horizontal mergers for both market definition and the analysis of potential competitive effects from the merger, while the second and third are used primarily in the analysis of potential competitive effects, the second in horizontal mergers and the third in vertical mergers. All three are discussed extensively by now in the economics and legal literature, so that an introduction inevitably gives inadequate attention to some corollaries and complexities.

R. Pittman
Antitrust Division, U.S. Department of Justice, Washington, DC, USA

Kyiv School of Economics, Kyiv, Ukraine

New Economic School, Moscow, Russia
e-mail: Russell.Pittman@usdoj.gov



B. Begović, D. V. Popović (eds.), *Competition Authorities in South Eastern Europe*, Contributions to Economics, https://doi.org/10.1007/978-3-319-76644-7_9

## 2 Critical Loss Analysis

Critical Loss Analysis (CLA) was introduced in 1989 (Harris and Simons 1989) primarily as a tool for market definition in merger investigations and has been used extensively since then in the analysis of both product markets and geographic markets. Subsequently it began to be applied, with appropriate amendments, to the analysis of competitive effects of mergers as well, with a focus on the analysis of the unilateral effects of mergers in markets with differentiated products. We will consider the two applications in that order.

### 2.1 *Critical Loss Analysis for Market Definition*

The standard methodology for market definition in merger analysis begins with the "hypothetical monopolist test": whether "a hypothetical profit-maximizing firm, not subject to price regulation, that was the only present and future seller of . . . [a set of products] likely would impose at least a small but significant and non-transitory increase in price ('SSNIP') on at least one product in the market . . ." (U.S. Department of Justice and Federal Trade Commission 2010). Even the broad implementation of this test requires the analyst to make a number of detailed choices and assumptions—some of which will be considered later—but for now let us make the exercise more straightforward by assuming that the hypothetical monopolist is restricted to charging a single price to all potential customers. (Note that this is a conservative assumption, in that it renders the analysis less likely to satisfy the test, since we are restricting the ability of the hypothetical monopolist to set the prices of each good at its profit-maximizing level.)

Algebraically, we assume that industry profits are currently set as:

$$\Pi_0 = (\mathrm{P}_0 - \mathrm{C})\mathrm{Q}_0 \tag{1}$$

where fixed costs are assumed sunk and irrelevant in the short term and marginal costs C are assumed constant, i.e. equal to average costs. The hypothetical monopolist of the industry would consider increasing price according to the following equation:

$$\Pi_1 = (\mathrm{P}_0 + \Delta P - \mathrm{C})(\mathrm{Q}_0 - \Delta Q) \tag{2}$$

and the critical issue is:

$$(\mathrm{P}_0 + \Delta P - \mathrm{C})(\mathrm{Q}_0 - \Delta Q) \gtrless (\mathrm{P}_0 - \mathrm{C})\mathrm{Q}_0 \tag{3}$$

Does the increase in profit from the price increase $\Delta$P on the sales that remain outweigh the reduction in profit resulting from the loss of sales $\Delta$Q? Simple algebra reveals the "critical loss" of output that would make the monopolist indifferent:

**Table 1** A 4-firm provisional market

| Firm | Current output | Capacity | Price | Variable cost |
|---|---|---|---|---|
| W | 100 | 105 | \$50 | \$30 |
| X | 80 | 85 | \$50 | \$30 |
| Y | 33 | 50 | \$50 | ? |
| Z | 30 | ? | \$50 | ? |

$$\frac{\Delta Q}{Q} = \frac{\Delta P/P}{M + \Delta P/P} \tag{4}$$

where M = $(P_0-C)/P_0$, the existing price-cost margin. If the loss of sales ΔQ resulting from the increase in price ΔP is higher than that which satisfies this equation, the price increase would not be profitable.

Of course, if we knew the elasticity of demand for the product, we would know the ΔQ/Q that would result from a given ΔP/P, and no further analysis would be required to answer the market definition question. But let's assume that we are early in an investigation, without the data required for estimating such a parameter. Then the critical loss calculation described above serves to frame a very specific question: if price increases by a certain amount, how much would demand fall? And in particular, where would it "go"? Or, in the language of the CLA literature, now that we know the "critical loss", what would be the "actual loss"?

Consider now a hypothetical merger investigation, and the information that might be available early in the investigation to the analyst at the antimonopoly agency seeking to answer the market definition question.[1] Suppose that the analyst has the following information, considered inexact but reasonably reliable.

Now suppose that firms W and X propose to merge, and our analyst wants first to analyze whether the product sold by these firms constitutes a relevant product market. Using the hypothetical monopolist test along with CLA, the question may be formulated as follows: would a hypothetical monopolist of this product raise prices by a SSNIP, say 5%?

Using the prices and costs of the merging firms shown in Table 1, and assuming that these represent the prices and costs of a hypothetical monopolist, we see that a price increase of 5% would equal \$2.50, so that the monopolist would gain \$2.50 on each unit still sold, but would lose \$50−\$30 = \$20 on each unit sale lost. Thus ΔP/P = 5% and M = \$20/\$50 = 40%. Then the critical loss for determining whether the price increase would be profitable is ΔQ/Q = 5/(40 + 5) = 1/9 = 11%. We therefore have the following question to investigate: if a hypothetical monopolist provider of this product raised price from \$50 to \$52.50, would sales be reduced by as much as 11%? And in particular—focusing on the demand side, as is the practice in US enforcement—to what other products might consumers of these products switch?

[1]Examples of the use of critical loss analysis in US and EC merger investigations are presented in Langenfeld and Li (2001), O'Brien and Wickelgren (2003), Amelio et al. (2008), and Hüschelrath (2009).

The relevant product market question asks to what degree customers will substitute away from the product in response to the price increase. Are there other products that are imperfect substitutes for this product but would become more attractive following a price increase? If the product is a consumer good, are consumers likely to be highly sensitive to price increases and to reduce their purchases of this good, allocating more of their budgets to other consumer goods, whether close substitute goods or unrelated goods? If the product is a producer good, are the firms that use this product as an input into the production of other goods able to substitute other inputs in the production process, and/or will they suffer their own losses of sales if forced to "pass through" this price increase of an input?

This is the basic version of CLA. It does no more and no less than focus the attention of the analyst on the precise (or somewhat precise, as will be discussed) question of how much substitution away from the products in the provisional product market would be necessary to defeat a potential anticompetitive price increase, and thus whether this choice of provisional product market represents the state of competition in the world as it exists or whether the provisional product market must be expanded to include the next closest substitute to constitute an actual market.

Once having identified the relevant product, a similar analysis would be applicable to the definition of geographic markets. To test whether the area that includes only the four firms in Table 1 is a relevant geographic market, for example, observe that the critical loss of 11% of their collective sales of 243 units is 27 units. If the hypothetical monopolist that raises price from \$50 to \$52.50 would lose sales of fewer than 27 units to producers outside of that area, the test is satisfied. If it would lose more than 27 sales, the area must be expanded to include those rivals to which purchasers switched. A number of variations and complications to this simple story should be considered.

### 2.1.1 Implicit Elasticities

In practice, the merging parties (and/or their lawyers and consultants) may argue that existing price-cost margins that look "high" suggest that a hypothetical monopolist would be unlikely to raise price much from its current level; after all, the argument may go, each unit lost in a reduction of output loses the entire existing margin—\$20 in our example—and the hypothetical monopolist would have to lose only a small amount of sales in order to regret its decision to impose a SSNIP.

However, as a theoretical matter, as Katz and Shapiro (2003), O'Brien and Wickelgren (2003), and Kaplow and Shapiro (2007) have pointed out, the estimated price-cost margin potentially contains information about the elasticity of demand facing the firms in the industry. According to the well-known Lerner Index, a profit-maximizing firm sets price where the price-cost margin equals the negative reciprocal of the elasticity of demand that it faces. In our example, the existing firms are earning profits of 40%, which implies a firm-level demand elasticity of −2.5. Industry-level demand elasticities are by definition smaller (in absolute value) than the firm-level demand elasticities of which they are made up. Thus a high operating margin, which implies a critical loss sufficiently small that merging firms may argue that it is unlikely to be realized, at the same time implies a small actual loss, since only firms facing a demand curve with relatively low elasticity could set prices and margins so high.[2] As Katz and Shapiro (2003) summarize it, "A high gross margin implies a small critical loss. But a high gross margin also tends to indicate a small actual loss."

### 2.1.2 Cost Estimates: Marginal vs. Variable, Constant vs. Fixed

The profit maximization derivations on which both the CLA and the Lerner Index are based use the margin between price (or sometimes marginal revenue) and marginal cost to analyze the incentives of either individual firms or the hypothetical monopolist. In general, however, business firms do not calculate "marginal cost" in the ordinary course of business; rather, they usually calculate "variable cost", and though empirical analysts often use the latter as a proxy for the former, there are good reasons, both conceptual and practical, why the two are not likely to be identical.

First of all, from a pure measurement standpoint, Fisher and McGowan (1983) and Fisher (1987) demonstrate just how different the accountants' treatment of factors such as advertising, research and development, and other typical fixed costs can be from the economists' definitions. A separate measurement issue concerns the multiproduct nature of most firms; even the most careful business accounts may not be kept at the level of individual products.

Second, and more conceptually, as noted by Carlton and Perloff (2005) and Pittman (2009), true marginal cost as the first derivative of total cost includes at least implicitly a rental value of capital, and this term may become especially important as firm and/or industry production approaches capacity. An inquiry into the likely effect of a SSNIP that does not factor in the possibility of a rising marginal cost curve—which of course we observe in any intermediate microeconomics text—may underestimate the attractiveness to the firm of reducing output, and therefore too quickly reject the proposition that a hypothetical monopolist would find it profitable to increase price and reduce output. Simons and Coate (2014) argue the related point that firms making decisions regarding profit maximization in the long term will not generally base their thinking on short run marginal costs, even if measured accurately.

Werden (2005) and Baumann and Godek (2009) also note that the issue is broader than just the distinction between (theoretical) marginal and (measured) variable cost. Even if marginal cost is measured accurately, by variable cost or otherwise, the assumption that it is constant over the range of output choices of firms and the

[2] As the Horizontal Merger Guidelines point out in Sect. 2.2.1, a high operating margin may also be an indicator of existing coordination among the firms in the market.

hypothetical monopolist may need to be examined. Approaching capacity limitations may be one factor; another may be differences in costs across firms, such that the hypothetical monopolist might not only raise price but also reduce output asymmetrically, focusing on cancelling production shifts at more expensive plants or even closing them down. To the extent that these complications lead the analyst to underestimate the marginal cost savings of lost sales, a price increase by the hypothetical monopolist will appear less profitable.

### 2.1.3 The SSNIP

As emphasized by Werden (2005, 2008), the details of the assumption of a SSNIP as usually practiced in the market definition exercise may be misleading in at least two ways, and these two may interact. First, the Guidelines ask whether a hypothetical monopolist *would likely* impose a SSNIP—a profit maximization question—whereas the more common practice is to analyze whether the hypothetical monopolist *could profitably* impose a SSNIP—a break-even analysis. The latter interpretation has the distinct advantage of not requiring the analyst to make assumptions about the shape of the demand curve in the industry (Langenfeld and Li 2001), but it may affect the conclusion nonetheless.

In particular, a break-even analysis of a "small" price increase—say 5% or 10%, the usual choices—may miss the possibility that a firm or hypothetical monopolist facing customers with varying elasticities of demand might find it unprofitable to raise price by a small amount that keeps most customers in the market regardless of their elasticity of demand, but find it profitable to raise price a great deal more such that elastic demanders are priced out of the market while inelastic demanders pay the higher prices (Werden 2005, 2008). Rejecting the profitability of a small price increase can lead to a decision to expand the size of the provisional market, when examining the profitability of a larger price increase might lead to the conclusion that the original provisional market was correct after all.

The analyst who finds that the application of a break-even SSNIP leads to a rejection of the provisional market definition may therefore want to check the robustness of this result by asking whether there are customers of the product with significantly different elasticities of demand. Are there customers with demand so inelastic that selling to them only, at an even higher price, would be a profitable strategy for the hypothetical monopolist? At this point, of course, one is moving away from the appealing simplicity of the break-even test.

### 2.1.4 Market Definition Is Not the Whole Story

It perhaps goes without saying—but we will say it—that market definition is not the whole story in merger analysis. In particular, market definition, especially as practiced in the US, is focused on the demand side—purchaser preferences and switching behavior. But in many investigations the supply side—including the strategic responses of rival firms—may also be important. In EU practice, some of this supply-side analysis is included in the market definition exercise, while in US practice most of it is subsumed under the rubric of the potential for entry by other firms into the product and geographic market.[3]

In our example, on the supply side the analyst would be asking questions like the following: Are there producers outside of the market that might reposition themselves (either in product or geographic space) such that customers could easily switch to new suppliers without losing much in the way of either utility or efficiency? Are imports (from other domestic geographic areas or from foreign companies) poised to enter the market, and are there good reasons like transportation costs, tariffs, or quotas that would limit the scope or scale of their entry? If these imported products are not being purchased by customers now, there may be good reasons why they would remain unpurchased even following a SSNIP.

## 2.2 *Critical Loss Analysis for Unilateral Effects Analysis*

CLA is used not only in market definition but also in competitive effects (and especially unilateral effects) analysis. In this case the algebra of the derivation of the critical loss becomes a bit more complicated, and the introduction of an important new term is required.

In particular, let us return to the industry setting of Table 1, but now instead of analyzing whether it would be profitable for a hypothetical monopolist of the entire industry to increase price by a SSNIP, we analyze whether the merger of two firms, say firms W and X, would provide the merged firm with the unilateral incentive to increase its own price only. We will simplify the analysis by considering the question of whether it would be profitable to increase the price of the good produced by firm W only; clearly the merged firm would consider the profitability of increasing the price of the goods produced by both firms.

Before the merger, firm W sets prices according to the same profit-maximization principles as the hypothetical monopolist, according to Eqs. (1)–(4), above. Prices were increased until just the point at which the loss in sales—both to other firms in the market and to the rest of the economy—outweighed the benefits of higher prices. After the merger, however, some of the losses from a price increase for the product of firm W are newly internalized by the firm—they are "recaptured" by firm X, now under the same control as firm W. Thus we have a new factor in the calculations, the

[3]See the *Horizontal Merger Guidelines* of the U.S. Department of Justice and Federal Trade Commission, August 19, 2010, at §4: "Market definition focuses solely on demand substitution factors, i.e., on customers' ability and willingness to substitute away from one product to another in response to a price increase or a corresponding non-price change such as a reduction in product quality or service. The responsive actions of suppliers are also important in competitive analysis. They are considered in these Guidelines in the sections addressing the identification of market participants, the measurement of market shares, the analysis of competitive effects, and entry."

diversion ratio $D_{WX}$, the share of the sales of W that are lost as the result of a price increase for W that are "recaptured" by firm X (Willig 1991; Shapiro 1996, 2010).

Thus the profit-maximization question facing the merged firm as it considers whether and by how much to raise the price of good W is now:

$$(P_W + \Delta P_W - C_W)(Q_W - \Delta Q_W) + (P_X - C_X)(Q_X + \Delta Q_W D_{WX}) \gtrless (P_W - C_W)Q_W + (P_X - C_X)Q_X \quad (5)$$

where $\Delta Q_W D_{WX} = \Delta Q_X$.

As with Eqs. (3) and (4), this translates into the critical loss of quantity W for the merged firm to raise price on good W (Langenfeld and Li 2001; Hüschelrath 2009):

$$\Delta Q_W/Q_W \gtrless (\Delta P_W/P_W)/[(P_W - C_W) + (\Delta P_W/P_W) - (P_X - C_X) \times (P_X/P_W)D_{WX}] \quad (6)$$

Comparing Eq. (4)—as interpreted for a single profit-maximizing firm premerger—and Eq. (6)—the calculation for the firm after merging with a competitor—shows that the difference is the last term in the denominator on the right-hand-side—and that because this is the subtraction of the product of three positive terms, it will tend to increase the size of the critical loss that would make a price increase unprofitable. Note also something that we will return to in the next section: the increase in the critical loss for good W following the merger—and thus the increase in the incentive of its producer to increase price—is a positive function of (a) the margin earned on the second good X, (b) the ratio of the price of the second good X to the first good W, and (c) the diversion ration of W to X—the percentage of sales of good W lost by a price increase that are recaptured by good X, now owned by the same firm.

## 3 Upward Pricing Pressure

Upward Pricing Pressure (UPP) might be considered a first cousin to the use of critical loss in the analysis of the unilateral effects of a proposed merger, with, among other wrinkles, a more direct focus on the potential efficiencies of the proposed merger and whether they are likely to outweigh the loss of competition in the price-setting of the merged firm.

In the previous section of the paper, we abstracted from the distinction between homogeneous and differentiated products, assuming that all firms charged the same price but that a single firm had the option to charge a different price. In this section we abandon this abstraction and embrace the distinction between these two types of goods that was such an important part of the revised Merger Guidelines in 1992. As Shapiro (2010) discusses at length, while the 1982 and 1984 Guidelines focused on the danger that a merger among competitors would increase the likelihood of collusion—either explicit or tacit—in the more concentrated market, thus focusing implicitly on homogeneous products, the 1992 Guidelines added a second focus on the likelihood that a merger among competitors producing differentiated products would provide incentives for the merged firm to raise price unilaterally, regardless of the behavior of competitors in response.

Thus a new emphasis was placed on the degree to which competing products were close or distant substitutes to each other—a concept implemented in the term that we introduced in the previous section, the diversion ratio $D_{WX}$ between two firms W and X, the percentage of sales of good W lost in response to a price change for good W that are "diverted" to good X. A larger value for this diversion ratio $D_{WX}$ clearly suggested a merger that would be more troublesome from a competitive standpoint, *ceteris paribus*.

However, the 1992 Guidelines, along with the subsequent literature, simultaneously added a new focus on another term in the denominator of Eq. (6): the price-cost margin earned in the production of good X. If this margin were "high", especially vis-à-vis the margin earned in the production of good W, the merged firm would be quite happy for sales of W to be diverted to sales of X; not so much if the margin earned on the production of X were "low". Thus increased attention came to be focused on the *product* $D_{WX}(P_X - C_X)$, the value to the merged firm of sales of W that were diverted by the price increase for W to sales of X, a parameter termed the "Gross Upward Pricing Pressure Index" (GUPPI) from the merger (Farrell and Shapiro 2010a; Moresi 2010). A corresponding term was calculated and considered for the merged firm's incentive to increase the price of good X.

## 3.1 How to Use GUPPI?

But how are we to interpret and use GUPPI? Any non-zero diversion from W to X accompanied by any non-zero margin on X would yield a positive value for GUPPI. One option would be to proceed with the CLA described in Sect. 2.2 above for the analysis of unilateral merger effects, plugging an estimated value for GUPPI into Eq. (6). Again, for an evaluation of the impact of the merger one would also perform the exercise in reverse, analyzing the incentives created by the merger for a unilateral increase in the price of X, taking account of recapture in the sale of W through the corresponding diversion ratio $D_{XW}$.

A second option would be to use GUPPI to calculate the likely price impact of the merger directly, abstracting from any possible efficiencies from the merger. Farrell and Shapiro (2010b) and Hausman et al. (2011) provide formulas for doing so that rely on the assumptions of a linear demand curve and symmetric cross-price elasticities of demand along with estimated values for six parameters: the prices and margins for the two goods and the two diversion ratios.

For good W, the post-merger profit-maximizing price change equals the following:

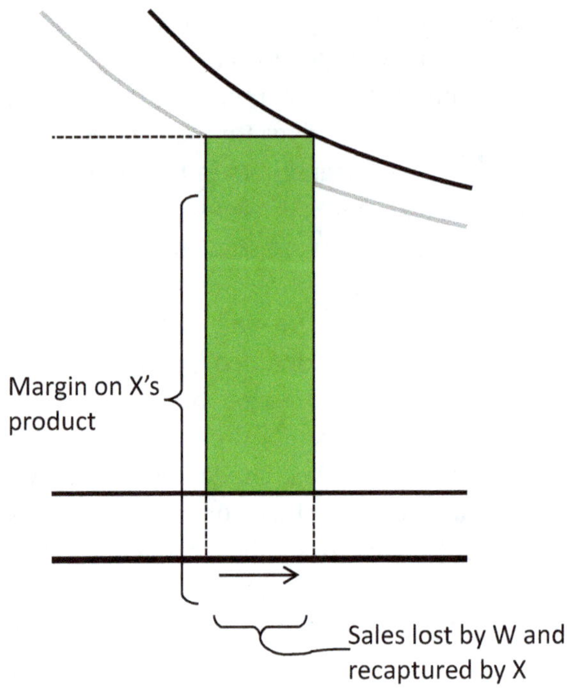


**Fig. 1** Value of diverted sales

$$\Delta P_W/P_W = [D_{WX}(P_X - C_X) + D_{WX}D_{XW}(P_W - C_W)]/[2(1 - D_{WX}D_{XW})P_W] \quad (7)$$

and correspondingly for good X. Again, what the formula makes most clear is one of the most important additions of the 1992 Guidelines to the 1982 and 1984 Guidelines: a significant incentive to increase price post-merger requires not only significant diversion ratios but also significant operating margins on the good or goods to which demand is diverted.

Figure 1 shows makes this point graphically. A price increase for the first good moves out the demand curve for the second good. The "value of diverted sales" is the rectangle that represents the *product* of (a) the volume of diversion from the first good to the second and (b) the margin earned on the second. Only if both the base and the height of the rectangle are of non-trivial magnitudes is the area of the rectangle "large".

Finally, as demonstrated in Werden (1996), information on diversion ratios and margins may be used to estimate the merger-specific marginal cost reductions ("efficiencies") that would be required to counterbalance the upward pricing pressure generated directly by the merger and so create a situation of unchanged pricing incentives for the merged firm.

## 3.2 *GUPPI to UPP*

A cousin of GUPPI is UPP, Upward Pricing Pressure, which adds estimates of post-merger marginal cost savings to the GUPPI calculations in order to calculate a measure of the "net" (of claimed or predicted efficiencies) incentives for the merged firm to increase prices. As suggested by Farrell and Shapiro (2010a) and then presented explicitly by both Farrell and Shapiro (2010b) and Schmalensee (2009), requiring now not only the assumption of linear demand curves but also estimates for the product-specific diversion ratios, prices and marginal costs, and claimed/predicted reductions in marginal cost, the formula for merger UPP for good W is as follows:

$$\Delta P_W/P_W = \{[2D_{WX}(P_X - C_X) - E_X\left(1 - (P_X - C_X)(D_{XW} - D_{WX})\right)] (P_X/P_W) + D_{XW}(D_{XW} + D_{WX})(P_W - C_W) - E_W[1 - (P_W - C_W))(2 - D_{XW}(D_{WX} + D_{XW})]\}/[4 - (D_{XW} + D_{WX})^2] \quad (8)$$

Again, there is a symmetric formula for the "upward pricing pressure" created by the merger for good X.

### 3.3 *The Diversion Ratio*

Of course, a key requirement for making use of all these concepts is the estimation of diversion ratios. Unlike prices and (variable if not marginal) costs, these are not to be found in the account books kept by the companies. How, short of complex econometric estimation, might these be approximated by the competition agency analyst?

A straightforward approach, often treated as a sort of default option, is to use the shares of competitors in a candidate or provisional market to estimate diversion ratios (Willig 1991; Shapiro 2010). In our numerical example outlined above, if we consider firms W, X, Y, and Z as the competitors in our candidate market, firms X, Y, and Z have 56%, 23%, and 21% respectively of non-W sales. Since these market shares reflect the preferences and choices of existing consumers in the market place, we might assume that those same preferences would drive diversion in these proportions in reaction to a price increase on good W. This approach is based on a number of assumptions (Willig 1991; Rybnicek and Onken 2016), including that we have an idea as to market definition—the latter a requirement that UPP analysis is designed in part to obviate (Farrell and Shapiro 2010a).

But there are often other good sources of information to guide the analyst in both evaluating the accuracy of market shares as indicators of diversion ratios and in judging how these estimates of diversion ratios might be adjusted to better reflect market realities. As Farrell and Shapiro (2010a) note:

> The diversion ratio might be estimated using evidence generated in the merging firms' normal course of business. Firms often track diversion ratios in the form of who they are losing business to, or who they can win business from. Consumer surveys can also illuminate diversion ratios, as can information about customer switching patterns (p. 18, footnote omitted).

In particular, interviews with, and documents supplied by, customers of the firms may yield subjective but informative information as to the particular qualities of differentiated products that make each a closer or more distant substitute for others as well as objective reports of past switching events and their rationales. In the latter respect, "natural experiments" may be especially informative: when product W became temporarily unavailable because of labor or transportation problems, what did its usual customers do in response? These additional sources of information can allow the analyst to calculate diversion ratios from an independent source or to better evaluate the diversion ratios estimated via market shares.

Finally, any estimates based on the within-market shares of diverted sales may be tempered by the recognition that some of the demand for good W will leave the market entirely in response to a price increase—thus each firm-level estimate may be multiplied by a factor that reflects the "aggregate diversion ratio"—the "fraction of the units that would be lost by an individual firm that are retained by the hypothetical monopolist" (Farrell and Shapiro 2010b).

## 3.4 *The Limits of UPP and GUPPI*

As noted above, both UPP and GUPPI may be used as indicators of the degree of competition likely to be lost from a merger; to provide a forecast of post-merger price increases by the merged firm; or to calculate the magnitude of merger-induced "efficiencies" necessary to remove the incentive for price increases following the merger. UPP and GUPPI, like critical loss analysis, are tools that focus attention on particular issues and factors that affect the profitability of a price increase by either a hypothetical monopolist (in market definition) or the merged firm (in unilateral effects analysis).[4]

That being said, it is also important to keep in mind that conclusions based on UPP and GUPPI—and CLA—are strongest when the analyst has also assessed the validity of the underlying assumptions as well as other questions not directly addressed by these tools. As one important example, none of these takes account of the possibility of the reactions of other firms to the possible price changes imposed by the merged firm. Such reactions could render the proposed merger either more or less harmful to competition and customers. For example, if competitors "accommodated" post-merger price increases by increasing their own prices, the merger harm

[4]Baltzopoulos et al. (2015) discuss the use of UPP in five recent cases reviewed by Konkurrensverket, the Swedish Competition Authority.

would be increased. On the other hand, if competitors repositioned their products in order to be closer substitutes to the products of the merged firm, that could increase the diversion to rivals, reducing the incentive for price increases and the harm to competition from the merger (Pakes 2010; Cheung 2016).[5]

## 4 The Vertical Arithmetic

Consider a proposed merger that is vertical rather than (or in addition to) horizontal. Consider, for example, a proposal by a manufacturer to purchase its supplier of a crucial raw material. How much should the antimonopoly agency be concerned about a loss to competition? In particular—though, as we will discuss below, the problem is potentially more general—how much should the agency be concerned about the potential for post-merger anticompetitive "foreclosure"—that is, the denial of access to important inputs to competing manufacturers?[6]

It is common in such a situation for competing manufacturers to contact the competition authority to express their concerns that if the raw material supplier comes under control of their manufacturing competitor, they will be discriminated against in supply in the future, whether with regard to price, service, or product availability. The reply from the merging firms will likely be that they would only be hurting themselves by treating a customer badly. How is one to evaluate the tradeoff that would face the newly merged, vertically integrated firm?

One analytical tool which could be presented to the competition authority by either party is a technique called the "vertical arithmetic" (Riordan and Salop 1995; Sibley and Doane 2002; CRA 2005; Moresi and Salop 2013).[7] As with critical loss analysis and upward pricing pressure, the vertical arithmetic offers no magical

[5]As Pakes (2010) also points out, there could also be post-merger repositioning by one or both of the merging firms, and this could either increase or decrease the harm to competition that would otherwise take place.

[6]Of course, a proposed vertical merger could also raise the possibility of the foreclosure of access to downstream customers from an upstream competitor—what Riordan and Salop (1995) and Baker (2011) term "customer foreclosure". Or, as in the case analyzed by Baker, it could raise both issues simultaneously.

[7]An interesting application was the analysis by Ofcom, the UK communications regulator, of the incentives of the British Sky Broadcasting Group to deny access to premium channels to its downstream competitors such as Virgin Media. For the Ofcom analysis, see especially https://www.ofcom.org.uk/__data/assets/pdf_file/0014/40451/annex8.pdf; for the Sky responses see https://www.ofcom.org.uk/__data/assets/pdf_file/0022/36616/1_sky.pdf and https://www.ofcom.org.uk/__data/assets/pdf_file/0021/50925/10_sky_annex_7.pdf. Application in a case brought by the FCC, the US telecommunications regulator, regarding similar issues in the proposed Comcast/NBCU merger is discussed in Baker (2011) and Baker et al. (2011), while application in a case brought by the Antitrust Division of the Justice Department, the proposed acquisition of the direct broadcast satellite assets of the News Corporation and MCI by Primestar, is discussed in Salop et al. (1998) and Rubinfeld (2000).

Fig. 2 A vertical merger

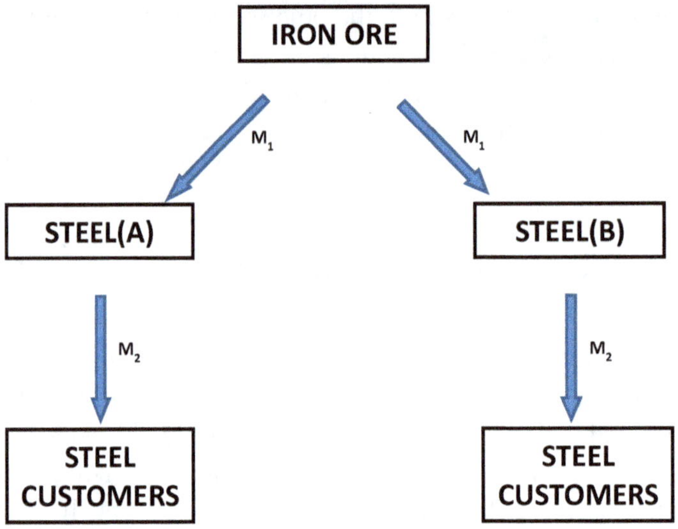


solutions, but it can be useful in focusing the competitive analysis on particular questions and issues.

Consider then a steel manufacturer A that is proposing to acquire its supplier of iron ore, as in Fig. 2. Assume that "steel" constitutes an antitrust product market; if the two firms both produced, say, "cold rolled steel", we would want to examine competition and foreclosure issues in that narrower potential product market instead or in addition to the broader one.

Let $M_1$ equal the percentage profit margin earned by the iron ore company in its sales to steel manufacturers A and B (we assume equal margins for sales to the two customers) and $M_2$ equal the percentage profit margin earned by steel manufacturers A and B in their sales to their own customers (also assumed equal across the two firms). Next we introduce $I_B$, the sales of iron ore to steel manufacturer B—A's rival—and $D_{BA}$, a downstream diversion ratio, the share of any sales of steel lost by steel manufacturer B that is recovered by steel manufacturer A (i.e., that would be recovered by the newly integrated firm after the merger).

Now consider the incentives of the newly integrated firm A in dealing with its steel manufacturer rival B. If the integrated firm refuses to supply iron ore to steel manufacturer B, it loses $I_BM_1$, its variable profits on those sales. However, from any steel sales diverted from the disadvantaged firm B to integrated firm A it gains $D_{BA}I_B(M_1 + M_2)$, the variable profits both upstream and downstream of the increased steel sales by A.

If $D_{BA} = 0$—if the none of the lost steel sales of firm B are recaptured by firm A—then the only result of A's decision to deny access to iron ore to B is the loss of its upstream variable profits $I_BM_1$—clearly an unprofitable strategy. On the other hand, if $D_{BA} = 1$—if *all* of the lost steel sales of firm B are recaptured by firm A—then the gains and losses upstream cancel each other out, and the integrated firm would gain downstream variable profits $I_BM_2$ from its decision to deny access to iron ore to B—clearly a profitable strategy. The breakeven point for the integrated firm's decision to deny access to its non-integrated rival is the point where $D_{BA} = M_1/$

$(M_1 + M_2)$—if A gains less than this fraction of B's lost sales, foreclosure is unprofitable in this example.

The importance of the variable margins at the two stages of production is quickly apparent. If the iron ore firm has been earning a very large margin on its sales to steel manufacturers—if $M_1$ is high, especially relative to $M_2$—then a vertical foreclosure strategy looks unlikely: the diversion ratio $D_{BA}$ would have to be very high to make such a strategy work, *ceteris paribus*. On the other hand, if the steel manufacturer A earns a very large margin on its sales to steel customers—if $M_2$ is high, especially relative to $M_1$—then a vertical foreclosure strategy looks more likely: even a small $D_{BA}$ can make the strategy work.

So we are back to the importance of a familiar pair of figures: margins and a diversion ratio. We discussed both the usefulness and imperfections of measured firm margins in the previous section. As in that section, we next face the question of how to estimate the diversion ratio—again, in this case, the share of steel sales lost by steel manufacturer B that would be recaptured by its competitor steel manufacturer A.

As with the discussion of the use of diversion ratios in the analysis of upward pricing pressure, a first, default approximation is to use the firms' shares of the sales of steel. Maintaining the assumption that steel constitutes a product market, if firm A has 50% of the market and firm B 20%, then a first approximation of the diversion ratio of sales from B to A would be $50/(100 - 20) = 0.625$. We could then, as earlier, discount this figure by the percentage of B sales that might leave the steel market entirely were B to cease being a supplier—likely a small number.

At that point we would consider other factors that might render A's market share either an over- or an underestimate of this diversion ratio. If A's current capacity utilization in steel manufacturing is very high, it might not be able profitably to take over much of B's sales. If other rival steel manufacturers have plenty of excess capacity, they might be more aggressive in taking the diverted sales themselves. (Of course, we should also consider the possibility that the integrated firm would foreclose their iron ore supplies.) Similarly, there may be steel imports that are not currently in the market but could potentially be available to customers of B.

The investigation of these types of questions may inform the analyst's estimate of the relevant diversion ratio. Then this estimated ratio may be combined with the two margin estimates to reach a more informed analysis as to the potential of anticompetitive input foreclosure from the vertical merger. Going further, Moresi and Salop (2013) introduce several variants on GUPPI that may be used in the analysis of vertical mergers—vGUPPIs.

Finally, we should emphasize that the vertical arithmetic, like critical loss analysis and upward pricing pressure, does not answer all questions. Perhaps most importantly, we have not considered the possibility that foreclosure might not only disadvantage B and advantage A but also lead to a rise in the price of the downstream good, steel; the analysis presented above is thus conservative in its evaluation of the incentives for the merged firm to engage in foreclosure (Baker et al. 2011; Moresi and Salop 2013). We have not considered the possibility that other current or potential suppliers of iron ore might step in to supply B, thus rendering a foreclosure strategy ineffective in harming B in the first place. (This reminds us of the broader point that vertical mergers are likely to be harmful to competition only in the presence of significant market power at *both* levels.) We have also not considered the likelihood that there are other, more refined anticompetitive strategies available to the vertically integrated firm than the rather crude instrument of absolute input foreclosure (Moresi and Salop 2013). The vertical arithmetic outlined in this paper is only one of many tools that the analyst employs in assessing foreclosure incentives and effects.

## 5 Conclusion

Critical loss analysis, upward pricing pressure, and the vertical arithmetic are three investigative tools that have come into widespread use in the enforcement of competition law within the last two decades, reflecting the increased role played by economic analysis in competition policy and law enforcement. Their value resides not so much in their ability to answer enforcement questions by themselves as in their usefulness in isolating certain important issues to be addressed and questions to be answered by the investigator and the decision maker. Furthermore, experience suggests that debates concerning whether they are applicable to a particular investigation as well as which assumptions inherent in their use are or are not satisfied may be as informative as the outcomes of the use of the tools themselves.

The enforcement agency analyst who is adept at using these tools will be well prepared not only for his or her opportunity to educate decision makers, tribunals, and courts as to the most important issues and questions regarding an investigation, but also for the presentations and arguments of the companies and their attorneys and economic consultants who come before the agency to urge their own point of view.

**Acknowledgment** The author is grateful for comments on this presentation from colleagues at the Antimonopoly Committee of Ukraine and participants in the Conference on Institution Building of the Competition Authorities in South-East Europe (Belgrade, June 2016) and on a previous draft of the paper from Xiaoling Ang, Beth Armington, Tim Brennan, Jim Foster, Rui Huang, Atsuko Izumi, Šarūnas Pajarskas, and Steven Salop. The views expressed do not purport to reflect the views of the U.S. Department of Justice.

## References

Amelio A, de la Mano M, Godinho de Mator M (2008) Ineos/Kerling merger: an example of quantitative analysis in support of a clearance decision. Comp Pol Newslett 1:65–69

Baker JB (2011) Comcast/NBCU: The FCC provides a roadmap for vertical merger analysis. Antitrust 25:36–41

Baker JB, Bykowsky M, DeGraba P, LaFontaine P, Ralph E, Sharkey W (2011) The year in economics at the FCC, 2010–11: protecting competition online. Rev Ind Organ 39:297–309

Baltzopoulos A, Kim J, Mandorff M (2015) UPP analysis in five recent merger cases. Konkurrensverket Working Paper 2015, 3

Baumann MG, Godek PE (2009) Reconciling the opposing views of critical elasticity. GCP Antitrust Chron, Sept

Carlton D, Perloff J (2005) Modern industrial organization, 4th edn. Pearson/Addison-Wesley, Boston

Cheung L (2016) An empirical comparison between the upward pricing pressure test and merger simulation in differentiated product markets. J Comp Law Econ 12:701–734

CRA (2005) "Vertical arithmetic": the use of empirical evidence in vertical mergers. CRA Competition Memo, Charles River Associates. http://ecp.crai.com/publications/vertical_arithmetic.pdf

Farrell J, Shapiro C (2010a) Antitrust evaluation of horizontal mergers: an economic alternative to market definition. BE J Theor Econ 10:9

Farrell J, Shapiro C (2010b) Upward pricing pressure and critical loss analysis: response. CPI Antitrust J, Feb

Fisher FM (1987) On the misuse of the profit-sales ratio to infer monopoly power. RAND J Econ 18:384–396

Fisher FM, McGowan JJ (1983) On the misuse of accounting rates of return to infer monopoly profits. Am Econ Rev 73:82–97

Harris B, Simons J (1989) Focusing market definition: how much substitution is necessary? Res Law Econ 12:207–226

Hausman J, Moresi S, Rainey M (2011) Unilateral effects of mergers with general linear demand. Econ Lett 111:119–121

Hüschelrath K (2009) Critical loss analysis in market definition and merger control. Eur Compet J 5:757–794

Kaplow L, Shapiro C (2007) Antitrust. In: Polinsky AM, Shavell S (eds) Handbook of law and economics, vol 2. Elsevier, Philadelphia

Katz ML, Shapiro C (2003) Critical loss: let's tell the whole story. Antitrust Spring 49–56

Langenfeld J, Li W (2001) Critical loss analysis in evaluating mergers. Antitrust Bull 46:299–337

Moresi S (2010) The use of upward price pressure indices in merger analysis. Antitrust Source, Feb

Moresi S, Salop SC (2013) GUPPI: scoring unilateral pricing incentives in vertical mergers. Antitrust Law J 79:185–214

O'Brien DP, Wickelgren AL (2003) A critical analysis of critical loss analysis. Antitrust Law J 71:161–184

Pakes A (2010) Upward pricing pressure screens in the new merger guidelines: some pro's and con's. Presented at DG competition authority, Brussels. http://scholar.harvard.edu/files/pakes/files/sdgcomp_0.pdf

Pittman R (2009) Who are you calling irrational? Marginal costs, variable costs, and the pricing practices of firms. https://www.justice.gov/atr/who-are-you-calling-irrational-marginal-costs-variable-costs-and-pricing-practices-firms

Riordan MH, Salop SC (1995) Evaluating vertical mergers: a post-chicago approach. Antitrust Law J 63:513–568

Rubinfeld DL (2000) The primestar acquisition of the News Corp./MCI direct broadcast satellite assets. Rev Ind Organ 16:193–209

Rybnicek J, Onken LC (2016) A hedgehog in fox's clothing? The misapplication of GUPPI analysis. Geo Mason Law Rev 23:1187–1203

Salop SC, Besen SM, Woodbury JR, Murdoch EJ (1998) An economic analysis of primestar's competitive behavior and incentives. Georgetown University Law Center and Charles River Associates

Schmalensee R (2009) Should new merger guidelines give UPP market definition? GCP. https://www.competitionpolicyinternational.com/should-new-merger-guidelines-give-upp-market-definition/

Shapiro C (1996) Mergers with differentiated products. Antitrust Spring 23–30

Shapiro C (2010) The 2010 horizontal merger guidelines: from hedgehog to fox in forty years. Antitrust Law J 77:701–759

Sibley DS, Doane MJ (2002) Raising the costs of unintegrated rivals: an analysis of Barnes & Noble's proposed acquisition of Ingram book company. In: Slottje DJ (ed) Measuring market power. Elsevier, Amsterdam

Simons JJ, Coate MB (2014) *United States v. H&R Block*: an illustration of the DOJ's new but controversial approach to market definition. J Comp Law Econ 10:543–580

Werden GJ (1996) A robust test for consumer welfare enhancing mergers among sellers of differentiated products. J Ind Econ 44:409–413

Werden GJ (2005) Beyond critical loss: tailored application of the hypothetical monopolist test. Comp Law 69–78

Werden GJ (2008) Beyond critical loss: properly applying the hypothetical monopolist test. GCP. https://www.competitionpolicyinternational.com/assets/0d358061e11f2708ad9d62634c6c40ad/Werden,%20GCP%20Feb-08(2).pdf

Willig R (1991) Merger analysis, industrial organization theory, and merger guidelines. Brook Pap Econ Activity Microecon 281–332

# Pricing Benchmark in Market Definition: Theoretical Background and Practical Application

**Siniša Milošević, Jelena Popović Markopoulos, Jelena Grahovac, and Aleksandra Ravić**

## 1 Introduction

The aim of this paper is to demonstrate the practical application of quantitative tests in the process of delineating relevant markets. The paper provides an application and comparison for four mutually complementary tests that are based on product price movements over time. Following the example of three products, the paper seeks to examine the empirical verification of the initial hypothesis that two out of the three selected products belong to the same relevant market.

The manner in which the relevant market is defined sets the estimated market shares and market power of business entities, hence precisely setting relevant market boundaries represents a precondition for further investigation of competition conditions in the given market.

The concept of the *relevant* market, as used in competition law, differs from the concept of the market as an economic category, and is predominantly narrower when compared. For example, business entities predominantly define the market as geographical territory where they sell their products, or even the whole industry sector to which they belong (European Commission 1997). On the other side, positive legal regulations governing the protection of competition perceive the relevant market vis-à-vis two, mutually complementary dimensions—the product dimension and the geographic dimension. This means that in each process of determining the relevant market, its scope is set by the assortment of products, on the one hand, and the geographical area where such assortment is sold, on the other.

The Law on Protection of Competition of the Republic of Serbia adopted the definition of the relevant market as applied in the European Union. The relevant

S. Milošević (✉) · J. P. Markopoulos · J. Grahovac · A. Ravić
Serbian Commission for Protection of Competition, Belgrade, Serbia
e-mail: sinisa.milosevic@kzk.gov.rs; jelena.popovic@kzk.gov.rs; jelena.grahovac@kzk.gov.rs; aleksandra.ravic@kzk.gov.rs

 
B. Begović, D. V. Popović (eds.), *Competition Authorities in South Eastern Europe*, Contributions to Economics, https://doi.org/10.1007/978-3-319-76644-7_10

product market represents a set of goods or services that consumers and other users consider interchangeable in terms of their characteristics, common purpose and price, while the relevant geographic market is defined as the area in which business entities are involved in the supply or demand, and in which the same or similar conditions of competition apply, appreciably different from the conditions of competition in neighbouring areas.

The paper consists of seven sections. The introduction defines the concept of the relevant market and presents the structure of the paper. The overview of different methodological approaches to defining the relevant market is given in the second part, while the third part presents the theoretical foundations of price-based tests. The following fourth part of the paper provides an overview of European Commission practice in the application of price tests. The fifth, and at the same time, the main part of the paper is dedicated to the practical application of price tests. The conclusion gives the summary of the paper's findings.

## 2 The Methodological Approach to Defining the Relevant Market

The key concept, on which the definition of relevant market is based, is the concept of interchangeability, i.e. demand-side substitution. In addition to demand substitution, the process of defining the relevant market may also require investigation of the possibility of supply substitution, which is beyond the scope of this paper. Different methodologies are used for investigating the possibility of demand substitution and, by extension, of defining the relevant market, while application of a specific one will depend on factors such as the nature of products for which the relevant market is determined and data availability. The actual procedure for defining the relevant market is case-specific, hence it may occur (although it is not common) that in some cases two products belong to the same relevant market, while in others they constitute two separate relevant markets.

Assessment of the relevant market primarily implies carrying out a qualitative assessment, followed by a quantitative one. The qualitative assessment of the relevant market represents the first step in the process of determining the relevant market. It refers to the logical assumption of the relevant market definition or other potential definitions, later tested by applying quantitative methods.

It is intuitive that chocolate prices will not be sensitive to changes in motor vehicle prices, because they are products that significantly differ in terms of characteristics, as well as in terms of usual purpose, thus under no circumstance can these two products constitute a single relevant market. Without qualitative analysis, significantly more time would be required to determine a relevant market. Therefore in practical terms, the pool of possible relevant market definitions is narrowed by carrying out the qualitative analysis.

The presence of similarity between the characteristics and the intended use of products indicates the existence of so-called functional substitution between them (Davis and Garces 2010). However, from the standpoint of competition, functional substitution is not sufficient, but it is significantly important to merit a look at the product prices, in addition to their characteristics and purpose. Therefore, for the mutual substitution of products, all three factors—product characteristics, intended use and price—are of equal importance. This is precisely the reason why in competition cases it is often necessary to carry out certain quantitative tests, in order to define relevant market, as precisely as possible. Quantitative assessment implies the use of different tests, based on time-series of observed product prices, in order to confirm or refute assumptions made during the qualitative assessment of the relevant market.

The hypothetical monopolist test, also called the "small but significant and non-transitory increase in prices" (SSNIP) test, is the best known and most common method for determining the relevant market. The methodological approach in defining the relevant market in the form of a hypothetical monopolist test was first introduced by the US Department of Justice in the Merger Guidelines, in 1982, while in 1992 became part of the joint Horizontal Merger Guidelines of the US Department of Justice and the Federal Trade Commission. In the EU, the hypothetical monopolist test was used for the first time in the Nestlé/Perrier case (No. IV/M. 190, 1992), and has been officially recognised in the Notice on the definition of the relevant market for the purposes of Community competition law, published by the European Commission in 1997. Modelled after the European Commission, the Office of Fair Trading of the United Kingdom included the hypothetical monopolist test for the first time in the market definition procedure in 1999.

The purpose of the SSNIP test is to identify the narrowest group of products (or geographic area) where the hypothetical monopolist could profitably implement the small (5–10%) but significant and more permanent (up to 1 year) price increase of its own product. The relevant product market question asks to what degree customers will substitute away from the product in response to the price increase (Pittman 2017). The procedure is basically iterative in nature and starts by identifying the closest substitutes for the observed product, progressively adding new products—potential substitutes, up to the point when shown that a price increase would be profitable for the hypothetical monopolist producing all products in a market defined in such manner. The test formulated in such way has a quantitative character, but its primary role is to offer a conceptual framework for analysing the nature of competition between products and services, and for assessing the competitive pressure on the potential relevant market (NERA 2001).

Despite the general consensus that the hypothetical monopolist test provides an appropriate analytical framework for defining the relevant market, its implementation is not always straightforward (Froeb and Werden 1991). In a situation in which there is no data on price elasticities, in order to see if and when the hypothetical monopolist would be able to profitably increase prices of its own products, it is necessary to assess the profit at different levels of product prices. This requires an assessment of cost function, or a rather heroic assumption that all average costs are the same. Because of limited data availability for the estimate of the hypothetical monopolist's cost function and difficulties in determining "competitive" price level subject to the assumed 5–10% increase, the test in effect is often reduced to a qualitative experiment and a not too formal econometric test that is rigorously implemented in all cases.

Reviewing the significance of the relevant market definition's concept and accepting new approaches in order to overcome information-related limitations, is based on the premises that the market definition is not an objective *per se* and does not necessarily have to be the first step in analysing competition conditions in all cases. Although there is still no universally accepted test for determining the boundaries of the relevant market (Kaplow 2013), the practice in recent years has increasingly turned towards information-wise less demanding tests, which exclusive rely on analysing (most often of available) data on prices. These tests are based on the logical premise that if two products belong to the same (relevant) market, their prices will move in similar manner over time.

## 3 Theoretical Foundations of Price-Based Tests

Horowitz (1981) and Stigler and Sherwin (1985) were among first to define the relevant market based on identifying similarities in product price movement over time. The authors depart from the idea that price-led arbitrage will disable diverse price dynamics in different price areas, if such areas belong to same relevant market. Four mutually complementary tests stand out among most utilised tests that are based on prices of goods and services, whose practical application will be the subject of this paper: the correlation test, the Granger causality test, the stationarity test (unit root test), and the cointegration test.

### *3.1 Price Correlation Analysis*

Price correlation analysis is based on the assumption that prices of products that are close substitutes move together, i.e. that exists a strong mutual correlation. It can be considered that products $i$ and $j$ belong to the same relevant market if there is a correlation between movements in their prices (Stigler and Sherwin 1985). For example, if the price increase of product $i$ occurs, instead of product $i$ consumers will purchase a substitute, product $j$, whose price remained unchanged. The increase in demand for product $j$ will lead to that product's price increase, hence causing the existence of a positive correlation in price movement of product $i$ and product $j$. As demonstrated, the price correlation analysis includes comparison of two price series that can be performed over time, in the case of time-series, or spatial comparison, in the case of structural series.

In other words, there are limits to which product prices may diverge within the same relevant market, because the demand-side substitution or supply-side substitution always bring them back to the equilibrium level. Therefore, we should expect that movements in prices of all products in a particular relevant market are correlated over time. The price correlation analysis demonstrates the strength of these links, i.e. the degree to which two price series are related. If a price of one product limits the price of another product, which is characteristic of affiliation to the same relevant market, both price movements must demonstrate similar patterns.

The correlation coefficient ranges from $+1$ (when two price series move together perfectly) to $-1$ (when two price series move in perfectly opposite directions). A high and significant correlation coefficient close to unity may indicate that the two candidate products belong to the same relevant market. A low or insignificant correlation coefficient may indicate that two candidate products do not belong to the same relevant market.

Price correlation analysis is subject to a number of limitations. A high correlation coefficient may suggest that markets should be widely defined when in fact the correlation is spurious. Spurious correlation occurs when two series seem to be correlated but actually are not. On the other hand, a low correlation coefficient may lead to a narrow market definition when in fact the two price series are related but subject to significant random disturbance that breaks up such correlation. Also, no unique criterion exists to determine whether a correlation is large enough. Despite these limitations, price correlation analysis can provide useful information for relevant market definition, if it is applied and interpreted appropriately.

## 3.2 *Stationarity Test*

If two products belong to the same relevant market, then limitations exist in terms of corridors within which their price movement may diverge. In that sense the unit root test, i.e. stationarity test, is used for investigating whether two products belong to the same relevant market (Forni 2004). If two products belong to the same relevant market, shocks that increase single product price against the other product will have a temporary effect. Substitution will occur, demand for the more expensive product will decrease, while demand for more affordable product will increase. The decline in demand for the more expensive product will cause its price to drop, while on the other side, the more affordable product's price increase will occur due to the increased demand for that product. In those conditions product prices always return to the long-term equilibrium level. For that reason the time-series of relative prices, i.e. the quotient or difference between prices of the first and the second product is always stationary, if such products belong to the same relevant market.

## 3.3 Cointegration Test

Using similar logic to when implementing the unit root test, investigating whether two products belong to the same relevant market may also be performed by applying the cointegration test. Two non-stationary time-series are said to be cointegrated if their linear combination is stationary. If the cointegration test demonstrates that price movement series for two products are cointegrated, then those products belong to a single relevant market, and vice versa (Coe and Krause 2008).

## 3.4 Granger Causality Test

Correlation in some cases may be spurious: the result of coincidence and not of a causative link between the observed occurrences, meaning that two products may belong to different relevant markets, yet have a high level of interconnectivity in terms of their price movement over time. For example, due to the strong correlation of prices of the two with the third product, indisputably out of the market. On the other side it may occur that no significant correlation between the observed products' price movements exists, but that they nevertheless belong to the single relevant market. This occurs when price alignment happens with a certain time-lag. This means that it takes a certain time following one product's price increase for the prices of its substitutes to increase as well. In this case, the correlation between price movements will be approximately equal to zero even though the products are a very close substitutes.

For those reasons the need arose for the Granger causality test, aimed at determining the existence of causality between prices of two products (Slade 1986). This test was named after Clive Granger, winner of the Nobel Prize in Economics (Engle and Granger 2003). The use of the concept of the Granger causality in competition law inquiries can be illustrated with reference to market definition. The intuition behind the test is obvious and based on a very simple idea: would it be possible to advance prediction of a single product price movement if we don't only look at the time-series of that product price movement, but also include in the analysis the time series of other product prices (Bishop and Walker 2010)? The first step is to fit a regression curve, by using the least squares method, to the time-series of the first product prices based on several shifts, i.e. lags. The second step is to add the time-series of the second product, also with several lags. Then we ask is the explanation for the first product price movement better if, in addition to those prices, we also include other product prices. The common statistical tests are used for enacting a ruling of "better" or "not better" explanation. Comparison between the mean squared errors is performed most frequently. If the explanation is "better", it improves the ability of predicting the first product price movement. In such a situation, the second product price is the cause of the first product price.

There are three kinds of relations in reference to the Granger causality. If we test the existence of causality between the prices of products X and Y, it is plausible that:

- the price movement of product X causes the price movement of product Y (unidirectional causality);
- the price movement of product Y causes the price movement of product X (unidirectional causality); and
- the price movement of product X causes the price movement of product Y, while simultaneously price movement of product Y causes the price movement of product X (bidirectional causality).

If two products X and Y belong to the same relevant market, it can be expected that the prices of product X cause the prices of product Y, and vice versa.

## 4 Summary of Case Studies

In its practice up to present, the European Commission has used price-based tests mainly for the purpose of defining the relevant market when examining proposed mergers. In the case of Nestlé/Perrier (1992), the price correlation analysis was used for the first time to define the relevant product market. In its merger notification, Nestlé defined the relevant product market as non-alcoholic beverages market, including bottled source water and soft drinks. The European Commission departed from the assumption that bottled source waters represent a distinct relevant market from soft drinks. Additionally, the assessment of the proposed merger considered whether there is a separate market for sparkling and flavoured waters within the wider, bottled water market. Based on the results of the correlation analysis, which demonstrated the high correlation between the prices for two types of bottled water and low correlation coefficients between bottled waters and other non-alcoholic beverages, the relevant market was defined as the bottled source waters market.

In the case of Gencor/Lonrho (1997), following the determining of a high correlation coefficient between the prices of gold and platinum, and due to indications of related "false correlation", the European Commission applied the cointegration test. This test demonstrated that long-term correlation between the prices of the selected product categories was nonexistent, i.e. the that prices of platinum, rhodium, palladium, silver and gold, have a tendency to move irrespectively of other(s), so that it can be reasonably assumed that this represents the case of separate relevant product markets.

In the case of UPM-Kymmene/Haindl (2001), based on the price correlation coefficient, the European Commission determined that two type of magazine printing papers, so-called wood-free coated paper (WFC) and wood coated paper,[1] make

[1]Such are Super Calendered (SC) and Coated Mechanical Reels (CMR), including Light Weight Coated (LWC), Medium Weight Coated (MWC) and Heavy Weight Coated (HWC) paper.

two separate relevant markets. Namely, the determined correlation coefficient was below 0.55, which constituted an insufficient argument for classifying all types of printing papers in the same relevant market. On the other hand, price correlation between certain types of wood coated papers was also tested, thus validating the determined correlation coefficient between the Light Weight Coated (LWC) paper and Super Calendered (SC) paper at 0.85, which indicates that both types of wood coated papers belong to the same relevant market.

In the case of CVC/Lenzing (2001), by applying the correlation analysis, the European Commission determined that it was not only viscose and lyocell fibres that constituted separate relevant markets, but that viscose fibres and fibres made of other materials, such are cotton, polyester and polypropylene, also did not belong to a single relevant market. Namely, the correlation coefficients between prices of viscose fibres and other fibres ranged from 0.04 for natural fibres, i.e. cotton-made fibres, to above 0.06 for polypropylene fibres from the lower price category, 0.24 for polypropylene fibres from the higher price category, 0.39 for polyester fibres from the lower price category, all the way up to 0.44 for polyester fibres from the higher price category. This European Commission opinion was completely contrary to the view of the parties to the concentration that all textile fibres, artificial (cellulose and synthetic) and natural, constitute the same relevant market.

In the case of Ryanair/Aer Lingus (2003), a price-correlation analysis was used to complement other evidence in determining the relevant geographic market. The takeaway from this example is that there is no agreed level or threshold that defines whether series move sufficiently together for two products to belong to the same relevant market. A partial, but generally accepted, response to this critique is the use of benchmarking techniques. As a benchmark against which to compare other correlations, one can use the correlation coefficient between the prices of two series that one is willing to state on a priori grounds are in the same relevant market. In this case the average correlation on six routes operated both by Aer Lingus and Ryanair was used as a general benchmark. According to this approach, the correlation coefficients of individual routes that were above the average correlation of 0.69 were used as a first indication that the merging parties are close competitors on these routes.

In the case of Arsenal/DSP (2009), the European Commission applied the price correlation and stationarity tests in order to define the relevant geographic market. Contrary to the view of the parties to the concentration that the relevant market in geographic terms was the global market, the European Commission concluded, based on the low correlation coefficients between continents and absence of stationarity of relative prices, that Europe, Asia, and North America represent separate geographic markets.

## 5 Practical Application of Price-Based Tests

We will demonstrate the practical application of price-based tests on the example of analysis of monthly time-series data relating to prices of three products, two different brands of edible sunflower oil and diesel fuel, in the Serbian market, during a 4-year period (2012–2015). For further ease of use, the products will be marked as A, B, and C, with C being diesel fuel. Each data-series had 48 observations. The prices of all three products were deflated using appropriate indexes.

Departing from the basic legal requirements in determining the relevant market (characteristics, common purpose, and price), already in the first step taken, it was noted that based on the criteria of characteristics and purpose, products A and B belonged to the same market, while product C represents the second, considerably different and separate market. Further empirical analysis dealt with the price movement of these three products with the aim of verifying whether products A, B, and C, whose retail prices move at approximately identical level, belong to the same relevant market. In addition to that, the purpose of the empirical work was to obtain an answer as t the existence of causality of the price of product A against products B and C, and if any, whether the causalities were unidirectional- or bidirectional in nature.

First, we will examine the graph presentation of time-series data of prices related to products A, B, and C. Already at first glance, such visual representation suggests that the prices of products A and B demonstrate similar dynamics, while the price of product C has a considerably different trend (Fig. 1).

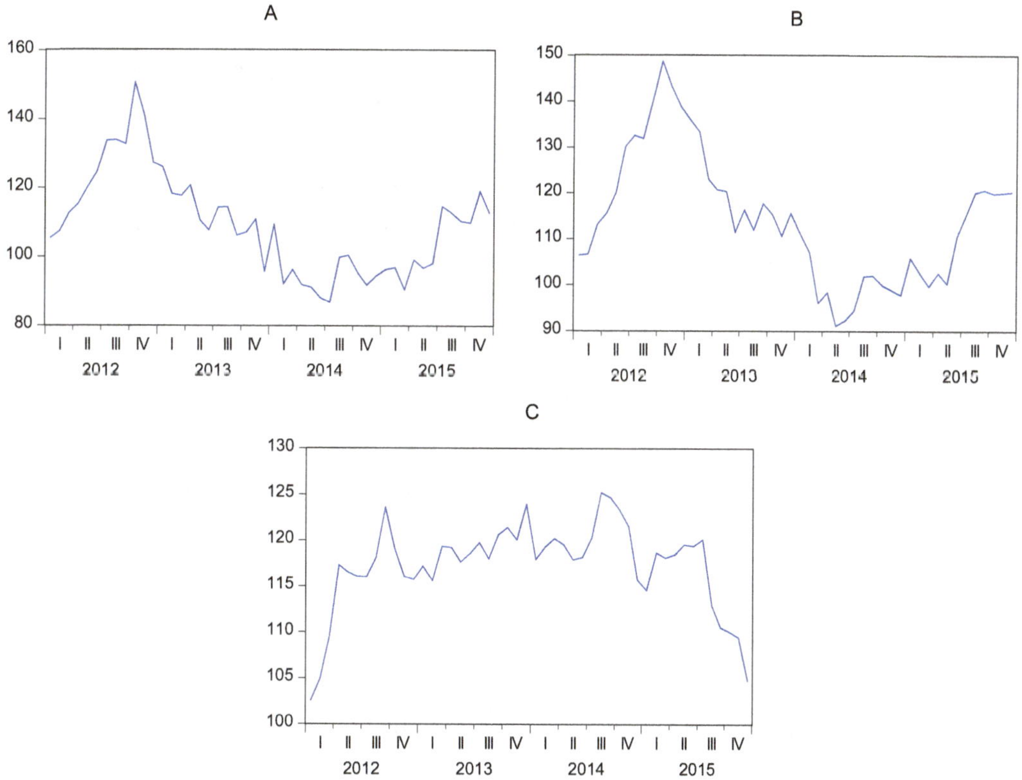


**Fig. 1** Movement of observed prices

### 5.1 Price Correlation Test

Further investigation analysed the correlation between those three data-series. The values of correlation coefficients and associated probabilities are presented in the form of Table 1.

Correlation analysis demonstrated a high and statistically significant correlation coefficient between products A and B (0.94), while the correlation coefficients of product C against products A and B have a negative sign, demonstrating low values (−0.17 and −0.14, respectively), and are not statistically significant.

The obtained results suggest that products A and B belong to the same relevant market, while product C belongs to another relevant product market, therefore confirming the preliminary conclusion reached based on the qualitative assessment of the relevant market, by analysing the characteristics and purpose of these products. The correlation analysis results should be interpreted with caution, particularly in situations when not all observed time series are stationary. Consequently, it is recommended to combine correlation analysis with other price movement tests.

### 5.2 Stationarity Test (Unit Root Test)

Next we implemented another price-based test, by investigating the stationarity of the time-series of relative prices, related to products A, B and C, whereas the relative prices are expressed as a difference in price between two products (Fig. 2).

Based on the graph presentation, already *prima facie it* can be concluded that the time-series of relative prices of products A–B is stationary, while the time-series of relative prices of products A–C, and B–C are non-stationary, which we will verify by applying the unit root test.

Firstly, we will test the stationarity of time-series by using the Augmented Dickey-Fuller (ADF) test, followed by the Kwiatkowski–Phillips–Schmidt–Shin (KPSS) test. Although in principle they lead to the same conclusions, the tests differ in the null hypothesis. Namely, the ADF test departs from the hypothesis on the presence of a unit root (lack of stationarity), while the KPSS test tests the null hypothesis that the time-series is stationary.

**Table 1** Results of the price correlation test

| Correlation coefficient associated probability | | PR_A | PR_B | PR_C |
|---|---|---|---|---|
| A | Correlation coefficient | 1.0000 | | |
| B | Correlation coefficient | 0.9367*** | 1.0000 | |
| C | Correlation coefficient | −0.1695 | −0.1379 | 1.0000 |

*Significant at $p \leq 10\%$
**Significant at $p \leq 5\%$
***Significant at $p \leq 1\%$

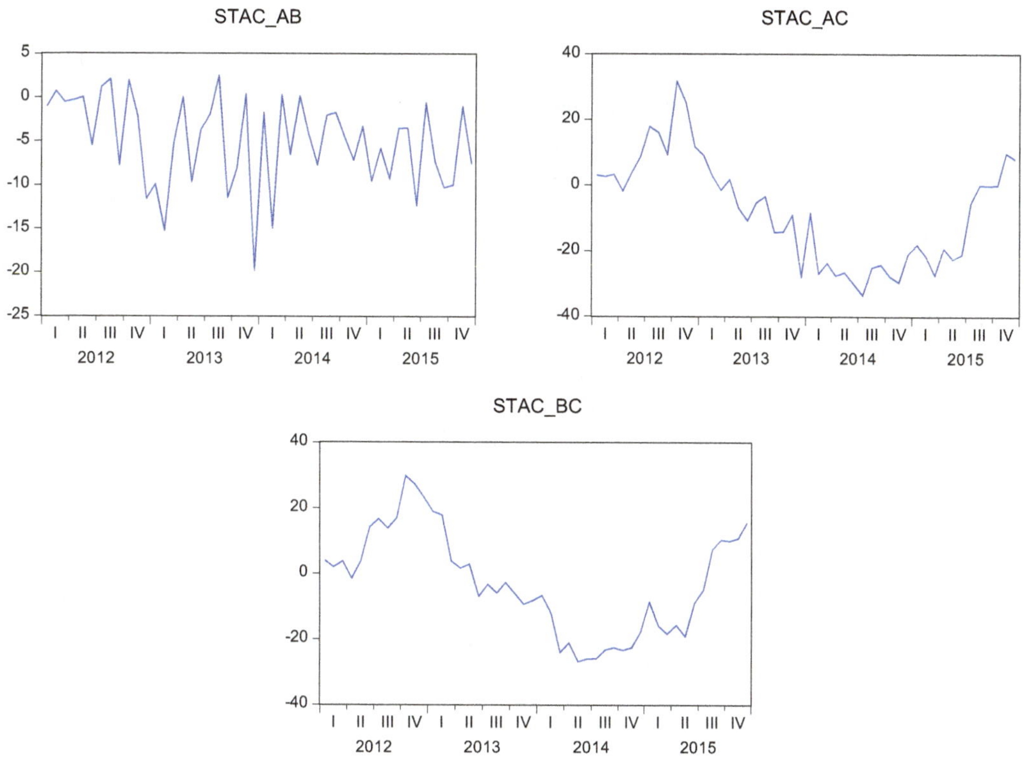


**Fig. 2** Movement of product price differences

**Table 2** Results of the ADF stationarity test for products A and B

| | t-statistic |
|---|---|
| ADF t-statistic | −7.5724*** |

*Significant at p ≤ 10%
**Significant at p ≤ 5%
***Significant at p ≤ 1%

By applying the ADF test to the time-series of relative prices of products A and B, we get the result as indicated in Table 2.

Based on the ADF t-statistic, which is below the critical value for all significance levels, we can reject the null hypothesis on the presence of a unit root, hence we concluded that the time-series of relative prices relating to products A and B is stationary.

Now we tested the stationarity of the time-series of relative prices of products A and C (Table 3).

The table demonstrates that the t-statistics is in the area of accepting the null hypothesis for all significance levels, hence we conclude that the time-series is not stationary. The identical result is also achieved when we apply the test to the time-series of relative prices of products B and C (Table 4).

By testing the stationarity of time-series of relative prices relating to products A, B and C, using the ADF unit root test, we concluded that products A and B belong to the same relevant market, while product C constitutes the separate relevant market.

**Table 3** Results of the ADF stationarity test for products A and C

| | t-statistic |
|---|---|
| ADF t-statistic | −1.6637 |

*Significant at $p \leq 10\%$
**Significant at $p \leq 5\%$
***Significant at $p \leq 1\%$

**Table 4** Results of the ADF stationarity test for products B and C

| | t-statistic |
|---|---|
| ADF t-statistic | −0.9788 |

*Significant at $p \leq 10\%$
**Significant at $p \leq 5\%$
***Significant at $p \leq 1\%$

**Table 5** Results of the KPSS test for products A and B

| | LM-statistic |
|---|---|
| KPSS t-statistic | 0.3516* |

*Significant at $p \leq 10\%$
**Significant at $p \leq 5\%$
***Significant at $p \leq 1\%$

By applying the KPSS test we arrive to almost identical conclusions, hence below, for illustration purposes, we will give only the result of testing the stationarity of the time-series of relative prices of products A and B (Table 5).

The critical value (0.352) is located in the area of acceptance of the null hypothesis, for significance levels of 1% and 5%, while the null hypothesis is practically located in the margins of the critical area, for the significance level of 10%. Based on the abovementioned, we conclude that the time-series is stationary.

## 5.3 *Cointegration Test*

The test that we have used in order to draw conclusions on the determination of observed products against the same or different relevant markets is the cointegration test. The purpose of this test is to investigate whether the linear combination of two (non-stationary) time-series is stationary, from which it is concluded whether products belong to the same relevant market.

In order to investigate whether the time-series are cointegrated, it is primarily necessary to estimate the regression equations for each pair of products (three equations in total), then to create the residuals and test whether the time-series of the residuals are stationary, by using the unit root test. Therefore, the cointegration test is actually reduced to testing the presence of a unit root in the residuals, obtained by estimating the regression equations, by using the ordinary least squares method.

**Table 6** Results of the cointegration test for products A and B

| | t-statistic |
|---|---|
| ADF t-statistic | −7.4955*** |

*Significant at $p \leq 10\%$
**Significant at $p \leq 5\%$
***Significant at $p \leq 1\%$

**Table 7** Results for products A and C

| | t-statistic |
|---|---|
| ADF t-statistic | −1.8884 |

*Significant at $p \leq 10\%$
**Significant at $p \leq 5\%$
***Significant at $p \leq 1\%$

**Table 8** Results for products B and C

| | t-statistic |
|---|---|
| ADF t-statistic | −1.5072 |

*Significant at $p \leq 10\%$
**Significant at $p \leq 5\%$
***Significant at $p \leq 1\%$

The result of the stationarity testing of the residuals obtained through the assessment of the regression equation of the A-B product time-series is presented in Table 6.

Based on the calculated value of the ADF t-statistics and associated probability, and comparing it against the critical values for different significance levels, we conclude that the null hypothesis on the presence of a unit root is rejected, i.e. that the time-series is stationary, which suggests that products A and B belong to the same relevant market.

For the estimated regression equation of the time-series of products A and C, and the related resulting residuals, we obtain a different result (Table 7).

The calculated value of t-statistic is not statistically significant and it is located in the area of accepting the null hypothesis for all significance levels, thus we cannot reject the null hypothesis on non-stationarity. Accordingly, we conclude that products A and C do not belong to the same relevant market. The identical result is also obtained if we test the stationarity of residuals obtained by estimating the regression equation of the time-series of products B and C, which is demonstrated in Table 8, thus we conclude that those products belong to different relevant markets.

## 5.4 *Granger Causality Test*

Bearing in mind that the previous test confirmed that products A and B belong to the same relevant product market, further examination referred to the causality of the price movement of these three products. The Granger causality test is applied to examine whether the time-series of product A prices causes the time-series of

**Table 9** Results of the Granger causality test

| Null hypothesis | Number of observations | F-statistic |
|---|---|---|
| No causality exists between product B and product A in terms of Granger | 47 | 9.5111*** |
| No causality exists between product A and product B in terms of Granger | | 11.1046*** |
| No causality exists between product C and product A in terms of Granger | 47 | 0.0168 |
| No causality exists between product A and product C in terms of Granger | | 0.6217 |
| No causality exists between product C and product B in terms of Granger | 47 | 0.4782 |
| No causality exists between product B and product C in terms of Granger | | 1.1437 |

*Significant at $p \leq 10\%$
**Significant at $p \leq 5\%$
***Significant at $p \leq 1\%$

product B and C prices, and if causality exists, whether it is unidirectional or bidirectional.

The causality analysis is preceded by a statistical analysis of the model from the aspect of the optimal number of lags. A single lag is included in the model, and the following results are obtained (Table 9):

The determined values of the Granger causality test and associated probability ($p < 0.05$) demonstrate that when testing the causality of products A and B, the null hypothesis on the absence of causality is rejected, thus it is concluded that the price movement of product A is caused by the price movement of product B, and vice versa.

On the other hand, in the case of product sets C-A and C-B, the null hypothesis on the absence of causality in the price movement relating to the observed products cannot be rejected ($p > 0.05$), which additionally increases the previous finding that product C does not belong to the relevant product market to which products A and B belong.

This result is consistent with the conclusions reached in all three previously applied price tests, as well as with the initial assumption based on the qualitative analysis of products' characteristics and intended use. Various brands of edible sunflower oil constitute a relevant market that is different and separate from the market to which diesel fuel belong.

## 6 Conclusion

The definition of the relevant market is one of the most fundamental concepts upon which all crucial issues of competition policy are based. Defining the relevant market is a widely applicable analytical framework that represents an initial step when analysing competition conditions and investigating potential infringements of competition. Properly determined boundaries of the relevant market enable identification of the market structure and market participants, as well as assessment of the competitive pressure that they face from one another.

There is a wide range of different methods and techniques that can be applied when assessing the relevant market, starting from the qualitative, which are based on product characteristics and their intended use, to the quantitative, which are based on the hypothetical monopolist test and price-based tests. Which of the methods will be implemented depends on the conditions under which the determination of relevant market is performed and on available data.

Tests that are based on the monitoring of time-series of product price movements are used when it is not possible to collect data for conducting other, more complex and information-demanding tests, such as the SSNIP test. Scientific papers published during last two decades and provide an abundance of examples of practical application of price-based tests, while the European Commission has used them extensively since 1992 in defining the relevant market, when assessing proposed concentrations.

Using an example of three products, we have demonstrated the practical implementation of price-based tests in the procedure of determining the relevant market. The performed tests and the results obtained aimed to empirically verify the initial hypothesis that different brands of edible sunflower oil belong to the same relevant market, while diesel fuel represents the separate relevant market. All four utilised tests confirmed the preliminary position obtained in the qualitative analysis, based on which we concluded that diesel fuel belongs to the separate relevant market, i.e. that it does not belong to the relevant market to which edible sunflower oil belongs.

This paper has addressed the issue of how price correlation and other price-based tests can be applied for a given data set of average monthly retail prices of two brands of edible sunflower oil and that of diesel fuel, over a 4-year period. However, the initial selection of products was done in a way that made the results of a preliminary qualitative analysis rather intuitive, and these were in a later stage confirmed by quantitative testing. It would be interesting to see how well the obtained benchmarks fits into another, similar data set, for example, by applying the same techniques to test the hypothesis that all edible oils (olive oil, palm oil, coconut oil, etc.) constitute the same relevant market.

**Acknowledgement** The authors are grateful to Dr Miloje Obradović, President of Serbian CPC, for his helpful comments and support and Prof. Zorica Mladenović and Prof. Aleksandra Nojković from the University of Belgrade, Faculty of Economics, for their helpful comments and inputs.

## References

Bishop S, Walker M (2010) The economics of EC competition law: concepts, application and measurement. Sweet & Maxwell, London

Case: ARSENAL/DSP, COMP/M.5153 (2009)

Case: CVC/Lenzing, COMP/M.2187 (2001)

Case: Lonrho/Gencor, IV/M619 (1997)
Case: Nestlé/Perrier, (IV/M.190) (1992)
Case: UPM-Kymmene/Haindl COMP/M.2498 (2001)
Coe PJ, Krause D (2008) An analysis of price-based tests of antitrust market delineation. J Compet Law Econ 4(4):983–1007
Davis P, Garces E (2010) Quantitative techniques for competition and antitrust analysis. Princeton University Press, New Jersey
Engle RF, Granger CWJ (2003) The Sveringes Resksbank Prize in economic sciences in memory of Alfred Nobel 2003
European Commission (1997) Commission notice on the definition of relevant market for the purposes of community competition law. Off J Eur Communities, 97/C 372/03
Forni M (2004) Using stationarity tests in antitrust market definition. Am Law Econ Rev 6 (2):441–464
Froeb LM, Werden GJ (1991) Residual demand estimation for market delineation: complication and limitations. Rev Ind Organ 6(1):33–48
Horowitz I (1981) Market definition in antitrust analysis: a regression based approach. South Econ J 48:1–16
Kaplow L (2013) Market definition alchemy. Antitrust Bull 57:915–952
NERANational Economic Research Associates (2001) The role of market definition in monopoly and dominance inquiries. Economic Discussion Paper, 2 July 2001, A report prepared for the Office of Fair Trading
Pittman R (2017) Three economist's tools for antitrust analysis: a non-technical introduction.
Slade ME (1986) Exogeneity tests of market boundaries applied to petroleum products. J Ind Econ 34:291–303
Stigler GJ, Sherwin RA (1985) The extent of the market. J Law Econ 28(3):555–585

# The Rationale for Using the Classic Cournot Mechanism in Merger Control

Bojan Ristić

## 1 Introduction

This paper aims to theoretically establish, justify and show the possibilities for the application of the classic quantity competition model within industries where firms before they start with the price competition, are required to choose some level of capacity. It is a model developed by French mathematician and economist Augustin Cournot in the nineteenth century, which can be considered as a reduced (short) form of such a two-stage game.[1]

The inspiration for this topic comes from the need to perform a more significant inflow of economic theory into the domain of horizontal merger control, which can be of assistance to authorities in charge of competition protection in gathering evidence for cases that they investigate. This is a particular area of competition protection policy, where the unilateral effects of horizontal mergers (hereinafter, mergers or concentrations) on the conditions of competition in the relevant market are determined ex-ante. Accordingly, a judgement is made whether the merger should be approved or blocked, and under what terms. Thus, a theoretical framework would be developed for the right *application* of the stated economic model. We hope that the mentioned authorities (hereinafter, commissions) would, therefore, gain a valuable tool for determining the short-term merger effects. The application of this model is considered especially useful for the horizontal merger simulation method.

This paper does not aim to suggest the perfectness of the tool it offers. On the contrary, it should be regarded only as complementary analytics which clarifies or questions other evidence, gathered by traditionally present analyses used by the commissions. First of all, we refer to the definition of the relevant market and the

[1] See Cournot (1897).

B. Ristić
Faculty of Economics, University of Belgrade, Belgrade, Serbia
e-mail: bristic@ekof.bg.ac.rs





B. Begović, D. V. Popović (eds.), *Competition Authorities in South Eastern Europe*, Contributions to Economics, https://doi.org/10.1007/978-3-319-76644-7_11

consequential judgement based on market shares and measures of market concentration.

Mergers can cause two types of adverse effects on competition. Those are the mentioned *unilateral effects*, which are in the focus of this paper, and the *coordinative effects*, which can be the subject of some further analysis. In any case, it is important to differentiate between the two.

The coordinative effects stem from the fact that concentration, by its nature, decreases the number of market players, thus increasing the market concentration, also raising the possibility for a *cartel* to be created and to endure.[2]

The focus of this chapter will be, as already mentioned, on the unilateral effects that exclusively refer to the entity created by horizontal merger. European legislation sees the dominant market position as an indicator of the possession of market power. In that sense, gaining a dominant position is considered as motivation for firms to obtain and strengthen their market power through such steps, at the expense of the consumers, rival companies and suppliers, which is considered to be an *abuse of the dominant position*. Thereby, to prevent the occurrence of such abuse, since it assumes already violated competition conditions, it is the task of the commissions to predict the unilateral merger effects.

The starting point is that unilateral effects are exclusively connected to the participants of the concentration, but not to their rivals. In this sense, these effects could formally be defined by applying the Nash equilibrium concept, which is at the heart of the Cournot model.[3]

This chapter consists of two connected and rounded parts. First, it is necessary to discuss the circumstances within which the Cournot model can be considered as a good approximation of reality. Therefore, there is a need to also consider its existing role in the domain of merger control. Second, having discussed and chosen the competition model, we will offer a short algorithm for its application in merger simulations.

It is worth emphasising once more that the foremost purpose of these parts is to indicate the economic philosophy behind the carried-out analysis to the *young commissions* (without sufficient experience, expertise and other resources necessary for carrying out merger control). The general aim is to indicate the possibilities of making positive breakthroughs towards an increase in the quality of the economic analysis that is being performed, which would decrease decision-making errors of the first and second kind, which are an inevitable part of this sphere of competition policy.

---

[2]For the definition of the coordinative effects see Begović and Pavić (2012, p. 97).

[3]See Werden and Froeb (2008, pp. 45–46).

## 2 The Rationale for Cournot Mechanism

The practice of this type is shaped by oligopoly theory, which lies at the very heart of the industrial organisation. The limitations inevitably faced in practice must be taken into account when considering the importance and the limits of the particular role of this economic theory. Practice is restricted by rigorous legislative norms (e.g. the short time-frame for collecting evidence), scarce resources (quantity of staff, accumulated knowledge, and insufficient financial funds), as well as limited availability of data needed to carry out the analysis. Because of this, it is logical to implement those economic tools, which under the given circumstances, reduce the space for making the stated errors.

A perfect simulation would assume that the applied competition model is fully compatible with the characteristics of the relevant market. In other words, there should be as many different game modes as there are different markets. However, economic theory does not differentiate an infinite number of competition mechanisms. Also, the limits of merger control practice can lead to a simplified appearance of reality, through the assumption of Cournot or Bertrand competition, depending on what is considered the key strategic variable—quantity or price. The approximation of reality always carries the risk of making a wrong decision. This is something that the authorities must be aware of when choosing the adequate set of instruments for the analysis.

It is evident that the possibility of mistake cannot be eradicated since forecasting social process outcomes always comes with a dose of unexplained variability. The interest of the authorities should be to minimise those possibilities by using sophisticated economic tools, which they are capable of implementing. On the other hand, another limiting factor must be taken into consideration: judges do not like "black boxes" containing evidence, which is something that the application of complex economic theories might resemble. Of course, this is the case when the analysed merger case gets its day in court.

By offering an answer to why the Cournot model of quantity competition should be applied, it is implicitly assumed that this model represents a good approximation of the market game within which a merger is taking place. Is this actually the case and when? The answer to this question has at least two components. First, the dilemma which competition model should be applied depends on the decision which strategic variable is considered to be crucial for the analysed market. Most often these variables are quantities and prices. However, firms use both strategic variables in their business. The Kreps and Scheinkman (1983) model (hereinafter, KS model) is proof that the outcome of the strategic interaction in which the firm would first choose its capacities and later engage in price competition with the aim to employ capacities, creates an outcome which coincides with the outcome of the Cournot model. That is why it is wise to use the Cournot model, and not the Bertrand model, in the circumstances described by the KS model. Second, it is a fact that merger control practice significantly relies on the Cournot model when establishing the relationship between the indicators of market structure (e.g. the number of firms within the industry, their market shares, and measures of market concentration) and the indicators of market performance (e.g. the Lerner index). Both of these reasons should be discussed in detail, as follows.

## 2.1 Cournot Mechanism as the Reduced Form of the Two-Stage Competition

According to available literature, it appears that as far as simulations are concerned, the question of choosing a competition model is still insufficiently explored. Typically, without going into detailed argumentation, it is pointed out that for homogeneous products the Cournot model of competition should be applied, while for the differentiated products the focus should be on the Bertrand model. A transparent approach to this issue can be found in influential papers, such as Werden and Froeb (2008), and Budzinski and Ruhmer (2009). By this simple division of authorities between the two models, it is implicitly presumed that in the case of homogeneous products the dominant strategic variable is quantity, while in the case of differentiated products it is price.

However, this division seems too strict in the case of limited capacities, where prices and quantities can be the variables of a single two-stage game, with the outcome which fits the classic Cournot model. Moreover, it turns out that in certain circumstances this result can be valid, for both the markets of homogeneous and of differentiated products.

The KS model was devised on the basis of the seminal Edgeworth (1925) model and the model that was later developed by Levitan and Shubik (1972), which introduce exogenously limited capacities into price competition. It introduces capacities limitations into price competition, but as an endogenous firm's decision. By making capacities endogenous within the frameworks of price competition, both variables, prices and quantities, are put in the context of one game, with the conclusions being fairly attractive to the topic of this paper. Namely, the price competition which precedes the firms' decisions regarding capacities will in certain circumstances have as a result the outcome of the Cournot model. This result significantly affirms the role of Cournot's competition as a tool for short-term predictions, which is exactly the case with merger simulations. In other words, it represents a theoretical basis for the application of the Cournot model, as its reduced form.

Therefore, the KS model assumes that the firms choose their capacities during the first period, while in the second period, starting from chosen capacities, they choose prices that will fully engage those capacities. It is assumed that the production for inventory is not possible. Once chosen, the capacities are binding for the firms, which introduces into the model the assumption of a significant leap in the marginal costs for every unit produced above capacity. The KS model proves that in the circumstances of limited capacities if firms believe that the result of the price competition will be such, regardless of the chosen capacities, pricing policy will fully engage them. As a result, firm's supply will be found at the intersection of the Cournot's reaction functions.[4] The example of homogeneous products duopoly originally proves this result, with the assumption of a negative slope demand function, non-decreasing marginal costs of production, and marginal costs of capacities. Also, the so-called *efficient rationing rule* is applied, which assumes that the lower price firm, up to the level of its pre-committed capacities, will serve the customers with the highest willingness to pay, while the more expensive one will be faced with residual demand, which excludes those customers. This rule maximises the consumers' surplus since the lower price is always achieved by the customers with the highest willingness to pay.[5]

To illustrate the rationale behind the KS model, similar as in Shy (1998), a simple example of two symmetrical firms, which participate in this two-stage game (firms 1 and 2) will be used. The inverse market demand is linear and given by the form $p = a - q$, where $q = q_1 + q_2$ and $a > 0$. The per unit costs of capacities for both firms are constant at the level $\hat{c}_1 = \hat{c}_2 = \hat{c} > 0$, while $a > b$. On the other hand, the per unit production costs are also constant and equal to zero, up to the level of installed capacities, i.e. $c_1 = c_2 = c = 0$, and are infinite for every unit above that level.[6]

Differing costs of capacities and costs of production is an important characteristic of the two-stage KS model. While the costs of production are crucial for the second game period and the selection of price, the total costs (costs of capacities increased by the costs of production) are essential for the selection of capacities in its first period. The costs of capacities are a function of the level of installed capacities, where every unit of capacity enables the production of one unit of output. If the firm does not intend to generate inventories in equilibrium, nor to have unengaged capacities, but to always use them for the measure of intended production, it seems realistic to expect that $q_i = k_i$. This continual following of the capacities with quantities can lead to the conclusion that the per unit capacity costs $(\hat{c})$ can be characterised as per unit production costs ($c$), which is *not* the case. The per unit production costs refer to the second game period. Thus, they are not directly connected to the decision concerning capacities if production is maintained within their limits. On the other hand, even related to capacities construction, total

[4]For the technical details of this complex model, which most certainly surpass the scope of this paper, see Kreps and Scheinkman (1983). For a rather intuitive interpretation see Shy (1998, pp. 112–115).

[5]For a detailed discussion of logic of efficient rationing see Davidson and Deneckere (1986), and Tirole (1988, p. 213).

[6]The assumption on zero costs of production is in accordance with the original interpretation of the KS model. Kreps and Scheinkman (1983) state that with slight complications in the proof, the conclusions of their model would not change even for non-zero production costs. The infinity of the capacity costs for every overrun unit secures their perfect rigidity. Maggi (1996) has shown that even without the perfect rigidity, the same conclusions, as in the standard KS model, can be reached.

capacities cost $\left(\hat{c}\, k_i\right)$ cannot be treated as fixed, since it depends on the decision concerning the volume of production. If the firm were to retract its intention to invest, this kind of costs would not occur in the first place. It is important to notice that the decision on capacities is introduced at the beginning of the game, so capacity costs still do not exist up to that moment. Thus, the price paid for the capacities cannot refer to fixed costs. Since the character of capacity costs is known, the issue of their definition is logically raised. A reasonable answer is given by Varian (2010), by defining the *quasi-fixed* costs, since there are none if the decision concerns the absence of investment, or they are fixed when the investment decision is final, i.e. irrevocable.[7] Quantities can vary within the boundaries of the installed capacities. So, a wrong notion that capacities can do the same should be avoided. The decision on their magnitude will be made by the firms' rational expectation regarding the optimal production volume for the set game. Furthermore, in the second period, when the decision on capacities is irrevocable, these costs can be predominantly characterised as *sunk*. It is logical to believe that in the short time-frame the firm is not able to return the payments caused by these costs. Due to the all stated features, firms do not even consider capacity costs while deciding on the equilibrium price.

At least in the short term, the selection of capacities in the first period of the game is a binding decision by which the firm's possibilities to vary prices are limited. In that manner, a wrong impression can be formed that this type of game is reserved only for the establishing industries, where the players are just entering the industry and forming their capacities in order to get into the price competition subsequently. To avoid this impression, the perceptions of the meaning of capacities, both the short and the long term, must be additionally clarified. This clarification seems crucial not only for understanding the first-period capacity costs, but also the circumstances under which this type of competition can be expected. The following example can serve as a practical illustration for this purpose.

The example concerns production in the domain of homogeneous alimentary products (e.g. sugar, edible oil, flour). In this case, capacities are determined on the annual level by the volume of planting of the primary raw materials. Usually, producers of the stated products are vertically integrated. This is, for example, very characteristic of sugar refineries, where in addition to the core business (sugar production), there is also a primary agricultural production of the main raw material, sugar beet. In such a system, the overflow of capacities determined by the planned planting is not possible without significant costs (when resources are obtained from external suppliers), which makes the choice of capacities quite rigid. A fact should also be added that the transport of sugar beet is not possible at longer distances due to the natural characteristics of this "sweet" root, which is also why longer warehousing is not feasible. All those factors make the arranged planting almost entirely fixed from the aspect of the processor, within a given year. In that context, the fixed capacities (buildings, processing machines, transport means, etc.) assume the real

[7]See Varian (2010, p. 373).

fixed costs, and as such, in the long term they are binding for the firm. On the other hand, every year, the choice of the planting volume, which depends on the sales plans for the final product based on expected price, withdraws quasi-fixed costs. Sugar refineries will not have this type of costs if they suspend the production for a year for some reason.

When it comes to sugar production, the infinity of production costs when production takes place above capacity can be observed through the fact that transport over longer distances is almost impossible. During transport, the quality of sugar beet decreases significantly. Therefore, all locations outside of the acceptable transport radius from the place of processing are excluded, and thus also importing of beets. During import, the entire profit would probably "drained-off" while waiting for the completion of the standard customs procedure.

Within the given example, it can be expected that the capacity choice is a simultaneous process. This phenomenon can be easily explained when it comes to sugar production since the simultaneousness is first of all the consequence of vegetation characteristics of the basic raw material. No firm can wait for the rival's decision on capacities since it would certainly be late with the planting, for which nature still holds the authority when it comes to determining the optimal period. It can be stated that by choosing capacities in this manner, the firm determines its short-run cost function. Alternatively, it could be said that by choosing the capacities, the firm *binds* itself to a certain short-run cost function, which is relevant for the two-stage game as a whole.

Within such a setting of demand and costs for $i = 1, 2$ and $i \neq j$, the outcome of the simultaneous Cournot game would assume reaction functions of both firms in the following form:

$$q_i(q_j) = \frac{(a - \hat{c})}{2} - \frac{1}{2} q_j. \tag{1}$$

According to that, the mechanism of the Cournot model will lead to the equilibrium outcome

$$q_1^* = q_2^* = \frac{(a - \hat{c})}{3}; \quad p_1^* = p_2^* = p^* = \frac{(a + 2\hat{c})}{3}. \tag{2}$$

The task is to show that the outcome of the two-stage game with capacities, and later with prices, will be equivalent to the stated outcome of the Cournot game. While solving the two-stage game, it is good to start with the second period, in this case, the pricing sub-game.

### 2.1.1 Second Stage—Pricing Subgame

Based on the efficient rationing rule, for the given capacities of Firm 2, Firm 1 faces the inverse residual demand, $p_1 = a - k_2 - q_1$. Within the pricing sub-game, the firms maximise their revenue functions, and also profit functions, since the capacity costs are not relevant for making a decision in the second period, while the production costs are zero. For example, if the capacities of both firms were to be given on the level $k_1 = k_2 = a/3$, the unique price which would fully employ the capacities would be $p_1 = p_2 = p = a/3$.

It can be noticed that this outcome would represent the solution to the Cournot game in the absence of any costs. From the first order conditions for the maximum of the revenue function $R_1 = (a - k_2 - q_1)q_1$, Firm 1's reaction function to Firm 2's capacities would be obtained, which could be written as

$$r_0(k_2) = \frac{a}{2} - \frac{1}{2}\,k_2, \tag{3}$$

In the same manner, bearing in mind the symmetry of the example, the reaction of Firm 2 would be

$$r_0(k_1) = \frac{a}{2} - \frac{1}{2}\,k_1. \tag{4}$$

It remains to be proven that the price $p_1 = p_2 = p = a/3$ is the pricing sub-game equilibrium, i.e. that under conditions of limited capacities the firms will not have the motive to determine any other price. Assuming that Firm 2 will precisely stick to the price $p_2 = a/3$, it is necessary to prove that Firm 1 will determine the same, i.e. that the price variations compared to the choice which would be made by the Walrasian auctioneer for the given quantities are not profitable.

Figure 1 helps in understanding the firms' choice in the second game period. It also demonstrates the way of forming the residual demand function, based on the efficient rationing. The left graph in the figure shows the given inverse demand, $p(q)$, while the right graph demonstrates Firm 1's residual demand, $p_1(q_1)$, assuming

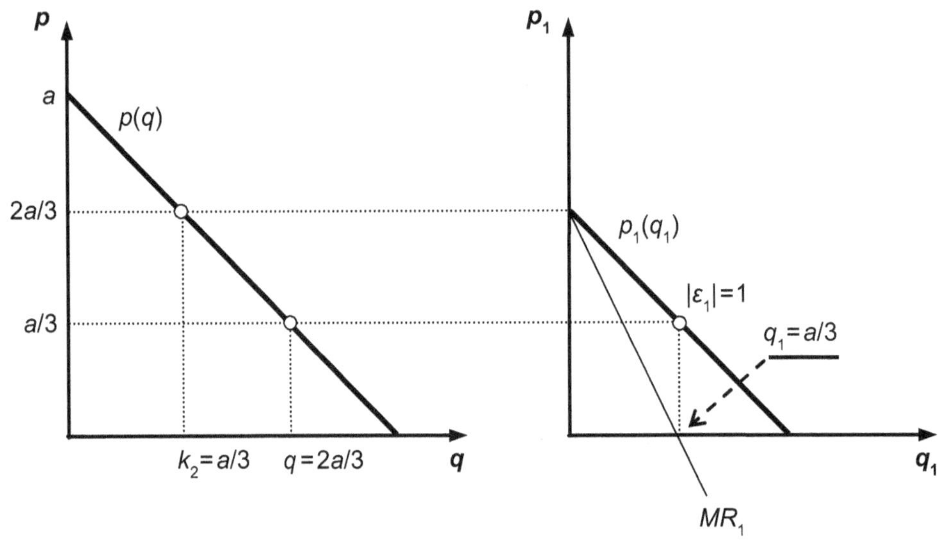


**Fig. 1** The pricing sub-game equilibrium and residual demand formation

a given efficient rationing rule for $k_2$. Firm 1's marginal revenues function, $MR_1(q_1)$, is a logical consequence of such obtained residual demand.

First, Firm 1 will not set the price below the level of its competitor, since it is not in the position to produce and sell more compared to the level of installed capacities, i.e. in this case compared to $k_1 = q_1 = a/3$. The inability to increase sales due to the price decrease assumes that the revenues will be lower if the price reduction occurs. The same quantity will be sold as before, but at a lower price. From Fig. 1 it is clear that for $p_1 < p_2 = a/3$ we have that $MR_1 < 0$.

Second, it is necessary to prove that a price increase by Firm 1, compared to the level $p_2 = a/3$, is also not profitable. It is worth noting that if Firm 1 sets the price $p_1 > p_2 = a/3$, it can count on the residual demand obtained from the application of the efficient rationing rule. Since the residual demand is obtained in a manner that the cheaper firm's capacities are subtracted from the market demand, formally $q_1 = a - p_1 - k_2$, it turns out that $q_1 = 2\,a/3 - p_1$. In the inverse form, the residual demand is $p_1 = 2\,a/3 - q_1$, so the function of the marginal revenues equals $MR_1 = 2\,a/3 - 2\,q_1$. It turns out that $MR_1 \geq 0$ for $p_1 \geq a/3$, which indicates movement on the elastic part of residual demand. This undoubtedly shows that a price increase would cause the decrease of the total revenues. Therefore, a conclusion can be reached that Firm 1 will not find it in its interest to raise the price above its rival.

It is obvious that it will not be profitable for Firm 1 to either increase or decrease the price compared to the price of its rival. Since the firms are symmetrical, the same conclusions would be valid even if the analysis were to be carried out from the perspective of Firm 2. Hence, it would be easy to check whether for any combination of *sufficiently small* capacities which satisfy the condition $k_i \leq r_0(k_j)$ for $i = 1, 2$ and $i \neq j$, the equilibrium price must fully employ such capacities. Formally, this price can be written as $p\,(k_1 + k_2)$. In the example, the previous condition could be reduced by claiming that the unique equilibrium price, $p\,(k_1 + k_2) = a - k_1 - k_2$, can be formed if $k_1 + k_2 \leq 2a/3$.

If $k_i \geq a$ for $i = 1, 2$, the capacities of both firms would be *sufficiently large* to be considered as unlimited. The firm with unlimited capacities, as a cheaper one, can flood the entire market. In that case, the firms would determine the zero price, just like in the Bertrand equilibrium. As an extreme case, far from reality, Bertrand solution for unlimited capacities is not of the KS model particular interest.

Finally, within the range between the sufficiently small and sufficiently large capacities, the firms would enter into the Edgeworth price cycles. The equilibrium solution, in that case, would assume the application of mixed (pricing) strategies since capacities are large enough to disable the unique price choice. By addressing issues related to solving the Edgeworth cycles, defining the equilibrium within the pricing sub-game gets significantly more complicated, which certainly exceeds the extent of this paper. Therefore, this issue will not be further addressed.[8] In any case,

[8]For a complete analysis of the pricing subgame, see Levitan and Shubik (1972) and Kreps and Scheinkman (1983).

even without the mixed strategies issue, it can be claimed that for sufficiently small capacities the firms will surely opt for the unique price to be fully engaged.

### 2.1.2 First Stage—The Choice of Capacities

In order to reach the equilibrium of the first stage and to answer the question which capacities will be chosen by the duopolists, it is necessary to add the price $p\,(k_1 + k_2)$ to their first stage profit maximisation problem. In other words, pricing policy is deliberate not to leave capacities unengaged. By solving these problems, every firm will reach its *capacity best-response function*. In this context, the capacity best-response function of firm $i$ for $i = 1, 2$ and $i \neq j$ is

$$r_{\hat{c}}\left(k_j\right) = \underset{k_i}{\operatorname{argmax}} \left[p\left(k_i + k_j\right) - c - \hat{c}\,\right] k_i. \tag{5}$$

Since $c = 0$, from Eq. (5) it is clear that the firm's objective function in the first stage corresponds to that characteristic of the Cournot model. The difference is that instead of production volume, capacities are used. In this sense, the capacity selection in the first stage of the KS model must correspond to the selection of quantities in Cournot's static equilibrium. It turns out that supply forming at the very margin of capacities is the optimal solution for both firms. In the example of linear demand and constant capacity costs, the capacity best-response function of the firm $i$ would be

$$r_{\hat{c}}\left(k_j\right) = \frac{\left(a - \hat{c}\,\right)}{2} - \frac{1}{2}\,k_j, \tag{6}$$

which corresponds to Cournot's reaction given in Eq. (1) for the supplied quantities at the level of capacities. It should also be noted that including the costs of capacities in the first stage of the game, leads to $r_0\left(k_j\right) > r_{\hat{c}}\left(k_j\right)$ for $b > 0$, so in the first stage equilibrium, the following is valid: $k_i \leq r_0(k_j)$, for $i = 1, 2$ and $i \neq j$. In addition to the fact that any combination that fulfils this condition would lead to price $p\,(k_1 + k_2)$, the *stable game equilibrium* would be achieved for $k_i = r_{\hat{c}}\left(k_j\right)$ and $k_j = r_{\hat{c}}\left[r_{\hat{c}}\left(k_j\right)\right]$, which precisely coincides with the equilibrium quantities within Cournot's game. Based on the capacity best-response function given in Eq. (6), $k_1^* = k_2^* = k^* = \left(a - \hat{c}\,\right)/3$ can be obtained, so we have that $p_1^* = p_2^* = p^*(2k^*) = \left(a + 2\hat{c}\,\right)/3$. If the firms intend to fully engage their capacities, which is logical even more taking into account that their construction assumes positive costs, the outcome of the two-stage game will coincide with the equilibrium of the classic Cournot model. Therefore, by completing this two-stage journey, we have returned to the very beginning of this analysis and the outcome given in Eq. (2).

An influential critique of the KS model, given by Davidson and Deneckere (1986), has proven that the model is vulnerable to the change of the assumption of the demand rationing, which is always necessary in the case of homogeneous products. This critique has certainly not lowered the importance of the KS model, but it has rather stimulated further research in the field of this significant result of oligopoly theory in the decades to come. Therefore, models given by Maggi (1996) and Schulz (1999) have proved that the KS model with differentiated products leads to the same outcome as Cournot's mechanism applied to differentiated products. Hence, applying the KS model in the differentiation issue has relativised the influence of former critiques, by also pointing out the significance of quantity competition in differentiated products markets.

The principal objection to the application of the KS model is based on the mere fact that the equilibrium capacity following mergers cannot be adapted within a reasonable time frame. Since the capacities are fixed prior to the merger (for both the merger participants and their rivals), the only thing that players can do after the merger is to raise prices unilaterally.[9] Although logical at first glance, such a sequence of actions seems to be too short-sighted. The aforementioned sugar industry example can give an illustrative argument. Obviously, prices are subject to the daily basis changes, but the choice of capacity, and therefore the short-term cost function, is binding to the firm. Even though the two variables (price and quantity) can be considered as endogenous to the firms in question, however, the dominant one in such cases is quantity. Application of Cournot's mechanism, as the reduced form of the two-stage game, seems entirely reasonable in this sense.

The previous discussion was aimed at developing the necessary philosophy of the Cournot model application within the economic analyses of the competition protection authorities, whenever the capacities represent the limitations of the firms' pricing policy. However, it is valuable to ask the question to what extent Cournot model is already present in the economic analyses of the commissions. The answer follows.

## 2.2 *Cournot's Mechanism and Traditional Unilateral Effects Reasoning*

By using the classic Cournot's mechanism as in Shapiro (1989), it would be useful to link market structure and market performance indicators. To establish this link, the oligopoly of $n$ firms would be used, with the market range defined by the inverse demand function $p = p(q)$, with $q$ equivalent to $q = q_1 + q_2 + \ldots + q_n$. The total costs function of the firm $i$, for $i = 1, 2, \ldots, n$, is $C_i(q_i)$, so the marginal costs can be expressed as $c_i = dC_i/dq_i$. Based on familiar logic formulated by Cournot, the equilibrium of the oligopoly game can be reached when each firm seeks to maximise its profit, moving along its reaction function for any given rivals' quantities. Since the reaction function is derived from the first-order conditions for firm's profit

[9]See Werden and Froeb (2008, p. 50).

maximisation problem, the equilibrium outcome of this game is obtained by solving $n$ first order conditions—one for each firm. Formally, the firm $i$'s profit function can be written as

$$\pi_i = p\,(q)\,q_i - C_i\,(q_i). \tag{7}$$

Differentiation of the previous term with respect to $q_i$, and with simple fact that $dq/dq_i = 1$, gives us

$$\frac{d\pi_i}{dq_i} = p(q) + q_i \frac{dp(q)}{dq} - \frac{dC_i\,(q_i)}{dq_i} = 0. \tag{8}$$

By additional rearranging, the previous term can be transformed into

$$p(q) - c_i(q_i) = -q_i \frac{dp(q)}{dq}, \tag{9}$$

which can be divided by $p$, and only the right side multiplied by $q/q$, in order to form the Lerner index—undoubtedly the best-known measure of a firm's market power

$$L_i = \frac{p\,(q) - c_i(q_i)}{p\,(q)} = \frac{s_i}{|\,\varepsilon\,|}. \tag{10}$$

By starting from the result of Cournot's competition, it can be concluded that the firm's profit margin is proportional to its market share and inversely proportional to the absolute value of the price elasticity of market demand.[10] Hence, the higher the market share of the firm, and lower the market elasticity of demand in absolute terms, the more market power it possesses. The previous statement is probably one of the fundamental premises in the economic analysis of the commissions. As a trivial rule, mergers of entities with larger market shares attract greater attention of the competition authorities than those with smaller shares. This also applies to all circumstances where it is estimated that consumers are insensitive to price changes in the absence of close substitutes, and consequently lack of competition in the analysed partial markets. In addition to these unambiguous conclusions, Eq. (10) can tell even more about other significant moments that characterise this quantity game.

1. In fact, each firm is aware that possesses *limited market power* since the market price is above its marginal revenue. In accordance with Eq. (8), firm $i$'s marginal revenue could be presented as $MR_i = p\,(q) + q_i p'(q)$, hence we have $p\,(q) - MR_i = -\, q_i p'(q) > 0$ for $p'(q) < 0$, which is always the case.
2. Cournot's equilibrium is *located between monopoly and perfect competition*. For $s_i = 1$ we have a monopoly market structure, while for $s_i \rightarrow 0$ the market structure tends to the standard definition of perfect competition.

[10]A somewhat different approach to this relationship can be seen in Pepall et al. (2011, pp. 72–74). For the case of differentiated products see Perloff et al. (2007, pp. 89–90).

3. *Market share* is directly proportional to production efficiency. Production efficiency is based on the firm's marginal costs. The implication of this point is particularly useful. If there are reliable indications that the shares asymmetry is accompanied by a difference in the profit margins, namely that larger firms are more cost efficient than smaller ones, which is the result of Cournot's competition—it makes sense to claim that Cournot model is an adequate approximation of such a reality.
4. Firms that are *less efficient* than some others can also survive in such markets, by paying this less efficient position with a relatively smaller market share. Unquestionably, this is not the case in the Bertrand model, where, as the result of the merciless price war, less efficient rivals would be wiped out of the market, since all firms are ready to lower their prices up to the level of their marginal costs.
5. In the case of *symmetric oligopoly*, where the firm has equal and constant marginal costs $c$, Eq. (10) becomes

$$L_i = \frac{p(q) - c}{p(q)} = \frac{1}{n\,|\,\varepsilon\,|}. \tag{11}$$

It is well known that the Lerner index can take values from the closed interval $(0, 1)$. As the market structure approaches perfect competition we have $L \to 0$, otherwise, if it approaches monopoly we have $L \to 1$. Equation (11) indicates that for $n = 1$ the market power is characteristic of a monopoly, whereas for $n \to \infty$ market power complies with the conditions of perfect competition. In other words, increasing the number of symmetric firms in the industry is followed by an increase in the intensity of competition. Most of the practitioners (case handlers), involved in merger control, would probably agree with the previous statement, even without a clear understanding of the logic of Cournot model.

6. An interesting conclusion can be reached by calculation the *weighted average of the Lerner's indices* of all individual firms, with their market shares used as weights. For this purpose, Eq. (10) can be transformed as

$$s_1 L_1 + s_2 L_2 + \ldots + s_n L_n = \frac{1}{|\,\varepsilon\,|}\left(s_1^2 + s_2^2 + \ldots + s_n^2\right). \tag{12}$$

Note that the term in the brackets on the right side of Eq. (12) is equal to the Herfindahl-Hirschman Index (HHI), probably the best-known yardstick of market concentration. It can also be said that the HHI is both necessary and sufficient when it comes to market concentration metrics. This is particularly mentioned because of the frequent, sometimes misleading and mostly unnecessary fascination of practitioners in the field of competition policy by concentration metrics based on various functional forms of market shares. The HHI, as the convex combination of the market shares, meets all the criteria for a representative concentration measure. By altering such functional form, we cannot provide more information as long as the inputs in the analysis are same—market shares. In the market concentration analysis, the use of the HHI alternatives does not contribute to the reliability of the analysis, and sometimes can even be methodologically wrong. A characteristic example of this is the use of the Lorenz curve, and Gini coefficient based on it, as a market concentration measure.[11]

Thus, Eq. (12) can be rewritten as

$$\bar{L} = \frac{HHI}{|\varepsilon|}. \tag{13}$$

It turns out that the industry-wide output-weighted average price-cost margin is directly proportional to the market concentration and inversely proportional to the market demand price elasticity. However, the previous statement, derived from the Cournot model logic, deserves special attention when it comes to the merger control practice.

Specifically, the level of pre-mergers market concentration and its post-merger increase should be subsumed as a *preliminary indication* of the potentially harmful effects of this business practice.[12] In accordance with the definition of unilateral effects, it is believed that with relatively high market concentration, prior to the merger and its increase after the merger, it is more likely that the merger will cause a significant decrease of competition. Such a merger case should certainly become a candidate for further in-deep analysis. One of the possible ways would involve using the merger simulation method based on the appropriately calibrated model of competition. It seems easy to conclude that for the purpose of this chapter we can nominate precisely the classic Cournot model as appropriate in a large spectrum of contexts. Later in this chapter, we will discuss the role of Cournot model in merger simulations by explaining its logic and mechanism. Unfortunately, in the case of the young commissions, metrics based on market shares and concentration measures is often the ultimate scope of the economic part of the analysis of merger effects.

We should notice that previous conclusions are derived from the assumption of product homogeneity in the relevant market. The reality is often more or less *differentiated* rather than *homogeneous*. From the point of view of the merger control practice, it turns out that the conclusions are the same, both for the homogeneous or differentiated products markets. The logic of reasoning based on the HHI is applied to all merger cases, without exception, regardless of whether the product market is homogeneous or not. The main explanation for this is the fact that the analysed forms in both cases must belong to the same relevant product market. Hence, a logical question arises. Why can't Cournot model be the backbone of the analysis in cases of differentiated products markets, when commissions already deduce as if it were so? Therefore, it would be useful to return to the KS model discussed in Sect. 2.1.

---

[11]Useful references for the issue of representativeness criteria for market concentration indices could be Hall and Tideman (1967), Tirole (1988, pp. 221–223) and Ristić (2012).

[12]For the rules of inference, based on the HHI, see European and American guidelines for the regulation of horizontal mergers, respectively, European Commission (2004), and the Federal Trade Commission and the U.S. Department of Justice (2010).

## 3 Cournot's Model and Calibrated Merger Simulation

By relying on certain axioms about the behaviour of the competitors, i.e. the type of competition, assumptions about the possible functional forms of demand and costs, and necessary data for calibration of the model parameters, simulations deduce the likely effects of the merger. Below we will present the main steps and logic of implementation of the simulation method, using Cournot's mechanism as the basis for the simulation.

It is presumed that the simulation was conducted subsequent to the implementation of the complete traditional economic analysis, in the abovementioned sense. Prior to the simulation we also presume that the commission has collected all available information, which specifies the nature of the relevant market, and that it has examined the strategic intentions of the parties to the concentration. In other words, in addition to the traditional analysis, we presume that the commission has collected all available qualitative evidence that can support merger simulation inference. Obviously perfect tools for merger control cannot be expected. This should be no surprise, bearing in mind that we are dealing with the specific social phenomena. Therefore, it is almost mandatory that the decision-making process be based on a wider range of analysis, in order to minimise regulatory errors. From an economic point of view, merger simulations are a natural step forward in enriching the evidence set, which does not necessarily have to be complicated or to require significant data or resources.

The simulation approach can follow four key steps,[13] namely: (1) the choice of the appropriate competition model, (2) selection of the functional forms for demand and costs, (3) calibration of the model parameters, and (4) calculation of the post-merger equilibrium and comparative static analysis.

In brief, the chosen model of competition is calibrated to predict market outcomes (prices and quantities), which can be observed in the present. This outcome is taken as the pre-merger equilibrium. By using the calibrated model, we can predict the unilateral effects of the merger simply, by comparing the equilibrium outcomes before and after the merger. Thus, through simulation, we are opposing the effects of the internalisation of competition with the expected merger efficiencies. Efficiencies can be manifested as the marginal costs reduction after the merger (e.g. as the manifestation of economies of scale, elimination of duplicate operations regardless of the production volume, rational use of resources, etc.).

Step (1) does not require any further comment since the preceding discussion provides the necessary erudition for its implementation. Therefore, we assume that we have the *relevant* market where it was quite *relevant* to choose Cournot's mechanism. Steps (2) and (3) require additional attention, while step (4) requires a concrete example, trivial for this discussion, so it will not be specifically addressed here.

---

[13]See for example Werden and Froeb (2008), Budzinski and Ruhmer (2009) and Davis and Garcés (2010, p. 401).

## 3.1 Demand and Cost Functional Form

When it comes to the *choice of the cost function*, whose shape is mostly unknown, it is easiest to assume the constancy of the marginal costs, at least to the level of the firm's capacities. How biased are we that way? Since the analysis is limited to the short time frame, this assumption cannot be regarded as too rigorous, and thereby it greatly facilitates the practical application of the simulation method. If it is unknown, the marginal costs vector could be obtained by the process of model calibration.

Based on the mandatory accounting reports, data on the average variable costs is available and can represent a reasonable approximation of the short-term marginal costs.[14] If needed, such data can be used as the benchmark for our merger analysis. The significant divergence of the calibrated marginal costs and this benchmark point may indicate that we have wrongly calibrated our model.

Of course, the simulation method does not limit the choice of the increasing marginal costs function. This possibility will be re-visited later in the discussion related to the model calibration.

Unlike the costs functions, the choice of the adequate demand model is a bit more complicated. Primarily, there is a significant difference in the definition of market demand for homogeneous and differentiated products. In the homogeneous product case, things are much simpler since the only necessary thing is to define a unique demand function for the entire market. In that case, sufficient information is the market demand price elasticity ($\varepsilon_0$), the relevant market aggregate supply ($q_0$), and the unique price at which the product is sold ($p_0$), all of them based on data observable prior to the merger. In the homogenous goods markets, it can be noted that theoretical rule of one price does not perform properly. This may be the result of action sales which firms often conduct in the short term in order to differentiate their products just by price. In such circumstances, practitioners should take the average price over a broader time horizon, which can be considered relevant for the analysed case.[15]

In the differentiated products market, each considered product will have its own demand function. Hence, it is necessary to establish a system of demand functions, which will include all products from the relevant market. In this case, in addition to direct demand elasticities for each product, a lot of additional information about all cross-connections between the products, i.e. cross-elasticities of demand, will be needed. In order to keep things as simple as possible when it comes to the logic of the functional form selection, the further discussion will be related to the homogeneous products case.

The market demand price elasticity can be econometrically estimated or can be obtained from the firms' records. If the firms tend to maximise their profits, even if they do not know the specific functional form of market demand they are facing, they

---

[14]See Werden and Froeb (2008, p. 69).

[15]For more information on the relevant time horizon and the choice of the dominant strategic variable for the purpose of merger control see Ristić (2015).

are probably aware of the possible price sensitivity of their customers—from their experience, or some other way. Also, this information, critical for a successful pricing policy, may come from engaging market research agencies to examine customer sensitivity to price changes. It should be noted that the same agencies may be engaged by the competition protection authority if needed.

Also, defining the higher order conditions of the demand function is of crucial importance for the outcome of simulations. Examples of linear and constant elasticity demand functions are typical for this type of analysis. For example, supply reduction is followed by a relatively larger price increases when it comes to constant elasticity demand function in relation to the case of linear demand. Apparently, predictions based on alternative forms of demand, with other things being equal, will vary. Hence, if precise information on the elasticity dynamics is missing, it is not superfluous to conduct simulations on all alternative forms. Model calibration represents the process of obtaining the concrete functional form of demand, based on the available information.

## 3.2 *Model Calibration*

Therefore, we will use the example of calibration given by Werden and Froeb (2008), which relies on Cournot model and the given information on the market price ($p_0$), the total supply in the relevant market ($q_0$), and the market demand elasticity ($\varepsilon_0$). A properly defined relevant market prior to the merger can provide such information. If we assume an inverse demand in the linear form $p = a - bq$ (for $a$, $b > 0$), based on the *definition* of price elasticity of demand, it turns out that the vertical intercept and the slope of this function can be expressed, respectively, as

$$a = \frac{p_0(|\varepsilon_0| + 1)}{|\varepsilon_0|}; \quad b = \frac{p_0}{q_0 |\varepsilon_0|}. \tag{14}$$

In order to obtain the marginal costs for all $n$ firms that belong to the scope of the relevant market, we will use the first-order equilibrium conditions already given in Eq. (8). If demand is calibrated in terms of expression (14), the first order condition can be rewritten as

$$\frac{d\pi_i}{dq_i} = p_0 - q_i b - c_i = 0. \tag{15}$$

By replacing $b$ with its calibrated term in the previous equation, the firm $i$'s marginal costs, for $i = 1, 2, \ldots, n$, would be

$$c_i = \frac{p_0(|\varepsilon_0| - s_i)}{|\varepsilon_0|}. \tag{16}$$

As expected, from the previous term, the firm's marginal costs are inversely related to its market shares. If constant, the marginal costs can be directly obtained from Eq. (16).

Since the parameters of demand and marginal costs are calibrated, the chosen model of competition is fully equipped and ready for short-term predictions of unilateral merger effects.

However, before running the model, its calibrated parameters must be tested whether they are logically consistent with the economic theory related to that particular model and compared to the available information from the set of abovementioned qualitative evidence, since the model is calibrated to explain actual reality. The question that should be asked is whether this model is able to do so. Undoubtedly, a key element in the checks is the marginal costs vector obtained in the calibration process.

If it turns out that the resulting marginal costs significantly differ from the marginal cost approximated by the other inputs to the analysis, it would be worthwhile to re-examine the key elements related to the calibration. Therefore, all variables exogenous to the model should be checked—first of all, the numerical value of the actual price elasticity. Attention should also be directed at the market shares because there is always a positive probability that the relevant market was not properly defined before the simulation. In that case, the analysis should start over from the beginning. Marginal costs should certainly be nonnegative values, while the resulting costs asymmetry should adequately correspond to the market shares asymmetry (larger firms—lower marginal costs, and vice versa).

## 4 Concluding Remarks

In this paper, we have shown that under the circumstances of limited capacity, prices and quantities can be variables in the same oligopoly game. Cournot model, as a reduced form of a two-stage capacity-then-price competition, turned out to be a good approximation of this reality. Moreover, it turns out that in practice Cournot model is implicitly implied in competition law, which seems to be a rarely known fact. The important role of Cournot model can be observed primarily in the context of merger simulation, applied to homogeneous products markets as well as to differentiated products markets.

Starting with the calibrated Cournot model, equipped to explain the observed equilibrium reality, as presumed, the next step is to reach the hypothetical post-merger equilibrium. The main novelty that needs to be incorporated into the calibrated model refers to the fact that merger reduces the number of players in the relevant market. In addition to this, expected post-merger efficiencies must also be taken into account, which will lower marginal costs of the merging parties. Expected efficiencies are the fundamental argument in favour of mergers, and it should be seriously taken into consideration in the simulation process. Without efficiencies, almost every merger simulation will show a significant decrease in the aggregate consumer surplus. In such an environment, it is the natural interest of the merger parties to show relatively biased expectations regarding the level of efficiencies that could be considered realistic. It is up to the commission to decide what level of efficiencies can be accepted, based on all the available information for the given case. Analysts are not prevented from applying the simulation method to alternate post-merger marginal costs scenarios, even for the extremely optimistic scenarios predicted by the merging firms.

However, the utilisation of the simulation method could be perceived as a complementary analytical tool for controlling concentrations, capable of decreasing the likelihood of common regulatory mistakes—false positive or false negative conclusions. It does not require significant additional time, data or other resources. If the relevant market was properly specified, all elements are most likely already available. The simulation method certainly allows a significant influence of economic theory in merger control, which is in line with the wave of the so-called "more economic approach" in European Commission practice, by incorporating the intensity of the competition and merger efficiencies into one comprehensive economic model.

At the same time, calibration could be seen as a low-cost, and sometimes the only alternative to a full-scale merger analysis, by using econometry, in equipping the selected economic model for estimating demand and cost functions. Of course, this does not exclude the possibility of conducting econometric approach, when authorities have enough time, reliable data and resources for such an endeavour.

The simulation method, based on an adequate economic model, can complicate the day-to-day life of judges and lawyers accustomed to the use of simple per se rules. Sometimes the simulation method may look like the black box generating evidence. Without sufficient understanding of the underlying economic theory, it can certainly become one.

## References

Begović B, Pavić V (2012) Uvod u pravo konkurencije. Pravni fakultet Univerziteta u Beogradu, Beograd

Budzinski O, Ruhmer I (2009) Merger simulation in competition policy: a survey. J Compet Law Econ 6(2):277–319

Cournot A ({1838} 1897) Researches into the mathematical principles of the theory of wealth. The Macmillan Company, New York.

Davidson C, Deneckere R (1986) Long-run competition in capacity, short-run competition in price, and the Cournot model. Rand J Econ 17(3):404–415

Davis JP, Garcés E (2010) Quantitative techniques for competition and antitrust analysis. Princeton University Press, New Jersey

Edgeworth YF ({1897} 1925) The pure theory of monopoly. In: Papers relating to political economy, Vol. I, Chapter E, pp 111–142. Burt Franklin, New York

European Commission (2004) Guidelines on the assessment of horizontal mergers under the Council Regulation on the control of concentrations between undertakings. Off J Eur Union (2004/C 31/03)

Federal Trade Commission and the U.S. Department of Justice (2010) Horizontal merger guidelines. Washington, DC

Hall M, Tideman N (1967) Measures of concentration. J Am Stat Assoc 62(317):162–168

Kreps MD, Scheinkman AJ (1983) Quantity precommitment and Bertrand competition yield Cournot outcomes. Bell J Econ 14(2):326–337

Levitan R, Shubik M (1972) Price duopoly and capacity constraints. Int Econ Rev 13(1):111–122

Maggi G (1996) Strategic trade policies with endogenous mode of competition. Am Econ Rev 86 (1):237–258

Pepall L, Richards D, Norman G (2011) Contemporary industrial organization: a quantitative approach. Wiley, New Jersey

Perloff MJ, Karp SL, Golan A (2007) Estimating market power and strategies. Cambridge University Press, New York

Ristić B (2012) O reprezentativnosti mera tržišne koncentracije i njihovom značaju za regulaciju horizontalnih spajanja preduzeća. Ekonomske ideje i praksa 1(7):77–90

Ristić B (2015) Simulacije horizontalnih spajanja preduzeća primenom Kurnoovog mehanizma konkurencije. In: Živković A, Molnar D, Stojanović Ž, Manić E (eds) Tematski zbornik radova – Ekonomska politika i razvoj. Ekonomski fakultet Univerziteta u Beogradu, Beograd, pp 53–87

Schulz N (1999) Capacity constrained price competition and entry deterrence in heterogeneous product markets. Working paper, Würzburg economic papers, No. 99-7, Universität Würzburg

Shapiro C (1989) Theories of oligopoly behavior. In: Schmalensee R, Willig R (eds) Handbook of industrial organization, vol 1. North-Holland, Amsterdam, pp 329–414

Shy O (1998) Industrial organization: theory and applications. The MIT Press, New York

Tirole J (1988) The theory of industrial organization. The MIT Press, Cambridge, MA

Varian RH (2010) Intermediate microeconomics: a modern approach, 8th edn. W. W. Norton & Company, New York

Werden JG, Froeb ML (2008) Unilateral competitive effects of horizontal mergers. In: Buccirossi P (ed) Handbook of antitrust economics. The MIT Press, Cambridge, MA, pp 43–104

# Difference-in-Differences as a Tool for Ex-Post Analysis of Mergers: The Case of a Merger in the Romanian Retail Market

**Radu A. Păun and Danusia Vamvu**

## 1 Introduction

This paper provides a broad overview of the analysis conducted by the Romanian Competition Council in the second half of 2013, following the authorization of a merger in the retail sector at the end of 2010. The implementation of the difference-in-difference methodology (henceforth DiD) represented the core of this analysis, and this is what this paper will focus on.

Following a brief introduction to the subject matter, Sect. 2 describes the DiD technique, both graphically and mathematically (i.e. the general regression model applied to the data). Section 3 discusses the main hypotheses that the DiD rests upon and presents some further details about the decisions we had to make when conducting this analysis, primarily due to the merger characteristics and data availability. Section 4 presents the main results, along with some comments, while Sect. 5 concludes the paper.

The importance of the ex-post assessment of a merger decision stems from its main objective, which is to evaluate whether the aims of the decisions of the competition authority were reached or not. It is essential (but not sufficient) that a competition authority can verify if a decision has achieved the goal that justifies the existence of the merger control policy. However, this is not sufficient, given that, in order to minimize the number of inappropriate decisions in regards to merger control, the competition authority needs to also understand the reasons underpinning the failure or success, with respect to reaching the goals of the decisions.

R. A. Păun (✉)
Industry and Energy Department, The Romanian Competition Council, Bucharest, Romania
e-mail: radu.paun@competition.ro

D. Vamvu
Research Department, The Romanian Competition Council, Bucharest, Romania
e-mail: danusia.vamvu@competition.ro



B. Begović, D. V. Popović (eds.), *Competition Authorities in South Eastern Europe*, Contributions to Economics, https://doi.org/10.1007/978-3-319-76644-7_12

Experience has shown there is not one specific way to evaluate the effects of a merger clearance, and this is mainly due to the fact that authorising mergers requires the prediction of the merging firms' future conduct, which most certainly complicates the analysis and gives relative importance to the industry's structure and performance during the merger process. According to Weinberg (2008), there are three main approaches that have been used to measure the effects of mergers on prices: case studies, merger simulations, and direct comparisons of prices before and after the process of concentration. Whereas the first two approaches rely on assumptions that have a vital impact on the outcome of the analysis, before and after comparisons of prices offer a much more flexible and reliable framework for analysis.

According to Buccirossi et al. (2006), in regards to the ex-post analysis of a merger decision, it is important to fully grasp the aim of such analysis, but a consensus on what should be the economic objective of the merger control has not yet been reached. The opinions of the competition economists are divided between those who think that all antitrust interventions should be aimed at maximising consumer welfare and those who believe that total welfare should be the standard. However, the European Commission clears mergers only if they are not likely to negatively affect final consumers.

The importance of assessing merger clearances in the retail sector is twofold. Firstly, it stems from the highly concentrated retail sectors, which are becoming even more concentrated due to merger waves occurring throughout European countries since the 1980s.[1] Secondly, supermarket mergers are a particularly important issue for antitrust authorities because food expenditures represent a large share of household budget (about 12.3%, on average, in European countries in 2015) and 6.7% of the GDP.[2]

Therefore, in 2013 the Romanian Competition Council tried to assess whether the effects of a particular merger that it cleared in 2010 were positive on consumers or not. A significant part of this assessment was the implementation of the DiD methodology. Authors such as Ashenfelter and Hosken (2010) and Aguzzoni et al. (2011) argue that DiD is the most suitable ex-post impact assessment methodology of a merger decision.

Simply put, for a specific merger case in the Romanian retailer market, this paper tries to answer the following question: has the decision under examination (i.e. clearance of the merger) protected consumer welfare, or would this goal have been better achieved had the Romanian Competition Authority adopted a different decision (e.g. to block the merger or to conditionally approve it)? In other words, we are set to find the best way to isolate, estimate and assess the effects of the cleared

---

[1]According to Allain et al. (2015), in 2004, $CR_3$ was 91.2% in Denmark, 79.6% in Finland, 81% in Iceland, 82% in Norway, and 91.2% in Sweden, while in 2003, $CR_5$ was 72.6% in France, 67.8% in Germany, 69.1% in Spain, 68.5% in Portugal and 63.5% in the UK. Furthermore, among the 100 retail mergers requests presented to the European Commission between 1990 and 2012, 89 were approved, 8 were approved subject to conditions, and only 3 were denied.

[2]http://ec.europa.eu/eurostat/statistics-explained/index.php/Household_consumption_by_purpose

merger on prices of the offered goods and see whether this was beneficial or harmful to end consumers.

As Jiménez and Perdiguero (2012) point out, the number of papers using the DiD approach to analyse the effects of mergers has grown in recent years. According to these authors, most of the studies using this methodology concluded that prices increased as a result of the merger (they also provide several examples of studies reporting significant price hikes). In their particular case, Jiménez and Perdiguero (2012) use evidence from an exogenous merger between two retail gasoline companies in a specific market in Spain and conclude that the concentration did not lead to price increases. By contrast, Connor et al. (1988) found cost and price reductions after a merger between US hospitals. In rail transport, Karikari et al. (2002) also noted reductions in prices, although this result depends on the type of goods, direction of traffic, and the type of transport.

In regards to retail merger analyses, Allain et al. (2015) assess the impact of a merger in the French supermarket industry on food prices and, by performing a DiD analysis on consumer panel data, they concluded that the merging firms significantly raised their prices after the merger, but nationally rather than locally. The increase of the competitors' prices was stronger in local markets where more merging firms operated and in which differentiation changed following the merger.

To conclude, empirical merger analysis of the retail sector seems to go in two main directions, with lively debates between the two approaches: on the one hand, some papers build structural models of demand and supply in order to simulate merger effects using pre-merger data,[3] whereas, on the other hand, some papers use both pre- and post-merger data on prices to directly estimate the effects of the structural changes and mergers.[4] The latter is the one we took in our analysis.

## 2 The Difference-in-Differences Technique

The main problem in trying to analyze the ex-post behaviour of the parties involved in a horizontal merger, by determining the effect of the merger on prices, lies in choosing an appropriate method that can control for all other factors that could influence prices. We are referring here primarily to the effects of any changes that may occur on the demand or the supply side (e.g. consumer preferences, income, cost level, taxation, etc.).

We chose the DiD methodology because it seems to be the best practice in assessing ex-post merger impact, it is often used by competition authorities such as the US Federal Trade Commission and the UK Competition and Markets

[3]For example, Smith (2004) simulated structural changes in the UK supermarket industry and found that retail divestitures reduced prices while mergers increased prices.

[4]The most relevant to our case are Ashenfelter and Hosken (2010), Ashenfelter et al. (2013), and Ashenfelter et al. (2015).

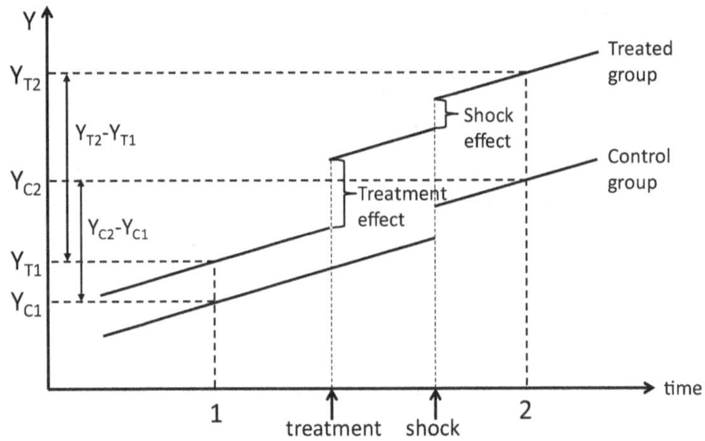


**Fig. 1** Choosing a representative control group

Authority, and is also recommended by consultants such as LEAR and Compass Lexecon. This technique greatly depends on selecting a representative control group, as well as choosing a suitable time window around the event (in our case, the cleared merger).

Using terminology that comes from medical studies, DiD involves the comparison of two groups of individuals: the treatment group and the control group.[5] In our case, "the treatment" refers to the takeover by retailer A of all the stores of retailer B.

A "before and after" analysis is limited in the sense that it only works if the trends of the treatment and control groups are parallel and if there are no shocks affecting the treatment group differently than the control group. In order to show this, we depicted the estimated effect and the real effect of the merger when choosing a reliable control group (Fig. 1) and an inappropriate control group (Fig. 2).

In general, in merger control one may look at the merger's impact on product prices, quantities, product quality, or range. In Fig. 1, any one of these variables is denoted by Y and is plotted on the vertical axis, whereas time is plotted on the horizontal axis.

In brief, the control group is meant to display the "normal" evolution of the phenomenon (e.g. product price, quantity, quality, or range) over time, both before and after the treatment (in our case, the merger). Apart from trend parallelism, this also implies that the control group is exposed to all the shocks that also impact the treatment group (and with the same magnitude). The only difference between the control and the treatment groups is the fact that the latter is also affected by the treatment (merger) under investigation. This means that the difference in time and across the two groups (i.e. the difference of the differences) will isolate the treatment effect.

[5]The treated group refers to those stores that are "treated" (the stores from the five potentially problematic areas in regard to the merger), whereas the control group "gets the placebo" (those stores not affected by the merger).

**Fig. 2** An example of an inappropriate control group

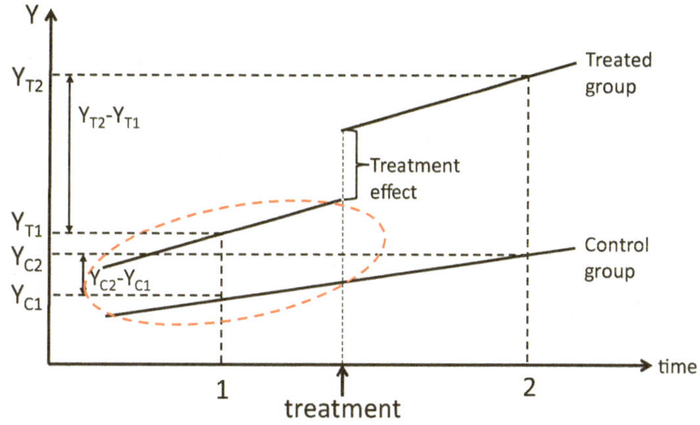


**Table 1** Mathematically formulated difference-in-differences technique

| | Before the merger | After the merger | Difference |
|---|---|---|---|
| Treatment group | $P_{1,\,1}$ | $P_{1,\,2}$ | $\Delta P_1 = P_{1,\,2} - P_{1,\,1}$ |
| Control group | $P_{2,\,1}$ | $P_{2,\,2}$ | $\Delta P_2 = P_{2,\,2} - P_{2,\,1}$ |
| | | | $\Delta\Delta P = \Delta P_2 - \Delta P_1$ |

It is apparent that when the trends of the treatment and control groups are not parallel, even in the absence of additional shocks, the estimated effect would be misleading (the difference of the two trends contaminates the estimated treatment effect). This is just one example of an inappropriate control group. Another could be a control group which is exposed to different shocks than the treatment group, or to the same socks, but with a different magnitude.

In our particular merger case, given the available data, we analyze the behaviour of the merger parties before and after the merger, in those locations that are potentially problematic due to the suspected opportunity to increase prices following the strengthening of market shares over a certain critical threshold.

More specifically, we are interested in the price dynamics of the involved parties in those areas that are identified as potentially problematic in comparison to prices from other stores, belonging to the same retailer, but in areas that are not affected by the merger. Consequently, in what follows, the variable formerly denoted by Y is replaced by P (Table 1).

The above table shows that for each product that we are interested in, we first calculate the difference between prices from the "before" and "after" periods, for the treatment and control groups ($\Delta P_1$ and $\Delta P_2$, respectively), and then the difference between these differences ($\Delta\Delta P$).

As indicated above, if the control group is correctly chosen so that its evolution is similar to that of the treatment group before the merger, and it is exposed to the same shocks (and with the same magnitude) as the treatment group, it can be reasonably assumed that the evolution of the control group observed throughout the post-merger period represents the "normal" evolution of the market. As a result, the difference between the differences isolates solely the treatment effect (the effect of the approved merger) on the treatment group.

**Table 2** Econometrically formulated difference-in-differences technique

| | Before the merger | After the merger | Difference |
|---|---|---|---|
| Treatment group | $P_{1,1} = \beta_0 + \beta_1$ | $P_{1,2} = \beta_0 + \beta_1 + \beta_2 + \beta_3$ | $\Delta P_1 = \beta_2 + \beta_3$ |
| Control group | $P_{2,1} = \beta_0$ | $P_{2,2} = \beta_0 + \beta_2$ | $\Delta P_2 = \beta_2$ |
| | | | $\Delta\Delta P = \beta_3$ |

The DiD analysis can also be achieved by estimating a regression model that is formulated as:

$$P_{i,t} = \beta_0 + \beta_1 \cdot Treated_i + \beta_2 \cdot Post_t + \beta_3 \cdot Treated_i \cdot Post_t + \varepsilon_{i,t} \tag{1}$$

where $i$ represents the store, $t$ is the time period (week, month, quarter, given case features), *Treated* is a dummy variable whose value is 1 if the store is part of the treatment group, 0 otherwise, *Post* is a dummy variable whose value is 1 for the post-merger period, 0 otherwise. The last term of the model represents the interaction between the two dummy variables described above, thus taking value 1 if the data corresponds to a store from the treatment group in the post-merger period.

Given the way the variables are defined in the regression model, the estimated coefficients are used directly in the DiD analysis, as shown in Table 2.

Therefore, the $\beta_3$ coefficient indicates exactly the impact of the treatment (the impact of the merger) on product prices and is thus what we are specifically interested in.

The main advantage of using the regression model for the DiD analysis is that it allows further investigation of the statistical significance of the estimated coefficient $\beta_3$, thus avoiding misinterpretation of the results.[6]

Another advantage, inherent to the regression analysis, is that $\beta_3$ will capture the *average* treatment effect, as it is estimated using data over two periods of time, before and after the merger, not just the two particular moments in time, denoted as 1 and 2 in the figures above. Consequently, the results obtained through the regression analysis are considered to be more meaningful than the punctual effect (which may depend on data particularities, mismeasurement, etc.).

Given the way that model (1) is specified, $\beta_3$ is also the average treatment effect across all stores in the treatment group (see discussion below).

The model presented in Eq. (1) can be extended by adding other variables that could explain the average price dynamics during the analysed time frames, thus obtaining more reliable results (i.e. avoiding the omitted variables bias). At the same time, the model extension can also be justified by imperfections of the control group: the addition of the right explanatory variables will allow slight differences between the treatment and the control groups, and will thus improve the estimate of the $\beta_3$ coefficient.

[6]While a result obtained using the tabular version of the DiD technique can still be representative, it might not be statistically significantly different from zero.

One example of an explanatory variable that may be added to the model is product quality, as changes in quality over time may lead to price changes and the effect may be different in the two groups. As indicated further, adding product quality into the model was not necessary in our particular case.[7]

Another example is the addition to the regression model of time dummies. By introducing time-fixed effects, one could account for seasonal changes of different magnitude in the two groups. Hence, an extended version of model (1) can have the form expressed in Eq. (2):

$$P_{i,t} = \beta_0 + \beta_1 \cdot Treated_i + \beta_2 \cdot Post_t + \beta_3 \cdot Treated_i \cdot Post_t + \beta_4 \cdot Time + \varepsilon_{i,t} \quad (2)$$

where *Time* is a vector of dummy variables, representing weeks, months, quarters, etc.[8] In most cases, the *Time* variable will probably represent the months of the year, hence this vector will comprise 11 dummies, one for each month.[9]

The model above could be further expanded by adding store-fixed effects (i.e. store dummy variables). This would allow for the intercept of the regression to vary across stores, and would attenuate possibly omitted variables bias, provided that the omitted variables are store-invariant (this is similar to adding time-fixed effects, the case in which the possibly omitted variables would need to be time-invariant).

Last but not least, a natural logarithm transformation could be applied to price data, so that the coefficient of interest ($\beta_3$) can be directly interpreted as the percentage change in product price following the merger clearance.

When fitting model (2) to data, the $\beta_3$ estimate will capture the impact of the cleared merger on prices for the treatment group as a whole. Adding time- and/or store-fixed effects into the model will allow variation of the intercept by time and/or store, but $\beta_3$ will still indicate the average treatment effect (average over time and for all stores in the treatment group).[10]

In our particular case, we decided to introduce into the regression model a dummy variable for each month of the year (hence subscript $t$ also represents a month) and to use price data in logarithm (for ease of result interpretation). Then, we ran a regression similar to model (2), separately, by product *and* for each store in the treatment group. This means that the $\beta_3$ coefficient of each regression indicates the

[7]This is fortunate because capturing product quality, especially in numerical form, in order to include it in a regression model, can prove to be an extremely difficult task. To collect such information, one may need to rely on consumer perception through carefully designed questionnaires.

[8]This choice should take into consideration case characteristics and should match the choice of $t$.

[9]One month needs to be omitted to avoid the resulting multicoliniarity, due to the fact that the regression model contains an intercept, $\beta_0$ which captures the impact of the omitted month on prices.

[10]Unless the time and/or store dummies are not interacted with the other variables in the regression model.

impact on product price in that particular store, part of the treatment group, relative to all stores in the control group.

As indicated in Sect. 3, we focused on 11 food product categories and the treatment group consist of five potentially problematic stores. Consequently, we ran 55 different regressions, thus the results presented in Sect. 4 comprise 55 different $\beta_3$ estimates.

## 3 Applying the Methodology: Main Assumptions and Decisions

In general, the DiD methodology may be used to compare prices (or other metric) of the products offered by the merger parties (the treatment group) to those offered by similar competitors (the control group), during two different time intervals, before and after the merger clearance. As indicated previously, if the control group is appropriately chosen (displays a trend similar to that of the treatment group and is exposed to the same shocks), this approach will isolate the effect of the merger over the parameter of interest (usually the price).

However, comparing the price evolution of the products offered by the merger parties with those offered by similar competitors might lead to a major problem: a false negative result. This is the case when the merging parties are influential enough that they might increase the price for their products and other players would follow suit. In this scenario, a DiD analysis may show no significant increase in relative prices between treatment and control groups only because they increased in a similar way. In a retail case, an approach that eliminates the threat of false negatives would be to compare the price of products offered by different stores from the same chain before and after the merger.

The first assumption we made is that, in what follows, all companies active in the retail sector (whether hypermarkets, supermarkets, or any other type of stores) provide products to consumers (predominantly individuals). This makes things easier for us since it means that the prices that we consider in the analysis are the shelf prices for the selected products.

An alternative view is that companies active in the retail sector provide a shelf listing service for various products, with the customers of this service being mostly legal entities (manufacturers or intermediaries for the listed products). Therefore, in this scenario, the analysis should take into account the listing price for the shelf products.

As mentioned above, the analysis that we use in this paper involves a comparison of price levels during two symmetrical time intervals, before and after the merger. The time periods analysed must be sufficiently long to allow for the full manifestation of the effects of the merger, and short enough to avoid any contamination effects from other changes that may occur in the market following the merger and which might manifest differently in the treatment and control groups, thus affecting the comparability of the two groups (e.g. the appropriateness of the control group). Some authors consider ideal to look at a 3-year interval starting from the date of the merger (2 years if the market is highly dynamic and innovative), while others use symmetric time intervals of 1 year each, before and after the merger, excluding from the analysis 1 year around the merger.

Another methodological aspect that should be emphasised refers to the actual nature of the analysed merger. More specifically, the papers that deal with ex-post merger assessment generally focus on two companies, call them A and B, which operated independently prior to the merger and as one following the merger, e.g. in the form of company AB. In our case, however, a retailer who was not present in contemporary retail market (Lidl) entered this market through the complete acquisition of another retailer (Plus). This means that, prior to the merger, we have data regarding the activity of Plus, whereas, after the merger, we have data regarding the activity of Lidl.

Even though the two brands operate in the same market segment of the retail sector (hard discounters), there are significant differences between them (in terms of commercial policy, product range, quality, etc.). Furthermore, consumer perception of the two brands is likely to be different, given, for example, the resources invested by the two companies in communication and marketing activities. This means that a price comparison between the two retailers is very sensitive and should be treated with caution.

This issue led us to look at the conduct before and after the merger of another retailer, Kaufland, which is part of Schwarz Gruppe, along with Lidl, and which could see the takeover of Plus by Lidl as an opportunity to raise prices, particularly in those areas where the position of the group was strengthened following the merger. This aspect becomes extremely important when discussing the appropriate choice of the control and treatment groups.

The merger analysis included the DiD assessment presented in this paper, but also the analysis of market evolution in some areas, the review of entries in the retail market and their development, the analysis of private labels and the analysis of the procurement market, all of which were performed within the Romanian Competition Council, by the Consumer Goods Department (while the DiD analysis was assigned to the competition authority's Research Department).

The first decision we had to make refers to the parameter (or parameters) that were to be analysed through the DiD. Even though, conceptually, one may look at different aspects that may be affected by the merger, such as product price, quantity, quality, or range, for obvious reasons most ex-post studies focus on merger impact on product prices. Consequently, our ex-post analysis of the Lidl-Plus merger focused also on prices.

The second decision refers to the definition of the control and treatment groups. As indicated above, comparing Plus prices before the merger to Lidl prices following the merger was not seen as an option, and we decided to analyse Kaufland prices instead. Discussions within the Competition Council showed the need to analyze the

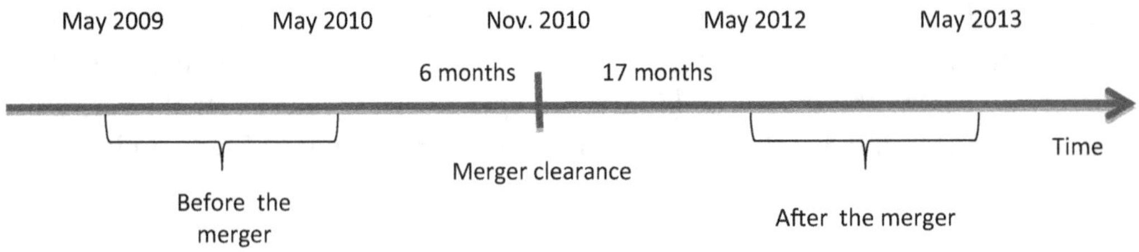


**Fig. 3** The time intervals used in the ex-post merger analysis

existing situation in five potentially problematic Kaufland locations[11] where the Schwarz Gruppe's position strengthened significantly following the takeover of retailer Plus by Lidl. Hence, the treatment group consists of five Kaufland stores. The control group is made of 11 other Kaufland stores, located in areas unaffected by the merger (i.e. areas where Plus stores were not present, or their presence was limited) and in cities of similar size to those from the treatment group.[12]

The third decision was related to the products that would be included in the analysis. We focused on 11 basic food product categories such as milk (regardless of fat content, the form of packaging, brand, pasteurization level etc., in order to compute the average price/litre), meat and sausage products (regardless of the form of packaging, brand, product type, in order to compute the average price/kg), non-alcoholic beverages (average price/litre), bread, tomatoes. The complete list of the product categories included in our analysis is given in Table 3. The analysis could have included non-food items and be dealt with them in a similar manner, so long as the selected categories are offered by both the treatment and control group.

The fourth decision we had to make referred to the time dimension of the analysis (Fig. 3). In this respect, given various restrictions, we ended up with the following two periods: May 2009–May 2010 (the "before" period), and May 2012–May 2013 (the "after" period). The time horizon covered by the data is somewhat narrower than ideal, covering two symmetrical periods of 13 months each. However, we do not believe that the DiD analysis was affected significantly, the only question that arose referred to the time window between the approval of the merger (November 2010) and the first moment following the merger for which we had available data (May 2012), which may be seen as slightly too wide.

In our view, it is essential that the "before" and "after" time intervals are similar in the sense that they contain the same months of the year, in order to isolate the seasonal price fluctuation. Additionally, by eliminating the time interval around the date of the merger (November 2010), we avoid the problem of the period in which firms begin coordinating their behaviour (through pricing), so that leaves us with only those periods underlying the uncontaminated prices, for both "before" and "after" time intervals. Finally, we assume that there were no significant changes in the market structure that would have altered the behaviour of the retailer after the merger

[11]Due to confidentiality issues, the five potentially problematic stores are referred to as K1, K2, K3, K4 and K5. Each of these Kaufland stores is located in a different town of Romania, with a population of between 50,000 and 85,000.

[12]For example, this means that no Kaufland store in Bucharest is part of the control group.

differently between the two groups, thus assuming that the two symmetrical periods before and after the merger are still comparable for the control and treatment groups.

Before going over the results of our analysis, we need to stress one particular aspect. Kaufland stores in Romania carry mostly the same range of products across the network, especially in the food department. As a result, by having only Kaufland stores in both the treatment and the control groups, we eliminate the possibility of different changes in product range or quality between the treatment and the control groups, as a result of the merger. In other words, if Kaufland made a change in the product range or the quality for the 11 product categories we monitored, for example by introducing private labels into Kaufland's offer, it made the same adjustment at all stores in its network. Consequently, the main parameter of interest for this ex-post analysis remains the product price.

## 4 Results

If Eq. (2) is fitted to price data for one particular product of interest, it returns one estimated $\beta_3$ coefficient, which would indicate the average effect on prices that the merger had for all stores in the treatment group, relative to the stores in the control group, for the two considered time periods.

Instead of adopting this approach, which would have implied running 11 OLS regressions (one for each product category we have chosen), we decided to run separate regressions for each of the five potentially problematic Kaufland stores in the treatment group and for each of the 11 product categories. By doing so, we allow for the estimated coefficients to differ from one regression to another, hence for the merger impact on prices to vary across the Kaufland stores in the treatment group. In other words, we have not estimated the average merger impact on prices for the treatment group as a whole, but rather the merger impact on prices at the store level. The coefficient of interest is still $\beta_3$ and represents the percentage change in the price of the product, due to the merger clearance.

Our decision has led to 55 separate regressions. Each of these regressions relies on 260–273 observations, with the exception of the five regressions related to fresh bread—this product was included in Kaufland's offer at the end of 2009, leading to a somewhat smaller dataset of 210–216 data points. $R^2$ adjusted for degrees of freedom (14) is above 0.6 in all regressions, except for those associated to cold cuts, where it ranges from 0.3 to 0.43, depending on the Kaufland store in the treatment group. For all regressions considered, the *F-test* of overall significance shows that the proposed regression models fit the data well (all *p-values* are virtually zero).

The coefficient of interest remains $\beta_3$ and represents the percentage change in the price of product category due to the merger clearance. Table 3 summarises the results.

Before running each individual regression, we visually inspected the price trends in the control and treatment groups before the merger, and identified six cases where trends were significantly different. For these six cases, which match the situation depicted in Fig. 2, the DiD analysis is not applicable. Consequently, these cases were marked by X in Table 3.

**Table 3** Results using DiD

| | K1 | K2 | K3 | K4 | K5 |
|---|---|---|---|---|---|
| Milk | −2.23% | −2.35% | −2.16% | −1.11% | −6.53%*** |
| Apples | +3.91% | −1.45% | +3.32% | +0.76% | −1.78% |
| Cold cuts | X | +2.04% | +0.31% | +3.11% | X |
| **Fresh bread** | **−0.50%** | **−1.36%** | **X** | **−0.09%** | **−5.94%*** ** |
| Poultry | −4.53%* | −7.29%*** | +1.08% | +0.57% | −4.88%* |
| Pork | −5.70%*** | −4.99%*** | −5.50%*** | X | −3.81%** |
| Potatoes | −2.62% | +0.86% | −3.96% | −3.13% | −5.38% |
| Eggs | +0.99% | +5.95%* | −5.18% | +5.80%* | −3.64% |
| Tomatoes | +0.80% | −6.96%* | +1.40% | −1.89% | −6.17% |
| Sunflower oil | +0.83% | X | −0.93% | +1.12% | +0.84% |
| Wine | −4.25% | X | −2.60% | +11.47%*** | −2.22% |

*The merger impact on price is statistically significant at 10%
**The merger impact on price is statistically significant at 5%
***The merger impact on price is statistically significant at 1%

The results for the "fresh bread" category should be treated with caution because the product was included in Kaufland's offer only at the end of 2009, which means that the time intervals before and after the merger are not similar. The lack of data for this product category starting from May 2009 until November 2009 affects the $\beta_4$ coefficient estimates for these months, ultimately distorting the coefficient of interest, $\beta_3$.

In addition to the six cases marked by X, Table 3 shows many price changes that are not statistically significantly different from zero (36 such cases). All in all, there are 31 price decreases following the merger and only 18 price increases. Moreover, taking into account only the estimates which are statistically significantly different from zero, there are ten such price decreases (20% of the 49 cases where the analysis could be performed under good conditions) and only three price increases (6% of the 49 cases). In other words, it appears that the situations where, for a specific product category in a specific Kaufland store, the price decreased relative to the price in the control group following the merger outnumber the situations where the relative price increased.

Consequently, the broad image Table 3 projects is one of some benefits being passed on to the Kaufland customers following the Lidl-Plus merger, and not of a general increase in Kaufland prices following the merger clearance.

## 5 Conclusions

The economic analysis of mergers remains one of the most complex tasks in antitrust enforcement, especially because mergers can have opposing effects for consumers: on the one hand they could generate efficiency gains (translated into lower prices) while, on the other hand, the elimination of a competitor may lead to unilateral or coordinated effects.

The approach we adopted in assessing this particular retail merger clearance used the DiD methodology. Given the information available, the DiD analysis can be implemented for some Kaufland potentially problematic locations, by comparing price dynamics at these locations with those in the control group (11 other Kaufland stores in the country). This analysis tested the hypothesis that Kaufland could decide to increase prices of products sold at those locations where the resulting shares rose above a certain critical threshold on account of to the merger clearance. The results indicate only isolated price increases following the merger (3 out of 49 cases), these situations being clearly outnumbered by relative price decreases following the merger (10 out of 49 cases).

This paper fits into a growing literature which attempts to evaluate whether approved mergers actually led to increased prices. When assessing a particular case on the Romanian retail market, we concluded that the retail prices of 11 food product categories remained primarily unaffected by the merger. Moreover, there are more cases of price decreases following the merger than there are of price increases. Consequently, the Romanian Competition Council's decision to approve the merger can be considered correct (in this case, increased market concentration was not detrimental to consumers).

## References

Aguzzoni L, Argentesi E, Buccirossi P, Ciari L, Duso T, Tognoni M, Vitale C (2011) The ex-post evaluation of two merger decisions, LEAR

Allain ML, Chambolle C, Turolla S, Villas-Boas SB (2015) The impact of retail mergers on food prices: evidence from France, Department of Agricultural & Resource Economics, UC Berkeley, Working Paper Series

Ashenfelter O, Hosken D (2010) The effect of mergers on consumer prices: evidence from five mergers on the enforcement margin. J Law Econ 53(3):417–466

Ashenfelter O, Hosken D, Weinberg MC (2013) The price effects of a large merger of manufacturers: a case study of Maytag-Whirlpool. Am Econ J Econ Policy 5(1):239–261

Ashenfelter O, Hosken D, Weinberg MC (2015) Efficiencies brewed: pricing and consolidation in the US beer industry. RAND J Econ 46(2):328–361

Buccirossi P, Ciari L, Duso T, Fridolfsson SO, Spagnolo G, Vitale C (2006) Ex-post review of merger control decision, LEAR

Connor RA, Feldman RD, Dowd BE (1988) The effects of market concentration and horizontal mergers on hospital costs and prices. Int J Econ Bus 5:159–180

Jiménez JL, Perdiguero J (2012) Mergers and difference-in-difference estimator: why firms do not increase prices? Research Institute of Applied Economics, Working Paper

Karikari JA, Brown S, Nadji M (2002) The Union Pacific/Southern Pacific railroads merger: effect of trackage rights on rates. J Regul Econ 22:271–285
Smith H (2004) Supermarket Choice and Supermarket Competition in Market Equilibrium. Rev Econ Stud 71(1):235–263
Weinberg M (2008) The price effects of horizontal mergers. J Compet Law Econ 4:433–447

www.ingramcontent.com/pod-product-compliance
Lightning Source LLC
LaVergne TN
LVHW080046210926
848481LV00011B/3288
* 9 7 8 1 0 1 3 2 7 3 4 4 5 *